all
**You
Need**
is
Ears

all You Need is Ears

GEORGE MARTIN
with JEREMY HORNSBY

ST. MARTIN'S GRIFFIN
NEW YORK

Published in the United States by St. Martin's Griffin, an imprint of
St. Martin's Publishing Group

www.stmartins.com

Designed by Omar Chapa.

Library of Congress Cataloging-in-Publication Data

Names: Martin, George, 1926–2016, author. | Hornsby, Jeremy, author.
Title: All you need is ears : the inside personal story of the genius who
    created The Beatles / George Martin with Jeremy Hornsby.
Description: Second St. Martin's Griffin Edition. | New York :
    St. Martin's Griffin, 2021. | Includes index.
Identifiers: LCCN 2020053710 | ISBN 9781250784049
    (trade paperback)
Subjects: LCSH: Martin, George, 1926–2016. | Sound recording
    executives and producers—England—Biography. | Beatles.
Classification: LCC ML429.M34 A3 2021 |
    DDC 781.49/092 [B]—dc23
LC record available at https://lccn.loc.gov/2020053710

Our books may be purchased in bulk for promotional, educational, or
business use. Please contact your local bookseller or the Macmillan Cor-
porate and Premium Sales Department at 1-800-221-7945, extension
5442, or by email at MacmillanSpecialMarkets@macmillan.com.

Second St. Martin's Griffin Edition: 2021

10 9 8 7 6 5 4 3 2 1

Contents

Prelude

HALLO. And hallo again.

That seems a fairly reasonable way of starting any autobiographical book, but in this case it is particularly apt, because 'Hallo' was the first piece of deliberately recorded sound.

It was in 1877 that Thomas Edison, trying to improve Mr Bell's new invention, the telephone, decided to use a short needle to vibrate at the back of the diaphragm, in place of Bell's piece of iron. Then, as Edison later described it, 'I was singing to the mouthpiece of a telephone when the vibrations of the voice sent the fine steel point into my finger. That set me thinking. If I could record the actions of the point, and send the point over some surface afterward, I saw no reason why the thing would not talk.'

He was right. He ran a strip of waxed paper beneath a needle, and shouted, 'Hallo.' When he ran the paper under the needle a second time, lo and behold, back came 'Hallo.' It wasn't exactly quadraphonic sound, but it was a start. Later that year he patented his phonograph, in which the recording groove was cut in tinfoil wrapped round a cylinder. He had proved *that* worked with the immortal line 'Mary had a little lamb'. The recording industry was born.

Today, a hundred years on, it is a curious fact that the history of sound recording has divided itself into four almost precise quarter-centuries.

The first twenty-five years, until just after the turn of the century, were occupied by a frantic international scurrying-around, with everyone trying to find effective means of bringing the new toy to the public. It was during this period that Emile Berliner invented the flat disc that we know today, and a machine for playing it on, which he called the gramophone.

But the first real breakthroughs came in 1901, when cylinder records were introduced, made of a hard thermoplastic, and in 1904, when the first double-sided discs were issued. That introduced the second quarter-century, which one might call the Acoustic Period. The search, now that a satisfactory *mechanical* means of reproducing sound had been achieved, was for improvements in the quality of that sound, in techniques both of recording and of playing the records. A great deal of work, for instance, went into finding the best theoretical and practical shape for the horn, whose size and design has a profound effect on the quality of the sound reproduction.

It was still mechanical reproduction, however—until 1925, when, bang on cue, the electric era of recording arrived. Now, instead of the diaphragm physically activating the recording needle, its vibrations were converted into electrical impulses to convey the message to the needle. When it came to playing the record, of course, the same thing applied in reverse.

Those techniques were refined and developed to the utmost over the next twenty-five years, up to 1950, which happened to be the year that a young innocent named George Martin joined the recording industry. It was exactly at that time that the fourth quarter-century was beginning, the era of electronic recording. That's where I was lucky. That was where God's timing for me was absolutely right. And that is why this book, as much as anything else, is the story of those twenty-five years of recording history.

The extraordinary thing is that the cycle is about to start all over again. As I write, we are coming to the very end of the quarter-century of recording by electronic tape. By the time this book is read, we will be into the next era—digital recording. But that is for the last chapter.

George Martin

1

CLASSICAL PRIMER

I was woken by the sound of a bell ringing demandingly in my ear. It didn't seem the best way to start the day, any day. For a moment, I wondered where on earth I was, then recalled that it was a bedroom in a Paris hotel, and it wasn't morning, but the middle of the night.

The immediate problem was to stop that infernal ringing, and reaching for the phone I whispered a sleepy and dubious 'Hallo' in its general direction.

'George, I'm sorry to wake you, but I just had to tell you the news.'

Brian Epstein's voice sounded very excited, and just a little drunk. It seemed early to be in that condition. I soon knew why he was.

'I've just left the boys celebrating, and they're as thrilled as I am,' he said, pausing for a moment to build up the suspense. I said nothing. It was too early in the morning or too late at night to formulate sentences. Then he said it.

'We're number one in America on next week's charts. It's quite definite. I've just been on the phone to New York.'

So that was it. At last we had made it, through the medium of a song called 'I Want to Hold Your Hand'. After a year of really hard graft we had finally breached the walls of the biggest record market in the world.

I forgot any idea of more sleep. That was no hardship. For the past year, sleep had been a rare enough commodity. I just lay there, thinking of what had been, and what might be to come.

But what mattered immediately were the two reasons why I had come to Paris with the Beatles. The first was that they were due to make their French début at the Paris Olympia, and I wanted to be there. The second was to make a quick record with them at EMI's Paris studio.

By the end of 1963, we had conquered England, musically at any rate. Now, as well as America, we were trying to make it big on the Continent. The EMI people in Germany, fired—who knows?—by some patriotic fervour, had insisted that the Beatles would get no big sales there unless they had a record sung in German. The boys thought this was nonsense, and I didn't believe a word of it myself, but equally I did not want to give the German EMI people any excuse for not selling Beatles records.

So, after some argument, I had persuaded John and Paul to re-record 'She Loves You' and 'I Want to Hold Your Hand' in German. The lyrics were provided by a German, who turned up at the recording to make sure their accents were all right. I didn't know about the accents, but I could see that the words were almost literal translations. 'Sie liebt dich, ja, ja, ja' sounded just like the sort of send-up Peter Sellers would have done.

The recording was set for a day that the boys had free from their rehearsals at the Olympia, and when I arrived at the studio I didn't really expect them to be there on time. Even in those early days they were not renowned for their punctuality. But after an hour had gone by I decided to ring their hotel.

None of them would come to the phone. Neil Aspinall, their road manager, had been deputed to do the talking, and he informed me that they had decided that, after all, they did not want to do the record and wouldn't be coming.

To describe my reaction as angry would be like calling Everest a good-sized hill. 'You tell them,' I yelled at Neil down a blushing Paris phone line, 'you just tell them I'm coming right over to let them know exactly what I think of them.'

I slammed the phone down. This was the first time that the boys had stood me up; and I was particularly irritated that they hadn't had the guts to speak to me themselves. I raced back to the Hôtel Georges Cinq, where they had an extravagant suite, and burst in on them in their drawing-room. The scene was straight out of Lewis Carroll. All that was missing was the White Rabbit. Around a long table sat John, Paul, George, Ringo, Neil Aspinall and Mal Evans, his assistant. In the centre, pouring tea, was Jane Asher, a beautiful Alice with long golden hair. At my appearance, the whole tableau exploded. Beatles ran in all directions, hiding behind sofas, cushions, the piano—anything that gave them cover.

'You bastards,' I yelled. 'I don't care if you record or not, but I do care about your rudeness!'

One by one, Beatle faces appeared from Beatle hiding-places, looking like naughty schoolboys, with sheepish smiles. There was a murmured chorus of 'Sorry, George'. If they wanted to be charming, as they did then, it was impossible to maintain anger for very long, and within a few minutes I had calmed down and joined the tea party—though in what guise it's hard for me to say: the Mad Hatter perhaps.

The following day we made the record. But of course they were right. Beatles records, in English, were to sell in their millions in every country, Germany included. Never again did they make a record in a foreign language.

And now, especially, there was no need to, because America had fallen. For me, it was a world away from the moment when I first placed a tentative forefinger upon middle C.

I guess I was six when we got the piano. I fell in love with it straight away, and went and made noises on it.

A piano then was what the television set has become now, not simply a piece of furniture but a focus for family gatherings, and we managed to acquire one through the good offices of Uncle Cyril, who was in the piano trade. He was the one who always played the piano at parties.

At Christmas there were family get-togethers of maybe thirty people at my grandmother's home in Holloway, London. At these gatherings she would recite ghastly poems—'The Green Eye of the Little Yellow God' and that sort of thing. To match her performance, my uncles would sing excerpts from *The Desert Song* and the like. All the grandchildren were expected to do something, a little dance or a poem, and my 'thing' soon became a tune on the piano.

My sister Irene, who is three years older than I, had started taking piano lessons from an 'aunt'—an uncle's wife's sister, actually—and I decided I wanted them too. By the time I was eight, I had persuaded my family that I was fairly musical, though none of them were, and I finally got my lessons: eight of them, to be exact. After eight weeks my mother had a row with the teacher, and I never had another lesson until I was in my teens.

So I just picked it up by myself. It was a rather jerky start to a life in music.

I was born in 1926, just before the Depression, and the first home I remember was a flat in Drayton Park, opposite the Sunlight Laundry. I call it a flat, but it was just two rooms on a top floor, with an attic room above. There was no electricity: we had gas lights on either side of the mantelpiece. There was no kitchen: my mother cooked on a gas stove on the landing. There was no bathroom: we had our baths in a tin tub.

The only water supply was a rounded corner sink on the half-landing, and the one lavatory on the ground floor was shared with the other three families in the house, but at least we didn't go short of furniture. My father was a carpenter, and he made us tables, and sideboards, and cabinets, and beds, and toys for Irene and me. But never chairs. For some reason he never made chairs.

He was a marvellous craftsman, and he loved wood. His life was a sensuous love affair with wood. He could see a piece of wood, pick it up, and spend ages just stroking it, just enjoying the feel of it. He was a very simple man, but he had huge talent in his hands. He was the most honest person I have ever known. During the Depression he was out of work for eighteen months. Eventually he got a job selling newspapers in Cheapside, in the City of London, and I remember going to see him, standing there in the freezing cold, and feeling very sorry for him.

I think he may have got that job through my mother's side of the family, which we always regarded as somehow the grander side. The men, my uncles and my grandfather, used to run the *Evening Standard* vans round London, and they earned quite good money for those days. I always regarded them as my rich relations.

I was the apple of my mother's eye. She was a Roman Catholic, and when I was five I was sent to join my sister at a convent school in Holloway. Three years later, I moved to St Joseph's elementary school in Highgate, which meant taking the number 11 tram from Drayton Park all the way up the hill to Highgate. That was probably the best part of it. Then, in 1937, when I was eleven, I won a scholarship to St Ignatius College in Stamford Hill. It was run by Jesuits, and boasted Charles Laughton as its most famous old boy.

Two years later war broke out. My school was to be evacuated to Welwyn Garden City, a place I had never heard of, but which I understood to be in the wastelands of the far north. My father was by then working as a wood machinist in east London. My sister had left school and gone to work as a clerk with the Sun Life of Canada insurance company, and they in turn were being evacuated to Bromley, in Kent. It looked as though the whole family would disintegrate, so my parents decided to remove me from the care of the Jesuits and follow my sister down to Bromley. There I was installed at Bromley Grammar School, which many years later was the school to which Peter Frampton went.

But if my education was proving a pretty movable feast, my interest in music continued uninterrupted. I had carried on with the piano on my own; once you are interested in something like that, you can find out about it without even going to the library and looking things up. A piano is a great tool for finding out about music, about the relationships between one note and another. I remember getting very excited when I discovered a new chord, and especially so when one day I realised that there was a natural cycle of chords. I found out how to get right through the whole lot and back again to where I started. I didn't realise it then, but I was lucky enough to have the gift of perfect pitch, and that must have helped. I was also able to work out, for example, that there were only three diminished chords in the whole range, and that they had different inversions.

I started playing things like 'Liebestraum', and various Chopin pieces, by ear. Where that gift came from, I don't know. There were certainly no professional musicians anywhere in the family. They just assumed 'George is the musical one . . . let him get on with it'.

Not that I was in a musical desert. At school we used to have concerts by the BBC Symphony Orchestra with Adrian Boult, and Bromley itself had a very large music society. They used to run dances, and I remember one in particular when the Squadronaires band came to play. I hung around the stage, and when one of them asked if I was a musician myself, I seized my chance and said airily, if brashly, 'Oh yes, I play piano, the sort of thing you're doing.'

I suppose they thought it was just adolescent bravado, and that they could always chuck me off again, but anyway they said: 'O.K., if you think you can do it, come up and try.' That was the only invitation I needed, and it was an unbelievable feeling to be sitting up there playing 'One O'Clock Jump' with them.

Music was pretty well my whole life. My only other outlet was a little tinpot amateur dramatic society called The Quavers, which was one of the Church's lay activities in Bromley. It was all good fun, performing in plays by Noël Coward and so on, and no one except the players took much notice. It didn't teach me much about drama; but The Quavers too used to run little dances, and some friends and I said that we would organise a band for them.

We called ourselves The Four Tune Tellers, and then we expanded and became George Martin and the Four Tune Tellers. Fame! My father made us a set of music-stands with a double-T design, and we played the standards by Jerome Kern, Cole Porter and so on, things like 'The Way You Look Tonight'. Quicksteps were always the most popular, and we always ended up with 'The Goodnight Waltz'. Our saxophonist was a boy called Terry Hyland, whom I met years later at London's Astoria. He was still playing saxophone.

We found one or two outlets for our talents other than The Quavers' hops, and got to playing one or two nights a week; with the money I earned I paid for piano lessons in Bromley with a Scot named Urquhart.

I was fifteen or sixteen. Mr Urquhart had a marvellous Bosendorfer piano, and it was then that I really woke up to music. I suddenly realised that I had talent—though, to be honest, the realisation was a mite unconfined: I used to romance about how, if I'd had the proper training, I would have been another Rachmaninov. I got that sorted out rather later, when it dawned on me that Rachmaninov's reputation was under no threat from G. Martin, but at the time I really fancied myself as a classical writer. The supreme achievement, I thought, would be to write music for films. Little did I realise what bloody hard work it really is.

But if those were my fantasies, the time had arrived for me to decide what to do in fact. End of school. Start of big wide world. While I had been at school, my parents were always trying to impress on me the importance of a job with security. I had always been good at mathematics and drawing, so now my mother suggested: 'Why don't you go in for architecture?'

My father said: 'Why don't you go in for the Civil Service? You'll never get chucked out of a job then.' To him that was, understandably, paramount, having suffered so much unemployment, but in both of them there was the feeling that they wanted me to do better than they had, an 'Our George is going places' mixture of parental pride and ambition.

But I was mad about aircraft, and what I, and a friend of mine, wanted to do was to become aircraft designers. He made it, I didn't. I tried to get into de Havilland, but they wanted £250 cash from anyone joining their apprenticeship scheme. It was 1942, and the aircraft companies were too busy trying to churn out the planes they already had. Their interest in aspiring young designers was, to say the least, minimal. In spite of that, I was accepted by one firm, Short & Harland in Belfast. But that would have meant leaving home to work in Northern Ireland, and I didn't fancy it.

So I didn't become an architect, and I didn't join the Civil Service, and I didn't become an aircraft designer. Instead, I went to work for Mr Coffin, in Victoria Street. Mr Coffin was a quantity surveyor, and the funereal quality of the work certainly lived up to his name. After six weeks, boredom got the better of my handsome remuneration of £2 5s a week, and I announced that I was leaving. Mr Coffin wanted me to stay. He even offered to up the ante, but I replied, in such tones of regret as I could muster: 'No, sir, I'm afraid it's not my cup of tea at all.'

From cups of tea metaphorical, I moved to cups of tea actual. I applied to join the War Office, who, after making me take an exam, accepted me into their non-uniformed ranks as 'Temporary Clerk Grade Three'. And that meant tea-boy. It was in Eaton Square. They were very nice people, and allowed me to file a few things as well as making the tea. The department was concerned with the financial side of the war machine, such matters as equipping a regiment with new field artillery, or authorising the spending of fifteen quid on a new canteen for the mess.

My work fell short of the heroic, but I lasted there for about eight months, until the day in summer 1943 when I walked into the recruiting office at Hither Green, near Bromley, and told them I wanted to join the Fleet Air Arm. They asked my name, and I got that right, so they said: 'Right, you're in.' I was seventeen.

I went home to Mother and announced: 'I've joined the Fleet Air Arm.' She was pale-faced and obviously upset. 'You haven't!' she said. But I had. I was sent first of all to HMS *St Vincent,* the training station at Gosport, and for the first eighteen months had no real leave, because we were getting ready to invade France and the whole of the south coast was sealed off. I couldn't go home, and my parents couldn't come to Gosport, but for some reason both they and I were allowed to go to Winchester. There, every three months or so, we would meet and have tea and cakes.

After a radio course at Eastleigh, I was suddenly, with what appeared unseemly haste, removed to Glasgow, and thence, without pause, on to a Dutch liner-turned-troopship, the *Nieuw Amsterdam,* bound for New York. The vessel was, to put it mildly, crowded. It was a cruise ship designed to take fifteen hundred passengers, and we numbered eight thousand. Three thousand of those were German prisoners being taken to Canada; they served us in the mess halls, which, like the kitchens, were going round the clock, with four sittings for every meal. Even sleeping was organised on a rota system, and we, being sailors, were given the night watch. We slung our hammocks on deck and 'slept' in the open— not that we got much sleep, because night was the time for cleaning the ship. From midnight to dawn we cleaned the decks and corridors. I discovered that two bars of soap on a wet deck made an excellent pair of skates, and we had races down the gangways until we were caught.

Two weeks in this floating dormitory-diner brought us to New York, from where, after a week of being amazed by skyscrapers, we went to Trinidad to do our flying training. By now I was a Leading Naval Airman, having started life as a Naval Airman Second Class—which in turn was, I suppose, a cut above Temporary Clerk

Grade Three. At any rate, we stayed in Trinidad until we got our wings, which meant our promotion to Petty Officer.

The first flight I ever made was in a Vickers Supermarine Walrus, a biplane amphibian which shook like mad. I was, I confess it, a degree scared, especially since it seemed to confirm all the worst of my anticipation. Something about my appearance, rather lean and pallid, had made me the butt of all the mickey-taking at Gosport, tactful stuff like: 'You're keen on aeroplanes! Never been up in one, have you? Cor, you'll be sick as a dog when you get up there! Terrible things!'

But I soon got to enjoy it, and it was certainly exciting, especially considering the wide assortment of aerial hardware to which we entrusted our lives. It was all quite zoological really. Apart from the Stinson Reliants, which were high-winged single-engined monoplanes, there was the Walrus, the Grumman Goose (also an amphibian), the Fairey Albacore, and the Fairey Swordfish, which carried one torpedo, and one Lewis machine-gun mounted at the back.

I was an observer, and in Trinidad we were taught air gunnery amongst other things, because the observer was not only captain of the aircraft, but was also supposed to be able to do everything else: radio, radio-telegraphy, navigation, and all the gunnery and torpedo-dropping. Actually, in a real battle we weren't supposed to do the gunnery, because there was a telegraphist-gunner who was supposed to look after that, but we had to be able to do it all the same, just in case he got shot; than which no thought could have been more sobering.

Happily, flying didn't entirely shut out my music. We organised a pantomime for the local theatre, for which I took care of the music, although the Trinidadian weather was hardly what one associates with pantomime time. And if there was a sing-song in the mess, it was always 'Give us a tune, Pincher', and I would duly oblige on what passed for a joanna. I didn't realise why Martins were always called 'Pincher', just as Clarkes are always 'Nobby', until I was told the tradition which says that it goes back to a certain Commander Martin, a naval officer of Nelson's era, who had somewhat cheekily 'pinched' a few vessels from the opposing fleet, thus augmenting the Royal Navy at a stroke.

From Trinidad, we returned to Greenwich for a fortnight's commissioning course, during which we were filled in on important military details like how to hold a knife and fork correctly. At formal dinners in the beautiful Painted Hall we were put through our paces in this vital contribution to the war effort.

The actual business of teaching us to be gentlemen was entrusted to an old officer who had a colonic obsession. He was forever telling us how important it was to go to the lavatory regularly and get one's bowels working properly. That, he insisted, was the basis of good health (the presumption being, I suppose, that one could not be an officer and gentleman and be unhealthy), and he lectured us on the subject incessantly. 'If your bowels are straight, your mind is straight.' Luckily, I had never had any trouble in that department, so I was able to feel secure.

Thus equipped with the manners of gentlemen, we were commissioned, and I immediately suffered. All my mates, with whom I had gone through all that training, were made Sub-Lieutenants. But I was still too young for that exalted rank, so was made a Midshipman. Unfortunately, a Midshipman got less pay than a Petty Officer, which I had been, and since they had back-dated our commissions to the time we had got our wings out in Trinidad, I actually had to refund them the difference. It seemed to me hard, to say the least, that I should have to contribute to the war effort financially as well as physically.

But it was typical of many points in my life; I always seem to lose out on deals like that. And even when, three months later, I eventually got my stripe, it still rankled.

From Greenwich we went to Burscough, in Lancashire, to learn the new wonder of radar, flying Barracudas (more zoology). It was a relief. In Trinidad there was no radar, and when you took off from an aircraft carrier you were on your own. Two and a half hours later you had to find the ship again, relying on your own navigational sense, and on the winds. You found your own winds, worked out what they were doing to the aircraft, and then navigated by dead reckoning. The result of failure in this enterprise was obvious, and we became extremely good at navigation!

As things turned out, I nearly didn't go to sample the delights of Burscough at all. My pianistic ramblings in the West Indies had been noted by the Entertainments Officer, with the result that when I came back to England I was invited to appear on a BBC programme called *Navy Mixture*.

So along went Midshipman Martin to do his thing. I played a piece I had composed for piano, a little three-minute item with the imaginative title 'Prelude'. Never mind, it was my first real 'guest spot'. Stanley Black conducted the orchestra, and the compere was a certain Petty Officer Jack Watson. The show was actually run by people in the Navy; they belonged to the DNE, the Department of Naval Entertainments, whose CO was the playwright Anthony Kimmins, adorned with the rank of Lieutenant-Commander. Also performing was a Lieutenant Jon Pertwee, who came up to me after the show and said: 'We liked what you did. Have you ever thought of joining DNE?'

'Not really,' I said. 'I'm just going up to my operational squadron. I'm a flyer, you see.'

'Yes, I know all about that,' he said, 'but I can offer you a job on the entertainments side of the Navy.'

'O.K., what is it?' I asked.

'It's a ship that's going to tour the Pacific in all the fighting zones, bringing succour to the wretched lads who have to fight. It's called the SS *Agamemnon*, and it's sailing from Vancouver. It's an amenity ship.'

'*What*', I asked in some disbelief, 'is an amenity ship?'

'Well, for a start it's got the capability of making three thousand gallons of beer a day. And it carries an entertainments party. The idea is that it goes around giving goodies to all the chaps, and entertaining them. You'd fit very well into one of our concert parties.'

I thought about the offer, and I must say it was quite appealing. But it would have meant leaving all my friends in the squadron, and chucking up the Fleet Air Arm altogether. So I refused it. I often wonder what would have happened if I'd accepted, because in retrospect it obviously had much more to do with my future career than flying bits of metal and wire round the sky.

The decision to remain an airman rather than become an amenity took me next to Ronaldsway, in the Isle of Man, where we did advanced exercises and formed into an operational squadron. We were going to be shipped out east, since the war was over in Europe. But while I was still in Ronaldsway the Bomb was dropped on Japan, and I knew that my little war was over, without my ever having had to fire a shot in anger. I was not, I confess, too disappointed. Our squadron was disbanded, we held a glorious and drunken farewell party and I was sent on indefinite leave—and went home to Mum.

But I was still in the Fleet Air Arm, and some time later a great chum of mine, who was on the Navy Appointments Board, asked if I would like to go up to Scotland to become a Resettlement Officer, hardly the most demanding of jobs. I accepted, and took the train north to Donibristle, in Fife, just above Edinburgh and hard by the Forth Bridge. There I was to spend fifteen months.

The squadron was 782, Royal Naval Air Service, and my job was to make sure that the ratings, as they were being demobilised, had jobs to go to. Failing that, I had to try to give them help in that direction, telling them about all the training schemes available to prepare them for the rude shock of entering the real world again.

I too, of course, now that the war was over, would have preferred to rejoin humanity straight away, but there was nothing I could do about it, so I had to make the best of a bad job, consoled by the comfortable wardroom life and the many good friends I made among the Wrens and my fellow-officers.

There was a choral society on the station, for whom I wrote little bits and pieces, and in whose choir I sang—without, I'm afraid, any great deal of accomplishment. Amongst the Wrens in the choir was a girl, their leading soprano, who had a very fine, Isobel Baillie type of voice. Her name was Sheena Chisholm, and our common ground of music led to a wider range of mutual interests.

It was just as well, because my job was by its very essence a self-eliminating one. So, as the number of men to be demobbed dwindled, I was given other jobs as well. I became the Transport Officer, and then the Release Officer as well. Thus it was that, in early 1947, I came to release myself from His Majesty's Forces.

But of what I was going to do with myself I had absolutely no idea. It was a case of 'physician heal thyself'. I had no education to speak of. I wasn't trained for anything. It was too late to become an aircraft designer. So there seemed only one possibility, and in what was really desperation I turned to music.

That was where my fairy godfather came into it.

Back in Bromley, when I had had the band and still considered that Rachmaninov and I were neck and neck, I had tried to improve myself by learning to read music. It was a very painful business, because I hadn't done it properly when I was young. In addition to the reading, I had been trying to write bits of music and put them down on paper.

Then, about three months after I'd joined the Fleet Air Arm, I went to a concert in Portsmouth given by a pianist called Eric Harrison. It was held in a hall in one of the Union Jack Clubs. After a pleasant evening listening to Chopin and Beethoven, I hung around until everyone had gone and then sat down to enjoy myself playing the piano, for which I hadn't had many opportunities. After about half an hour of this, I was suddenly aware that there was someone else in the room. It was Eric Harrison.

'What was that you were playing?' he asked.

'One of the things I've been writing myself.'

'Oh, you compose, do you?'

'Well, I try to,' I said, 'though I haven't had much training.'

'I think you should do something about it,' he said.

Somewhat taken aback, I asked him: 'Like what, for example?'

'Well,' he said, 'you should send some of your compositions to the Committee for the Promotion of New Music.'

'I'm afraid I didn't even know there was such a thing.'

'It's a little non-profit-making organisation,' he told me. 'They hold monthly meetings. My namesake, Sidney Harrison, is on the committee. He's a very nice man, and I'm sure he'd help you.'

So I thought about it, and finally plucked up my courage and sent him a Debussy-like composition I'd written, called 'Fantasy'. But I had no real hopes of hearing very much as a result, so I was amazed and delighted when I got a very long letter from Sidney Harrison in reply. It must have run to three foolscap pages. He thanked me for sending him the piece, and then went into a detailed criticism and analysis of it. Not that he tore it to shreds. He simply told me what was wrong with it, that it was very derivative, that I must try to do something a little more original, and so on. At the same time, he was very encouraging. 'You must go on doing more of this,' he wrote. 'Go on writing more music, and keep sending it to me, and we'll correspond.'

That is exactly what happened. Sidney Harrison became my fairy godfather by post. I would send him a piece of music, and he would write back saying things like: 'Good idea. Try and get to know your marine band, and write pieces for them to play.' We never met, but the correspondence went on throughout my Fleet Air Arm career.

He always wrote somewhere in his letters to the effect that 'You really must try to take up music seriously'. So now, with the decision almost taken for me by lack of an alternative, I thought it was about time to go to see Sidney Harrison in the flesh. I told him about my doubts, but he was adamant. 'No,' he said, 'you really must study music as a career, because you've got talent.'

'But look, I'm twenty-one,' I said. 'Can I really take up music now?'

'Of course you can,' said Sidney, who was a professor of piano at the Guildhall School of Music in London. 'You can go and study for three years at a music college. I'll tell you what to do. You come along to the Guildhall, and play your compositions to the principal, and if he likes them as much as I do, you're in.'

My interview with the principal, Edric Cundell—arranged of course by Sidney—took place in February 1947. I played my bits and pieces to him. He asked me a few questions. Then he said, 'Very well. Come and start next year.' By that he meant the next scholastic year, beginning in September.

I thanked him, of course, but I also gave voice to my fundamental worry. 'It's fine to be coming to study at the Guildhall, but how on earth do I pay for it?'

'You should know, being a Resettlement Officer. As a man serving in the Navy, you're entitled to further education. We'll apply for a grant for you.'

So, with my government grant in the offing, I released myself from the Navy and looked around for a job to fill the months until September. The 'job' which turned up was with the Iron and Steel Federation in Park Lane, and was of such total boredom that my stint with Mr Coffin seemed almost sparkling in retrospect. It was an exercise in patience, checking over the fascinating details of wage sheets and hours worked. The only way that I could keep my mind alive was by trying to do it as efficiently as possible. Silly me. I had forgotten that the New Order was upon us.

One day I managed to check seventy-two of these sheets, and at 5.30 I duly stacked them all on my desk. Immediately, an irate colleague rushed up to me.

'Are you trying to be funny?' he asked.

'What do you mean?' I said, finding little that was comical about the place, let alone me.

'Do you know that the average in this place is about thirty of those? Are you trying to make us look like idiots?'

I bit my tongue back from the obvious retort and said simply: 'No. I was just trying to keep my mind alive, that's all.'

He stared at me hard and disbelieving, and then uttered the awful threat: 'You'd better watch it, mate.'

It was my first real introduction to the complexities of labour relations, and I duly slowed my pace down to match my fellow-workers. After all, I might aspire one day to the awesome task of a certain senior member of the office staff. This individual's taxing responsibility was to separate pink, white and blue slips into piles. There was only one snag to this, as far as he was concerned. He was colour-blind. So every now and again the tedium was relieved when the wretched man held a pink slip aloft and shouted, 'Blue!', to which we would respond, 'No!'; and again until he got it right.

I was living at home with my parents during this period of high intellectual activity, but sadly things started to go terribly wrong between my mother and myself. We had always been very close, and my absence in the Navy had been a great strain on her. It was over my friendship with Sheena, an ex-Wren by now. My mother took great exception to her, saying that she was only after me for the wrong reasons, which was rather silly considering the little that I had to offer anybody at that time. But it became an obsession with my mother, who was obviously only doing what she thought best for me. Then, one day, I found that she had been opening my let-ters. A furious row ensued, and with the impetuosity of youth I promptly left home. I went to stay with some friends at Winnersh in Berkshire.

I was still there with them when I finally said my *adieux* to the Iron and Steel Federation and its pink slips, and walked through the door of the Guildhall School of Music, armed with my grant of £160 a year. But I was only to stay at Winnersh during my first term, because on 3 January 1948, my twenty-second birthday, Sheena and I got married.

In a way we were driven into it by my mother's attitude. It was almost a statement of defiance. My mother did come to the wedding, but sadly our relationship had become distant. She had had a bad fall the previous year, and had hit her head, and I think she wasn't really herself, the person to whom I had always been so close. Three weeks after we married, she died in hospital of a cerebral haemorrhage.

I was shattered. My grief was compounded with a sense of guilt. It was hardly an auspicious start to our marriage. On top of that, Sheena had nervous dyspepsia, and a kind of agoraphobia—she couldn't bear to be alone outside, wherever she was. That problem was compounded by the difficulty of finding an inside for her to be in. Houses were impossible to get, and the only way to find a flat was to wait on a council list for ages. In desperation, I put an advertisement in all the London papers in the areas round Willesden. It read: 'Down to earth with a bump. Fleet Air Arm officer unable to find anywhere to live.' As luck would have it, the ad was seen by a man whose son was in the Fleet Air Arm, and he offered us a place in Acton. It was cheap, and it was terrible, and it was our first home.

I stayed at the Guildhall for three years, studying composition and all that goes with it—conducting and orchestration, musical theory, harmony, counterpoint and so on. I took piano, of course, because that was the natural instrument for me, but one also had to learn a second, and it was suggested that I should take up a wind instrument.

So I thought about all of them, and finally settled on the oboe, a decision reached for a variety of reasons. For a start I wasn't very fond of brass. Then, too, there was the sheer question of economics. After all, my three years would soon be up, and if I was going to get a job quickly I wanted something that I could master well enough to play professionally—and preferably an instrument where there wouldn't be too much competition! Everybody played the clarinet, so it came down to a choice between the oboe and the bassoon. The oboe was both cheaper and less cumbersome to carry around, and good oboe players were in very short supply, so orchestras were likely to settle for someone like myself. So the oboe it was: one of the most difficult instruments to play, the one they call 'the ill wind that nobody blows good'.

My wife and I were living on a £300 married student's grant, and I helped to eke that out by writing bits of music and playing the oboe in the evenings. I would never have been a great performer, though. I haven't the temperament for it. I was always terribly nervous, and still am when I have to perform. I had been frightened enough when I had had to go and play my piano pieces in front of Edric Cundell; but at least I knew them. The oboe exam was something else. It was in front of two of the country's most eminent oboe players, Terence MacDonagh and Peter Graeme. There were just the two of them in the room, and me, and I was terrified. Sheer terror made me sweat so much that it was running down my fingers and they slipped on the keys. There was no controlling it. That oboe became like a live eel in my hands.

All the same, when the time came to leave the Guildhall, I had to earn a living somehow, and I did it by playing the oboe. I got various engagements, but it was freelance work and I really wasn't very good. I used to play with bands in the parks, up on the bandstand confronted by rows of old ladies in their deckchairs, who always seemed to get up when I started playing. I couldn't really blame them. I was unfamiliar with a lot of the music, and when it came to something like the overture to *The Silken Ladder*, with its complicated oboe part, I was pretty well lost. I used to get about two pounds ten shillings for each performance, and you could say that in my musical life it was my stint as jobbing gardener.

Fame and fortune as an oboe player lay on no discernible horizon, and it soon became clear that I would have to take a day job as well. So I went to work at the BBC Music Library, at Yalding House in Great Portland Street. It demanded a modicum of musical ability, sorting out scores and so on, but it was still very much a clerk's job—grade unspecified.

Then, in September 1950, after I had served the Corporation for a couple of months, I got a letter from a man asking me whether I would like to consider working for him. His name was Oscar Preuss, and the letterhead proclaimed that he was with EMI, at an address in Abbey Road.

2

PALATES AND PALETTES

SINCE a great deal of this book is about music, this seems a good point to pause and describe my feelings about music in general, and writing music, and orchestrating music.

If I had to pinpoint one piece which really turned me on to music as a child, it would have to be Debussy's 'L'Après-midi d'un faune'. I was fifteen when I heard it played by the BBC Symphony Orchestra, with Adrian Boult conducting in my school hall. Listening to it, I couldn't believe that human beings were making such an incredibly beautiful sound. I could see these men in their monkey-jackets, scraping away at pieces of gut with horsehair and blowing into funny instruments with bits of cane on their ends. But the mechanical things I saw simply didn't relate to the dream-like sound I heard. It was sheer magic, and I was completely enthralled.

My curiosity aroused, I got hold of the miniature score of the work, looked at it and saw how it was done. I saw which bits were on flutes and which on clarinets, I saw where the French horn came in, the special *sforzando* effects on the strings, and so on. I looked at it, I analysed it, and today I know exactly how that piece of music works, and precisely why it is so clever. And in spite of knowing those things technically, I still think it's the most magical, wonderful piece of music.

But although today I can write music like that myself, I didn't do it first. Debussy did. The real wonder of music and orchestration is that you can actually *paint* sound, yet no modern artist worth his salt tries to imitate Botticelli. Classical music was my first love, and I am often asked what I am doing working in the pop field. 'Isn't it something of a comedown?' is the typical question. But the typical answer is 'No!', for various reasons.

To start with, the 'classical music' that people refer to when they use the term is old music, music that was written at least fifty and more often at least a hundred years ago. Of course, there is contemporary 'classical music'. But to most people it sounds extremely dissonant, and I personally don't know anyone outside the profession who really enjoys listening to it.

To be fair, most composers writing contemporary 'classical music' are in a cleft stick. They can't use the styles which have already been evolved, because then they're accused of being romantic, or sensuous, or derivative. So the only way to go is to write new sounds—and remember, even the twelve-tone scale is old-fashioned now, and almost regarded as romantic itself. The result is that the modern 'classical' composer either writes stuff that most audiences can't stand, or reverts to writing symphonies that could have been written by Brahms. And what's the point of that? So 'classical music' becomes a one-way street; and that's where pop music has come into its own, because it can be truly creative.

What's more, many 'classical' composers have obviously been popular. Schubert, for instance, wrote 'pop' music in that his songs were sung for the pleasure of ordinary people. Even Beethoven wrote for bands and so on. At the same time, one has a certain reverence for them simply because they laid the groundwork of our basic musical culture. But if Bach were alive now, I'm absolutely sure that he'd be working at music in the same way that we do in the business today. Above all, he was a worker and a craftsman, and he didn't enjoy much reverence in his time. He was really hardworking; he trudged hundreds of miles to try to meet Handel, because he'd heard so much about this famous man who was the toast of London and a friend of the king. (Poor old Bach never did meet him; he missed him by a day.) He lived comfortably, but never in luxury, which was hardly surprising since he fathered twenty children by his two wives. There was no choice but to work hard, running a choir, playing the organ, and constantly writing music for his patron, the duke of wherever it happened to be at the time.

The duke would say: 'I need a cantata for Sunday week because it's the wife's aunt's birthday.'

Bach would say: 'It's going to take me a while to write it, your dukedom.'

But that never helped, because the reply would inevitably be: 'Sorry about that, Johann, but I do need it for that day, and you do want to eat next week, don't you?'

So Bach would go home and think: Oh, hell! What *am* I going to write now? Ah, I know. There was a good little tune in that string quartet I wrote three months back. I can take that out and give it to the sopranos. He would literally do this, pinching his own material, rearranging it, and then saying to himself: That'll do. He'll never know I wrote it before.

And when he presented the duke with his cantata, sure enough, that worthy wouldn't recognise it, and would be delighted. 'Great. You've done it again, Johann. Terrific.'

Bach would just keep churning it out, writing away like a film writer of today who has a deadline to meet—and God knows, Bach had plenty of those. So whether or not he'd have a regular number-one spot in the hit parade today, I'm quite certain that he'd be in there pitching. The one thing he wouldn't have been doing is punk rock, because he was musical and punk rock wasn't—it was a separate phenomenon altogether.

Of course, there are composers working in the 'classical' style today, and very successfully; but usually for special reasons. Take Khatchaturian, who died recently after a life of writing extremely popular 'classical' music. I suppose I call his music 'classical' rather than anything else because he wrote symphonies, and because he wrote for orchestra rather than rock group. But one of the main reasons for that is that in Russia they regard the development of electronics in music, pioneered by the West, as being bourgeois and decadent. They have few rock groups, and what there are are carbon copies of ours; that's why there's such a demand for our rock records behind the Iron Curtain. So, if any musician is going to be encouraged in Russia, it won't be in that direction, but into the footsteps of Tchaikovsky, Borodin, and so on. Naturally a Khatchaturian, if he has any talent at all, will tend to write for symphony and ballet orchestras.

Now that's fine, because they have an outlet for that music. But in the West, sheer economics operate against large orchestras. In the ordinary way, no one can afford to have an orchestra playing his or her music. Composers do get commissions, of course, but the outlet for the big orchestral style is almost invariably in film music. The hard fact is that if, as a composer, I say, 'I only write for symphony orchestra,' the response is bound to be: 'Hard luck, mate. You'll never hear it played, will you?' Havergal Brian proved that with the enormous list of symphonies he wrote, only a few of which have ever been performed.

The same constraints apply in the recording of music. When I started at EMI, my job was to make recordings of classical music. But it was the move into creative pop work that made the job truly worthwhile, and infinitely more interesting. It's possible I won't be remembered for it in a hundred years' time, but it's certain I won't be remembered for making yet another recording of Beethoven's Fifth Symphony. So many recordings have been made of that kind of work that there's no way of contributing anything new.

There isn't a single classical performer who is creating music in the way that a lot of the pop performers are.

Much of pop music depends on arranging and orchestration—things which are very difficult to teach. The old man who taught me at the Guildhall used to give me exercises. He would say: 'Now, next week I want you to take the second movement of Beethoven's Hammerklavier Sonata and score it for a symphony orchestra.' I would spend ages scoring what would be one movement of a symphony, but the trouble was that I never heard it played, so I never knew what my orchestration would sound like. But he had the experience to know, and he would look through it and say: 'Oh, yes, very good. I like that. I like the way you used the strings there. But I wouldn't put the bassoon on the third there. That makes it too thick on the bottom.' He would tell me what I should and shouldn't do—but, since I never heard it, I could never truly assimilate his teaching. Today, I can hear something in my mind, but I couldn't then.

Of course, I had written and played my own pieces on the piano, but that was different altogether. It was a sort of musical doodling with the fingers, which turned into something. But that's the fingers doing the writing for you, and of course you hear it as it happens. I can sit and ramble on the piano for hours and not play anything. It's like automatic writing—the fingers just go their own way. That isn't cerebral composition.

Nor is it orchestration, which is different from composition in any case. Orchestration is a matter of giving colour to lines that are already there, and that is simply a question of experience. There are certain things which, if you do them one way, will produce a particular sound, but which with only slight modification will sound completely different. No amount of lecturing will ever tell you the right method so that you will be able to apply it automatically. Of course, there are certain basic rules you can follow in order to avoid falling straight into a musical manhole, but the actual craft, the technique of being a first-class orchestrator, can only be won by experience. It has nothing to do with music in its pure form. Composition is a cerebral exercise of musical line and harmony, and whether it's performed on a synthesiser or by a hundred-piece orchestra, it's still the same music. The basic design doesn't change.

What orchestration does is to give it life. And however you choose to do that colouring changes totally the way in which the audience receives the basic line.

This struck me forcibly when the Beatles came along. There were many people who couldn't assimilate their tunes, because they couldn't hear the music for the noise. They thought that the Beatles were a noisy and objectionable group, much as people (with greater reason) thought of punk rock. The average middle-aged person heard them and said, 'Gosh, what an awful noise!', and didn't listen to the music, or the harmonies, or the words.

It wasn't until they became more popular, when artists like Mantovani started recording orchestrated versions of their songs with pleasant, syrupy sounds, that that same middle-aged person started to say: 'Oh, that's a nice tune. That's the Beatles, is it? They do write good music, don't they?' What that person was hearing was exactly the same tunes, the same harmonies, the same basic lines—done in a way that the middle-aged ear could assimilate.

But as time went on, it became more than a mere matter of tunes and harmonies. We actually developed into a composition team, a creative team building musical images which no one else had done before or was doing then. I'm not saying that the results were the equivalent of Bach's Mass in B Minor, but at least they were creative, they weren't sterile, they weren't reproductions of anything that had been done before.

Orchestration is clothing. You could take a Beethoven string quartet, which to some people would be as dry as dust, and you could dress it up in a different way. It would be the same music, but now those people would enjoy listening to it. And of course that's exactly what happens; every couple of years or so, someone dresses up a classical piece in some new finery, and, lo and behold, it gets to the top of the hit parade.

In orchestral classes at the Guildhall I also had to do the reverse—that is, take an orchestral piece and translate it for piano. Of course, a lot of well-known composers have done that. Rachmaninov turned Mussorgsky's 'Pictures at an Exhibition' into a piano piece, and it's now a famous part of the repertoire.

The astonishing man was Ravel, of whom we always think in terms of lush orchestrations. He was a very fine pianist, and—with the exception, I think, of his Piano Concerto—he always wrote his compositions as piano pieces first of all. Then he orchestrated them. I find this very curious. If I'm writing an orchestral piece, I write straight for orchestra. But Ravel, who was one of the greatest orchestrators of all time, and the musician I admire most of all, performed what I think was an extraordinary operation on almost everything he wrote.

But every man has his own best way of working, as no doubt did the other masters of orchestration like Debussy, Tchaikovsky (who first started using the orchestra in a descriptive fashion), and in this century Stravinsky, who really knew how to handle an orchestra.

Today, orchestration has become a highly developed art, particularly in the film world, where you find many fine orchestrators. When I started, I might be doodling a little piece on the piano and think: That might be rather nice on clarinet. But if I'm writing a film score now, I would come to a particular section and think: Ah, I'd like to use a nasty trombone sound there, or, This is a part where it doesn't need any strings at all, just a percussive element. I tend to think of orchestration in terms of painting a picture. An artist can do a brilliant outline sketch in sharp charcoal—Picasso, for example, did the most beautiful line drawings. But when it comes to orchestration, what you do is to fill in all the subtle colourings, making the picture into a three-dimensional form.

It wasn't until long after I left the Guildhall that I started to get a clear mental picture of how that sound picture would turn out. I had to write a lot and actually hear orchestras playing what I had written. And even then, the fact is that every time you write a score, no one can be absolutely certain how it will sound. You may have an idea in your mind's ear, but you never know for sure. So you learn to take risks, risks that spring from the imagination—the cornerstone of good orchestration.

But of all that I knew nothing, as I donned my old naval great-coat and cycled off to Abbey Road for my interview with Oscar Preuss.

3

ABBEY ROAD

IT WAS my fairy godfather at work again, as I was about to discover after I had parked my bike outside the huge old white-painted mansion in Abbey Road that had been converted into the EMI studios.

Oscar Preuss had a large, homely office in the front of the building, with thick carpet, easy chairs, coal fire and grand piano. He sat at an old roll-top desk in the corner by the window, facing his secretary, a young and attractive girl with a distinctly cool manner—towards me, at any rate.

My first question to him was, naturally: 'How did you get hold of my name?'

'I've been looking for an assistant for a while,' he said. 'I mentioned it to one of my colleagues here, Victor Carne, and asked him if he knew anyone suitable. He told me that he didn't, but that he would ask around.'

Victor Carne, it turned out, was a great friend of Sidney Harrison, and when he had asked Sidney if he knew anyone, Sidney had replied: 'There's a young man who's just finished at the Guildhall. His name is George Martin.' So Victor, a fascinating man who was a great friend of Gigli, and who did all EMI's operatic work, told Oscar, and Oscar told me I'd got the job, at the princely sum of £7 4s 3d a week, which was just £1 8s 10d more than I'd been getting as a music student.

Oscar was the head of Parlophone, which was just one of the labels under the EMI umbrella, along with HMV, Columbia, and Regal Zonophone. All these labels had existed before the war, but when it came, some of them were cannibalised to help the others. Parlophone had been the one that had suffered the most. It had originally been a German label, with music taken from the Lindstrom catalogue, and its trade-mark, which people often take for a pound sign, is in fact the German L. But that was coincidental to the fact that all Oscar's top performers, like Victor Sylvester and Rawicz and Landauer, were taken from Parlophone and put on to the Columbia label. Parlophone had been reduced almost to extinction, but now, in 1950, Oscar was trying to build it up again, though it was still weak.

He did the lot. He was administrator, and at the same time made all the records. The label was a one-man band, but it encompassed the whole world of music. It had classical records, jazz, light orchestral, songs, dance music with performers like Ivor Moreton and Dave Kaye, piano music, Billy Thorburn's 'Organ, Dance Band, and Me', and occasional comedy records like the classic 'The Laughing Policeman'.

With all that on his plate Oscar certainly needed his assistant, whom he proceeded to toss in at the deep end. With my background I was regarded as very 'twelve-inch'—a reference to the old 78 r.p.m. shellac records of those days, which had popular music on ten-inch and classical on twelve-inch discs. 'Right,' said Oscar, 'the first job you can do is to look after the classical end.' I suppose, with my being a classical musician, it seemed logical enough.

I was put in charge of a group of musicians called the London Baroque Ensemble, conducted by Dr Karl Haas. Dr Haas was a lovely old man, a doctor of music. He had suffered badly in the war, was never very well, and in addition was always broke. But if he had any money at all on him, he would be off out to buy me presents like boxes of liqueur chocolates, or take me out to lunch. He would borrow from one person in order to be able to give a present to someone else, and then probably vice versa.

His generosity was matched by the problem his name could cause. I remember him coming to see Oscar one day; the commissionaire from the door came in and said: 'Mr Preuss, there's a man outside who calls himself Mr Arse. Is that right? Mr Arse?' It's wonderful what you can do with aspiration—or the lack of it!

The good doctor was a musicologist rather than a great conductor, and he had a tremendous knowledge of baroque music, at a time when it was still very unfashionable. He had persuaded Oscar to make recordings of baroque music with his group, which was in fact a get-together of the top musicians in London—playing mainly in the studio, though I think they did give occasional concerts. They were mostly woodwind players, and it was fascinating for me, an oboe player of moderate achievement, to be recording people of the stature of Frederick Thurston on clarinet, Dennis Brain on French horn, Jack Brymer, Terence MacDonagh and Geoffrey Gilbert.

We recorded things like the Dvorak Serenade for Wind, Mozart serenades, a lot of Bach and marches by Beethoven: pieces which today have become very popular, but were then virtually unheard of. The recordings were mono, of course, since stereo didn't exist, but I was still very proud of what we achieved. And whenever we used small string sections, they were invariably led by Jean Pougnet, a charming hulk of a man. His favourite pastime was chopping up timber at his country home, and his huge hands looked quite incapable of making the nimble and beautiful sounds which he coaxed from his violin.

Apart from the pleasure of hearing how woodwind should really be played, I also gained from these sessions an early lesson in recording. By careful placing of the instruments, it was possible to record using only one microphone. The natural acoustics of the studio gave the recordings their fine sound, and I learned that to obtain a natural sound one should use as few microphones as possible, a principle which I believe still holds good today.

It was while the Ensemble was in full swing that Dr Haas went one day to a party. There he met Peter Ustinov, who at that time used to do impressions of opera singers and so on as his party piece. He discovered that Ustinov was not only very keen on baroque music, but was knowledgeable about it as well. So he decided to form the London Baroque Society and invited Peter to be the president. Karl was the conductor, I was the secretary—and that *was* the London Baroque Society: just the three of us. We would meet from time to time at Abbey Road, have a nice lunch, chat about music in general, and decide what the Ensemble would record. There was a certain eighteenth-century elegance about it all. That was how I came to meet Ustinov, and later to record him.

When I entered EMI in 1950, I was entering a world in which there was already a great deal of controversy. Long-playing records had been pioneered by CBS in America, and in June of that year Decca had issued their first. But the big-wigs at EMI stupidly refused to acknowledge that this was going to be a viable form of recording. They said that no one would want the tedium of having a very long-playing record, that it would be too expensive, and that they would be content to stick with their 78 r.p.m. singles.

I couldn't understand it at all. I was making classical records, and nothing was more annoying than having to chop up pieces of music into tiny fish-finger lengths of four and a half minutes each. I had to plan the music that was to be played, going through the score and deciding where to make the breaks. They were quite arbitrary, sometimes even in the middle of a movement. When the music had no natural break, I'd have to have the last chord on the first side played again to start the second side, to stop it sounding peculiar. It was absurd, but it had to be done, because we were limited to an absolute maximum of four and three-quarter minutes. Different producers would have different breaks for the same piece of music, which would also depend on the tempo at which the conductor was taking the orchestra, and it became a matter of some fascination to hear where other people were making those breaks.

It was good fun, but it wasn't good business. Yet EMI issued a statement saying that they would give six months' notice of any departure from standard records. The man responsible for that catastrophic decision was Sir Ernest Fisk. I say 'catastrophic' because they lost two years, and I believe the decision was fundamental to their subsequent loss of the repertoire from Columbia Records in America. In 1953 they were to lose that catalogue to Philips, and in 1957 they also lost the RCA-Victor catalogue to Decca, after an association of fifty-seven years. Sir Ernest Fisk was an Australian, and a cycling fanatic who delighted in nothing so much as pedalling round Hyde Park, and he will go down in history as the chairman who delayed the entry of EMI into the long-playing record market, bicycle or no bicycle.

What history may not record is the day I nearly got the sack as a result of not knowing what he looked like, since he worked at the head offices down at Hayes. I was working with a choir in the Number One studio at Abbey Road, which had a big organ in it. The organist was late, keeping me waiting, the engineers waiting, and the choir waiting.

I didn't know this particular organist. At twenty past ten in the morning, when the session should have been well under way, I went upstairs and waited around for the unknown musician to turn up. Through the door came a man with a domed head, dressed in a black coat and striped trousers and carrying a music case.

I rushed up to him in a fury and said: 'It's about bloody time. Do you realise we've been waiting for you? You've been keeping everyone waiting for the last twenty minutes.'

'What *are* you talking about?' he asked.

'You know perfectly well what I'm talking about,' I said. 'The session was due to start at ten, and you've kept us hanging about.'

'Do you know who I am?' he asked coldly.

A terrible doubt started to tug at the back of the Martin mind. 'Yes, you're the organist . . . aren't you?'

'No, I am not the organist. My name is Fisk, and I am the chairman of this company.'

Ghastly silence. It looked as though I had a great future behind me. I made grovelling excuses and attempted to sink through the floorboards, trying to make myself as anonymous as possible. For the next few days I was in fear and trembling, because I really had been very nasty to him. Happily I heard no more, so I suppose I should thank him for that.

The group managing director, by contrast, went by the nickname of 'the Japanese General'. His conversations were sparse in the extreme. I rarely spoke to him, since Oscar did most of the direct communication with 'God', but if I did pick up the phone when he rang, he would simply say: 'Mittell here.' Then there would be silence, but a silence pregnant with the unspoken demand that one should speak. So one spoke. Then there would follow another long silence. He just wouldn't say a word.

I think that at this time, although the record companies possessed quite a sizeable part of EMI's earning power, the entertainment industry was still regarded by the board as slightly suspect. My impression was that they would rather be making bicycles than gramophone records. And I think they were terrified at the capital expenditure involved in going into LPs. But they had no excuse for not knowing their potential value, for the simple reason that everyone told them so—Oscar, Leonard Smith and Norman Newell on the pop side of Columbia, and Walter Legge who ran Columbia's classical side.

Walter Legge was the prima donna of the classical world in those days. He was married to Elisabeth Schwarzkopf, and he had a hand in running the original Philharmonia Orchestra, which obviously did him no harm. They were just two of the many artists who recorded under his direction. He was something of a maverick, and I always admired him, since he did bring a breath of fresh air into the fuddy-duddy company that was EMI at that time.

No less extraordinary a man was Oscar Preuss himself. I suppose when I joined him he was about sixty; he had begun at the age of fourteen or fifteen as an engineer apprentice, not all that long after Edison had started it all. He made diaphragms and needles for the early types of phonograph, including the old cylinder machines, because in those days the engineer who did the actual recording used to make his own machinery. He had risen over the years until finally he had become head of Parlophone, so he had an enormous amount of experience.

For my first month or so at Parlophone, my training consisted of dogging his footsteps and trying to absorb as much of that experience as possible. Then, after a while, he started to ease me into doing things on my own. He might say: 'George, I might not be in on the dot tomorrow. You start the session off, will you?' And I *would* be there on the dot, and get the musicians and engineers organised, so that we would have our first take done before Oscar would breeze in and say: 'That's no damned good; we'll do something about it.' I had to steel myself to introducing myself to musicians and then more or less informing them that I was in charge. I've no doubt that in those early days they regarded me as a bit of a whipper-snapper, but I had the authority (even if no great salary!) and they had to tolerate me.

One of the most terrifying of all those sessions was the first time I recorded with Sidney Torch and the Queen's Hall Light Orchestra. It was in the Number One studio at Abbey Road, which is a cavern of a place about half an acre in size. Even with the fine old Compton pipe organ in place (on which, apparently, Fats Waller had made his only organ recordings), the floor was still vast. Oscar had told me that he wouldn't be in until 11 a.m., which was an hour after the session was due to start. I think he did it deliberately to see how I would cope. My main recollection is of the long, almost unending walk across the floor of the studio, and through the assembled forty-five-piece orchestra to where Sidney Torch stood on his rostrum. It must have been rather like the feeling a batsman has when he first walks to the crease at Lord's.

'Good morning, Mr Torch,' I squeaked in a piping voice. 'My name is George Martin, and I'm Oscar's assistant, so I'll be starting the session.'

I was almost wetting myself with fright at the apparent impertinence of it, but luckily Sidney was quite nice about it. He smiled benignly and said that that was O.K., and more or less indicated that if I didn't get in his way, he wouldn't get in mine.

After that we were to get on pretty well, but he could be irascible in the extreme. I have seen him, when the orchestra were not bending to his will, fling his baton right across the studio (a long throw!) and shout: 'For Christ's sake, gentlemen, do get it right!'

Meanwhile, I had to learn fast, and learn from my mistakes. One of the earliest of those was right at the start, in 1950, when I was sent to see a film in which Mario Lanza was singing the theme 'Be My Love'. Being still very classically minded, I was wholly offended by this man's singing, just belching it out with brute force and bloody ignorance. I hated every minute of it, and wrote a scathing report which read rather like something from the pen of an avant-garde music critic. I said that it was a corny song, that it had every cliché in the book, and that it was too calculated.

So we did nothing about it. What I had overlooked, in my asperity, was the simple possibility that it could be a hit song. And, of course, it was.

Another lesson came when Oscar started giving me jazz sessions to handle as well as the classical and light music ones. The band in question was Humphrey Lyttelton's, and as they ran through one of their numbers I found myself becoming very critical of the bass player. All we seemed to be getting was a dull thud.

I watched this player for a while, and then said to him: 'Do you think you could play the notes more clearly?'

After a silence, short but shocked, he made a reply which is unprintable, but the gist of which was that he considered I knew little about it—which was true.

Undaunted, I floundered on: 'It sounds as though you're playing with boxing gloves on.'

This was also true, but Humph exploded. Calling me names of which I had not previously heard, he stomped out of the studio.

Clearly I needed help of the highest order. I sought out Oscar in his office and told him what had happened. This immediately prompted a second explosion, this time from Oscar. 'You go and get Humph back into the studio, and you apologise to all concerned,' he ordered. And then the twist of the knife: 'If you lose us Humph, you've lost yourself your job.'

Outside in Abbey Road I found my disgruntled artist wandering up and down. Eating great dollops of humble pie, I told him how sorry I was to have been so stupid, and eventually persuaded him to carry on with the session; thus ensuring, though I didn't mention it at the time, my continued employment.

Later, Humph and I were to become firm friends, and we made many records together, such as 'Bad Penny Blues'. But the lesson was learned. Musically I was right. Diplomatically I was wrong. Tact is the *sine qua non* of being a record producer. One has to tread a fine line between, on the one hand, submitting to an artist's every whim, and, on the other, throwing one's own weight about. I had to learn how to get my own way without letting the performer realise what was happening. One had to lead rather than drive. I think that now, as then, that is probably the most important quality needed in a record producer.

Another, lesser, quality was the ability to hold one's liquor. This was particularly necessary when dealing with Scottish artists. Parlophone had a corner in the Scottish market. It was *the* record label for Scotland, with its output of eightsome reels, jigs and so on. Oscar used to record Robert Wilson, and there were the accordion duettists, Mickey Ainsworth and Jimmy Blue, whom I would have to go up to Scotland to record.

They were great whisky drinkers. We would start recording at ten in the morning, and after an hour and a half or so they would say sorrowfully: 'We're working up a terrible thirst, George. Let's have a wee drop.' So we would leave everything and proceed to the bar on the corner (it being Scotland, there always was a bar on the corner). There they would order their tots, always doubles, of neat whisky. It was never your ordinary Johnnie Walker or Bell's, but always Pride of Methlane or something like that, unknown brands with the effect of firewater. I would have to partake of these tots with them, which they would sling down the bar-top towards me like desperadoes in some Western movie. As for their own drinks, no sooner had the glass reached their hands than it was downed, and would be slung straight back at the barman with the urgent request: 'Ah, let's have another one.'

The curious thing was that it never affected them. They would get rid of half a bottle each during a session, and the only result was that their fingers flew over the keyboards even faster. Matching them in this ability was Annie Shand, a pianist who had a little band in Aberdeen. I recorded her in the Aberdeen Theatre, and halfway through the session she suddenly stopped and started to delve into her handbag, from which she produced a large whisky bottle. 'Would anyone here like a wee tot?' she asked, as she unstoppered the medicine. 'Wee' of course meant 'extremely large', as indeed was her handbag, which she kept specially as a kind of personal bar. To Annie, whisky was the natural food of life.

On top of these lesser lights, we had the great Jimmy Shand (no relation to Annie) under contract. I did a great deal of work with him, and became steeped in Scottish music—you couldn't help doing so. Scottish dancing was very popular in those days, in England as well, and Jimmy would even get me at it. Each time I went up there we would record about eighty-four titles, twelve or fourteen a day, and stockpile them for the year, issuing a few every month.

Jimmy was a shy and retiring man—and, unusually for a Scots

musician, teetotal—who spoke with a decided Fife accent. He was very kind, though rather suspicious of people in general, a product perhaps of a general Scottish distrust of 'foreigners'. But we had one great thing in common. I had acquired my first powered vehicle, in the shape of an old Ariel VB600 side-valve motorcycle and sidecar. It turned out that Jimmy, who delighted in all things mechanical, was particularly fanatical about motorbikes. He had a beaten-up old machine which he tended with great love, and his great outlet, away from the incessant sound of his own music, was flying round the Fife countryside at something like ninety miles an hour with his cap on back to front.

Then there was our 'Latin American' Scot, Roberto Inglez, whose real name was Bob Ingles. He had truly taken his coals to Newcastle, because he was the biggest seller of Latin American music records in Latin America. He used to play what he called 'one-finger piano', very low down in the register, and had very lush orchestrations, rather more sophisticated and schmaltzy than Edmundo Ros, using strings and even the French horn, which Dennis Brain used to play for him.

His exotic 'cover' could be better than he thought. One day he was doing a session in the Number Two studio at Abbey Road, when there was a visit from some girl dealers, being shown how records were made. They were standing wide-mouthed and wide-eyed in the control room, when over the mike came Bob's thick Glaswegian accent.

'Oh,' said one of the girls, 'he really is foreign then, is he?'

Bob was one of the first people whose records I tried to 'plug'. Oscar had decided as part of my early education that I should do some record promotion, which meant going to the BBC and trying to get records played. I was hardly a dazzling success. I took one of Bob's records to Jack Jackson, and tried to persuade him to play it on his 'Saturday Night Show', the one with Tiddles the Cat. He was very kind to me, but regrettably unmoved by my persuasion. 'Bring me stuff by Guy Mitchell, or Mitch Miller, or anyone like that, and I'll be interested,' he said. The trouble was I didn't *have* anyone like that to offer, and said so.

'Look, son,' he said, 'I don't want to be unkind to you. If you can bring me a record that's suitable for my programme, I'd love to play it. But Roberto Inglez! I mean . . . !'

I felt immensely crushed.

One man who did play my records, on 'Housewives' Choice', was Godfrey Winn, and I became quite friendly with him. I remember taking him to lunch one day, at some plush restaurant in Ebury Street, and drawing five pounds in expenses to pay for it. As usual, I rode there on my motorbike, to save on taxi fares.

After lunch he offered to give me a lift back to the studios in his conveyance, which was a Bentley or something of that ilk. What could I do? Having lashed out the fiver on the meal, I could hardly improve my efforts to impress by confessing that I had arrived on a motorbike—though nowadays, of course, it would be regarded as rather chic. 'No problem,' I said. 'I'll easily get a cab round the corner. Thanks all the same, Godfrey, but there's really no problem.' It wasn't enough. Kind man that he was, he insisted on finding a cab and seeing me into it, whereupon I had to go through the charade of tapping on the glass behind the driver and saying: 'St John's Wood studios, please.'

A hundred yards up the road, with Godfrey safely out of the way, I had to bang furiously on the glass again, shouting: 'Let me out! Let me out!' I've no doubt the driver thought I was mad. But I couldn't let the EMI image down.

That was important, and may have been one reason why I was no good at record plugging. I was a sheep among wolves, and didn't even realise it. In those days there was a great deal of scandal surrounding the plugging business, and all sorts of people were taking backhanders. But that was not Oscar's style. He was a very upright person, and the question of backhanders never came up, so that I was never really aware of what was going on. Besides, my image of EMI was that they, too, were very upright.

To work for EMI then was rather like it must have been at Rolls-Royce in the 1930s. They were terribly proud of their 'By Appointment' sign, of the dog-and-gramophone label of HMV, and so on. They paid abysmally, but then you were supposed to be privileged to be a member of the company, as in the BBC today but more so.

As for formality, it was rather like working in the Civil Service. Everyone wore a suit and a tie; there was no slopping around in jeans as there is today. You couldn't even take your tie off in the studio, and the engineers wore white coats which made them look like surgical assistants. I remember one, Peter Bown, now at the top of his profession, who only had one suit, and that was the demob suit a grateful nation had bestowed on him; he had to wear the wretched thing to work every day.

This code applied to artists too. Even the jazz drummers would be playing in collars and ties. It was a rather stupid sort of snobbery, which could have ludicrous results. There was the occasion when Eddie Fisher, an enormous star, arrived at the main entrance. He was due to make a record, but he was wearing his American army uniform. Unfortunately he wasn't an officer, so the commissionaire sent him round to the back door. That was the status of 'other ranks' in those days!

But the big stars didn't often get treated that way. There was much more glamour about them then. They came in great big cars, and their refreshment was smoked salmon and champagne. You knew when a star was coming to the studio—there was a feeling in the air. And when someone like Jane Morgan came, she would look absolutely fabulous. She would be immaculately made-up, in a glittering fur and decorated with diamonds. That has all gone now. The big stars shuffle in wearing old jeans, looking no different from anyone else.

Often, the big stars were entertained, when they arrived, by Oscar's secretary, Judy Lockhart-Smith. One who always expected his tot of whisky was Robert Wilson, the Scottish tenor. Unfortunately our nightwatchman also fancied a drop and, having taken it, would add water to the bottle to make up the level. Judy, unknowing, poured Wilson a glass of this diluted liquid one day, and he took one sip and spat it out. He couldn't believe his own taste-buds!

Judy, as I said earlier, remained distinctly cool towards me for a long time. I found her attractive, but a trifle snooty and obviously upper-crust, and her first glance at me had been as though I was something the dog had brought in. In spite of her youth, she was very much the old-timer, and I was the sprog. We worked together in a kind of uneasy truce, with a fair helping of mutual apathy, which was an unlikely start for two people who were later to have a marvellous marriage.

But she got on well with our performers, and on top of her normal work would go and turn the music over, during recordings, for people like Kentner, Gerald Moore, Yehudi Menuhin, Rawicz and Landauer, and Solomon, the pianist. Not that that was always happy. Another of our performers, Ray Martin, had a little dachshund who wandered into the studio one day while Solomon was recording a sonata. Unfortunately, the beast wasn't studio-trained, and deposited a small pile of excreta beneath the piano. Solomon put his foot on the loud pedal, and—squish, right in it. He stalked out of the studio and refused to do any more recording that day.

That was the sort of trouble you never got with Sir Thomas Beecham. He was a lovely man, who lived nearby and who frequently recorded with us. On these occasions he would go for lunch in McWhirter's, the workers' restaurant next door, rather than the posh one up the road. It served very basic food—three shillings and ninepence for lunch, and an extra threepence if you had the joint. On one occasion he went in there and asked the serving lady if he could see the wine list. 'No wine, dear,' she said. 'I'll go and get you a nice drop of Tizer.' He didn't mind, because he was that sort of man. With Malcolm Sargent it was quite different. It always had to be the smoked salmon sandwiches and the champagne. He had his star status and liked to be kept separate from the 'peasants', whereas Beecham enjoyed being one of them.

Sargent's nickname, of course, was 'Flash Harry', and I remember one day, during a rehearsal of one of Beethoven's works, someone put the music for 'I'm Just Wild About Harry' on his rostrum while he was out of the studio. He came back, picked it up and said: 'I suppose this wouldn't be referring to one very famous conductor not very far from here, would it?'

Another conductor I worked with was Charles Mackerras. I had met him much earlier when we both got gigs playing the oboe in the stage band of *Don Giovanni* at Sadler's Wells. The band had to march across the stage and play in a balcony in full view of the audience, but conducted from the orchestra pit. We had to dress up in wigs and doublets and so on, and got extra money for doing so, for which I was only too grateful. There were two oboes in this band, Charles Mackerras and myself, with the difference that he was very good. Beside his, my playing was, to put it kindly, mediocre, but he was very friendly and very helpful. He was also learning to be a conductor with Sadler's Wells at that time, and in his spare hours he was collecting all the Gilbert and Sullivan music, of which he was a great fan.

Then, when Arthur Sullivan's music came out of copyright, he made the brilliant move of assembling various pieces from the different operas, arranging them for orchestra, and co-operating on the production of a ballet based on Sullivan's music. Its name was *Pineapple Poll;* it was a tremendous hit, and was promptly recorded by Len Smith on Columbia, using the Covent Garden orchestra.

Oscar was furious. 'You knew Charles Mackerras,' he told me accusingly. 'Why didn't you get *Pineapple Poll?*'

Lamely I replied: 'I knew he was doing something, but I didn't think twice about it.'

Oscar tried to recover the situation by recording it with the Sadler's Wells orchestra, also conducted by Charles Mackerras, but it wasn't nearly so good a recording.

The fact that we were allowed to do it at all was typical of EMI. Although we were all in the same building—Len Smith actually had the office opposite us—the different labels were still rivals. Every month, these rivals would meet at what was called a 'supplement meeting', to discuss what they were going to record the following month. The meetings were so called because the titles in question would be included in a supplement to the catalogue. Oscar was terribly suspicious of Columbia's Walter Legge, and would never reveal at these meetings what he was going to record on the classical side, until Walter had said his bit. He had good reason. If he chose to say: 'I'm going to record the Sinfonia Concertante by Dittersdorf next month,' then as likely as not Walter Legge would say: 'I'm awfully sorry, old chap. I did that last month. I haven't issued it yet because I've been keeping a stockpile of that and a couple of other pieces.' It would be rubbish, of course, but Legge would have thought that it was a good idea to record the piece, and he would walk out of the room and make a couple of quick telephone calls, and the whole thing would be fixed up. Eventually, Oscar got wise to this trick.

In addition to this, each label would have a monthly publishers' meeting. That was how we got to hear most of the new songs. They didn't have facilities for home recording then, of course, and it was generally their pluggers who came to see us, booked by Judy at fifteen-minute intervals, and sang and banged out their latest numbers on the grand piano in our office in the old Tin Pan Alley style. We would make notes and keep copies of the songs. It was great fun, like the old music hall, and was in the tradition of George Gershwin, who had done the same thing when he had been a song-plugger—not like the highly polished demo-tapes you get today.

These meetings would take place in the morning, and in the afternoon I would hold recording tests in Studio Two. Every half-hour there would be someone new to test—and in those days Judy knew much more about pop and jazz than I did. She used to take herself off to Paris and go to the Blue Note club, and was really into the whole scene.

But for most of the time, the business was far less dramatic than it is today. It was just another job, though an interesting enough one, and people outside didn't know or hear much about it. Certainly there was no feeling, as there is now, that everyone wanted to be a record producer.

Even the rivalry between the different EMI labels was usually pretty gentlemanly. We didn't go snooping into each other's files to find out what was happening. There was more of a parallel with British Leyland, where you might find someone who felt that he was 'once an Austin man, always an Austin man'. It was 'once a Columbia man, always a Columbia man'.

Oscar guarded his pigeon, Parlophone, like a mother hen, if that's not mixing the ornithology. No one could touch Oscar's Parlophone. On the other hand, there were some people who had been shoved around from label to label, and, since Parlophone had lost so many artists during the war, Oscar would still record for Columbia those he had handled in the past. Robert Wilson, for example, whom he recorded, was actually an HMV artist.

But there were certain fixed rules. For example, Parlophone would never record a musical show. That had to be on HMV. This differentiation between the labels extended into the shops. Today, records can be sold anywhere. Then, they could only be sold in record shops, and those shops had separate dealerships, one HMV, one Columbia, and so on. What's more, HMV were incredibly proud of their dealerships. They were so restrictive that HMV records could only be sold by HMV-accredited dealers, and they would only allow one in each town. They dished them out as sparingly as Rolls-Royce dealerships, and it was felt that you were highly honoured if you were allowed to put the sign of the dog and gramophone above your shop.

But it was stupid, because they were deliberately restricting their own trade, and in the end it broke down and they started selling HMV records through other outlets. That led to a huge row within EMI, and one man, who wanted to stick to the old ways, felt strongly enough about it to resign over the issue. It may seem silly in retrospect, but it emphasises the strength of feeling that people had in wanting to maintain their own individuality.

One of my first essays in this search for identity came in 1952, when I suggested to Peter Ustinov, my colleague in the London Baroque Society, that we make a record together. At that time, Peter was the *enfant terrible* of British actors, our answer to Orson Welles. Because he was always amusing people with his funny little pieces of mouth-music and so on, we decided to make a double-sided single, 'Mock Mozart' and 'Phoney Folk Lore'. The first was a mini-opera done in three minutes by Peter, and I labelled it 'The voices and noises of Peter Ustinov'. There was a harpsichord accompaniment by Anthony Hopkins, and Peter himself sang all the parts—the sopranos, the altos and the tenors.

For those days, that was pretty adventurous. We didn't have multi-track recording, of course, so in order to produce the four-part ensemble he had to sing with himself. We did that by dubbing from one tape on to another, mixing as we went. And of course it was all mono. Technically, it meant that we lost generations, the geometric quantities by which the signal-to-noise ratio rises. Perhaps I should explain at this point, for the non-technical, that the quality of recording on a tape is determined by the fineness of the molecules on the tape coating itself. The signal-to-noise ratio is the amount of good recording you get on a tape, compared with the background noise—the hiss, the rumble, the crackles—which derives from the sheer physical passing of the tape across the recording head.

That ratio deteriorates as you do more and more recording. So, while on the first recording the noise, let's say the hiss, may be perfectly tolerable, it becomes worse if you then re-record that on to a second tape. And so on. In fact, each time you do it, you worsen the signal-to-noise ratio to the power of two; you square it each time. If you do two recordings, the noise is four times louder. If you do three, it's nine times louder. In the case of the Ustinov record we made four recordings, and therefore it was sixteen times louder. But most people aren't aware of that noise, and I don't suppose those who bought the record even knew it was so high—though today's hi-fi maniacs certainly would.

The other big problem was that, although the idea of singing with himself was fine in theory, when I got Peter into the studio I found that he couldn't sing against another line, even his own. He was a 'follower', as many people are. The whole point of singing the parts in sync with himself was that he had to hear the previous voices he'd done and then sing a different line—but he would start 'following' himself on the previous lines.

So we had to do it in little bits. I would rush back and forth from the control room into the studio, saying things like: 'Now look, Peter, sing this bit—te dum te dum te dum—and start when I give you a hand signal like this.' That way he would remember it; I would give him the signal, and it would fit in.

It was a complicated, and long, and tedious process, but in the end it worked well. And the other side was far simpler, with Peter doing his standard 'party pieces' of imaginary folk songs. But then it came to the monthly supplement meeting at EMI, and when we arrived at 'Mock Mozart' every eye turned towards me in something akin to horror.

'What's this, George?'

'Peter Ustinov!!??'

'What do you think you're up to, George?'

'It doesn't make sense. No one's ever made a recording like this before.'

Oscar backed me up, but they all clearly thought I was mad, and I had to argue with everyone there to convince them the record had a chance. It was touch and go whether it would be released at all; but happily I had my pay-off. A week after it was issued, the manager of the Oxford Street shop rang me up and said: 'That Peter Ustinov record—did you make it?'

'Yes,' I said, wondering what new attack I would have to face.

Instead he said, 'Can you help me get some new supplies? I've already sold two hundred, and I can't get any more.' (That manager, incidentally, was Ron White, now managing director of EMI's publishing house.)

So I was able with great glee to go back to my masters and tell them: 'You didn't press enough records.' I think they had originally only pressed three hundred. But by the time they had pressed more, the demand had dropped anyway. That was another lesson well learnt. Of course, by today's standards, three hundred records sounds pitifully few. But a lot of records then only sold perhaps a hundred and eighty; that was still an economically viable number since the costs of recording were not high, while the retail prices of the records were very high indeed.

On top of that, we wouldn't actually pay someone like Peter an advance. He, in fact, got a royalty of 5%, which was the highest we ever paid in those days. Then again, the studio costs were negligible, since the studios were there anyway. The largest expenses on that recording were the hire of the harpsichord, at about fifteen pounds and a similar fee to Anthony Hopkins for playing it. So one only needed to sell two or three hundred records at seven shillings each in order to break even.

Making a record with someone like Peter was an exception anyway, since most artists, especially singers, were under exclusive contracts to the record companies. Important artists would have contracts for about two years, with probably an option for a further three. What they got out of it was a guarantee that they would have records out every so often. Some would get an advance on royalties, but they would have to be pretty good to get that, since EMI was as mean with its artists as with its permanent staff. The average royalty was a penny a record, for a single, with a top royalty of 5%. So the artists' commitment to the company was pretty low.

The variety of those artists was enormous. In the same week I might be recording Bob and Alf Pearson, of 'My Brother and I' fame, Dick Bentley and Joy Nichols from 'Take It from Here', the Covent Garden orchestra, Tommy Reilly and his harmonica, Eve

Boswell, and Charles Williams, who conducted the Queen's Hall Light Orchestra as well as Sidney Torch.

Charles, who wrote 'The Dream of Olwen', I remember particularly for the windfall he once had. He wrote a number of pieces for background music, and got regular payments for his compositions through the Performing Right Society. Suddenly, for no apparent reason, one of these payments was a vast sum, something like £5000. It turned out that one of his pieces, a semi-religious kind of tune, had been picked up by a television station in America for use as their signature tune. No one had told him!

Or I might be recording Freddie Randall and his Jazz Band, because, far from the hallowed halls of classicism, I now found myself recording all Parlophone's jazz artists, despite my early contretemps with Humph. There was Graeme Bell and his Dixieland Jazz Band, Joe Daniels and his Hot Shots, Jack Parnell—and Johnny Dankworth and his Seven.

In fact, one of the first hit records I ever made was with John. It was called 'Experiments with Mice', and was based on the 'Three Blind Mice' tune. He and Cleo Laine were to become very close friends of mine, and I did a lot of recordings with him. Cleo, who wasn't married to him at that time, was the singer in the band. The nice thing about John and Cleo is that they've been in the business as long as I have. They, like me, have seen all the rough ends of it. They've done a lot of touring, have been through all the financial ups and downs, and now have emerged as great artists on the world stage. A delightful irony is that in the early days Cleo was always considered to have too good a voice to be successful; it's a double pleasure to see that sort of talent winning through.

John was a fanatically hard worker, but that could have funny consequences. He was once preparing some sort of jazz concerto for Matyas Seiber at the Festival Hall, and working with Dave Lindup, his arranger, who always went with the band on tour. Because they had this work to complete, John booked into a hotel room, and asked specially if he and Dave could share a room, so that they could work overnight. The clerk looked slightly doubtful, probably nursing private suspicions about the lives of musicians, but they went upstairs and thought no more about it.

That night they started work as soon as they got back from the gig, and at about four or five in the morning Dave turned to John and said: 'I'm falling asleep. I can't do any more. I've just got to have some sleep.' So he undressed and fell into one of the room's twin beds, while John went on working.

By about seven in the morning John, too, started to feel a bit tired, but it was too late to go to bed, so he just packed it in, showered, dressed, and went down to breakfast. It was only when he got to the toast and marmalade that he realised that not only had he asked to share a room with Dave, but also, as the staff would quickly notice, only one bed had been slept in. They got some very odd looks as they left that morning.

John, for obvious reasons, was always very upset by racialist remarks, and would lay into anyone who made them. But he can still laugh at the day he went to a local greengrocer's to buy some fruit. He saw some nice-looking grapes, and told the man: 'I'll have a couple of pounds of those grapes. They look jolly good.'

But when the crate was taken out, he noticed 'South African' on the side, and thought to himself: Why should I have those? So he said: 'No, hang on a minute. Those grapes come from South Africa, don't they? On second thoughts, I don't think I'll have them.'

The man looked at him coolly and replied: 'Well, perhaps you're right, sir. You never know what nig-nog's been handling them, do you?'

Following 'Experiments with Mice', the next big record we had with John was 'African Waltz'. It was written by a budding young songwriter, of whom nobody was taking a great deal of notice, called Galt MacDermot. We were to do a number of his other songs, including 'I Know a Man' with Rolf Harris. This, of course, was long before he wrote the show which made him a millionaire—*Hair*.

He was just one of the people who were always hanging round publishers' offices in Denmark Street, trying to sell their songs.

In those days, this was literally what happened. Today, everything is controlled by the record companies, and even the publishers are owned by them. But then, the publishers were a very strong force. If they took up a songwriter, or accepted one of his songs, it was their plugging, to the record companies and the radio people, which gave it a chance of being a hit. If you didn't have a publisher behind you, you might as well not bother to write at all. So songwriters would literally hang around the publishers' doors, hoping for an interview with the people running them, as in later years they did with the record companies. I was continually fending off people—I still do, I suppose—because if you listened to absolutely everything that people brought to you, there wouldn't be any time to make records. Today, what we generally do is to have a lot of people who listen to the stuff and recommend it if they like it. And if it's something very special, we listen to it all ourselves.

Another reason why the publishers were so strong was that there was not a rash of singer-songwriters as there is today. The writers and the performers were two different types of people. The performers were always looking out for good material, and the writers were always trying to get their songs played by great performers. So a songwriter would try to get himself accepted by a publisher who had the necessary clout to go to a big artist.

In turn, the artists were desperate for number-one songs, and they would blame us if they heard about someone else getting one which they felt they should have had. For example, Norman Newell, who handled the pop side of Columbia, made a hit record of 'Moon River' with Danny Williams. We on Parlophone didn't record it at all, so it would have been quite possible for Eve Boswell, one of our artists, to round on me and demand: 'Why didn't I see "Moon River"? Why haven't I recorded that?' And she would have had every justification for doing so.

In fact, 'Moon River' was the subject of a great gaffe on the part of my assistant, Ron Richards. I sent him to see the film to report if there was any good music in it. He sat all through it, and then sent me a memo saying that 'there was some incidental music, but nothing worthwhile'!

But we all make those mistakes. As I became more entrenched in the business, I started to get to know the journalists, disc jockeys and so on, and one I was particularly friendly with was Noel Whitcomb of the *Daily Mirror*. A buzz had started going round the business about some kids playing in coffee bars, and Noel and I decided to go and have a look. So, one evening in 1957, we went to the 2i's coffee bar in Soho, to see a new act, Tommy Steele and the Vipers Skiffle Group. We sat with our coffee and watched this genial young man bounce on to the stage with his guitar over his pelvis, and my immediate impression was that he was a blond cardboard imitation of Elvis Presley. Noel thought the same. Tommy had a lot of energy, but his voice didn't sound too great—what little I could hear of it: for the Vipers were extremely loud and he wasn't.

By today's standards the act was positively matronly, but for those days it was quite shocking, rather like musical masturbation; the pelvic gyrations quite turned me off, especially as I was still thinking only in terms of voices. Noel agreed, 'There's nothing there', so I let Tommy Steele pass.

On the other hand, I liked the group, and thought they had great guts, so I signed them to a recording contract, and made a lot of successful records with them. But passing over Tommy Steele was obviously a big goof, especially since Decca came down the following day, signed him up, and made a great star out of him. I remember confessing to Sir Joseph Lockwood, who by then had taken over EMI, that I had turned down Tommy Steele, and he was clearly very upset by the revelation. I should have kept quiet. In fact, I have recorded Tommy since then, and we became good friends, but that doesn't wipe out the original mistake.

On the other hand, people can get blamed unfairly. The classic example is Dick Rowe, of Decca. He became known as 'the man who turned down the Beatles', and he carries that cross to his grave. But it is quite unfair, because in fact everyone in England had turned down the Beatles. The only difference with Dick Rowe was that he had enough nous to give them not one, but two recording tests. He really was considering taking them. So instead of being indicted for turning them down, he should be praised for giving them such serious consideration when others were turning them down out of hand.

By about 1954 I was doing virtually everything on Parlophone, and Oscar was doing very little. Lockwood had become chairman of EMI, and that was like a breath of fresh air in the company. For a while he was terribly unpopular, because he was a ruthless man. But he certainly pulled EMI up by its bootlaces and made it work.

In July of that year I passed my driving test and launched into the four-wheeled world. The vehicle in question was a 1935 Austin Ten Cambridge saloon, which cost me a whole sixty pounds. It was hardly immaculate, but in those days it was good enough to take the test in, and I was so elated about passing that, when I got back to the office, I offered to drive Oscar home to Arkwright Road in Hampstead, not far from the studios.

He graciously accepted and at six o'clock we set off. We were driving happily along the Finchley Road, and approaching the traffic lights by the John Barnes department store, when, like the good driver I was now proud to be, I changed down from top gear into third. As I did so, the gear lever, which was floor-mounted and quite long, with a spherical knob on top, came completely away in my hand.

With some aplomb, I trust, I handed Oscar the amputated limb of my new toy and said: 'Would you mind holding that for a moment?' Then I steered gently into the kerb. I was irretrievably stuck in third gear. I was humiliated. And Oscar went home by taxi.

If I was unhappy with that early motoring experience, I was even less content with the way things were going at EMI. For a start, there was the question of wages, or the lack of them. After three years, my pay had risen to a pauperly £13 9s 3d, which meant that after deductions I took home £12 6s 8d. EMI always paid very badly, believing that because they were giving you an interesting job you should subsidise them. Even Oscar was never well paid, and after fifty years' service with them, during which he had invented a number of things they used, his pay-off was an *Encyclopaedia Britannica*. That was all he had to show for it.

So it wasn't surprising that when, during 1954, Frank Lee of Decca offered me a job at £1200 a year, I was only too keen to accept. My first daughter, Alexis, known as 'Bundy', had been born the year before, and my economic life was so tight I had real cash-trickle problems. I went to C. H. Thomas, the managing director of EMI Records and said: 'I've enjoyed working here, thank you very much, but the money just isn't good enough. So I've accepted another post.'

Now, I said this with no feeling at all that I was laying the basis for a haggle. I didn't see it as a way of screwing more money out of them. In those days I had a rather scrupulous moral attitude to that sort of thing, which, on reflection, may have been a bit naive on my part.

But Thomas, worldly-wise, clearly saw it otherwise. 'Don't you think you're being rather unfair?' he asked.

'How?'

'In not allowing us to compete,' he said.

'I don't think that comes into it,' I said, determined to allow my naivety to show. 'If you wanted to pay me more money, you would've done.'

'Well,' he said, 'I don't want to lose you, so I'll match the offer.'

In fact, I think he only gave me £1100 in the end, which didn't quite match it, but it did go with a promise that when Oscar retired I would take over Parlophone, if Thomas had his way. I think this is what tipped the scales for me, since it was by no means certain what would happen after Oscar departed, and I had told Thomas that I didn't want to become some old fuddy-duddy, a mere cog, and that I wanted to do something while I was still young. So I accepted, and had to ring Frank Lee at Decca to tell him I wasn't coming after all. Not surprisingly, he was rather upset.

But although I stayed at EMI, there were other reasons for my not being too happy with them. My diary for that time contains a note for a memo I was sending to the management. It says: 'The first concrete case is that of our last year's best-seller, Ron Goodwin. He is particularly bitter about the exploitation, in that to date, of his last three records we issued—and he's only made six in all—only one has ever been heard on the air.

'This factor, coupled with the unfortunate representation of Parlophone in America, which to British artists is far worse than no representation at all, has made Ron decline to sign the option on his contract, which is due at the end of November. The loss of such an artist would be catastrophic.'

I was doubly upset because Ron had become a good personal friend, so much so that he was later to be the best man at my wedding to Judy. He was an up-and-coming arranger who had been introduced to me by Dick James in 1953, the year after I had started recording Dick. Dick was a band singer, as Eve Boswell was, and was one of the first artists I recorded as my own, rather than Oscar's. I made some successful records with him, like 'Robin Hood', but having a family he didn't like touring the country, and eventually gave up singing in music halls and became a song-plugger working for the publisher Sidney Bron, father of Eleanor. In 1953, however, he was still singing, and suggested using young Ron Goodwin (now one of our best film composers) as the arranger for his records.

I was equally upset about what happened with another friend, Kenneth McKellar. A similar diary note says: 'We have lost the services of a brilliant young Scottish tenor, whom we recorded two years ago. I am certain that with the right backing he could have been as big a success as Robert Wilson. I am certain that the company will, in a very short time, be regretting his departure.

He prefers the Decca label because they are so much more alive in supporting and publicity.

'In explanation he complained: "It isn't so bad on HMV or Columbia, but you never see any evidence of Parlophone in any of the leading record shops." Although we outwardly deny this, I firmly believe this to be true.'

This note was at the end of 1954, but I had first met Kenneth in 1947, when he was studying forestry at Aberdeen University, where my first wife used to sing in the choir. While I was at the Guildhall he was at the Royal College of Music in London, and often used to come to stay with us in Acton, where I remember him helping me to build a fireplace.

After I joined Parlophone I persuaded him to come and do a recording test at Abbey Road. He had a very fine voice, and between 1951 and 1955 I recorded eight titles with him; none of them was very successful, partly because of general lack of backing, and partly, I suppose, because of Oscar's ties with Robert Wilson. Wilson was still the king in Oscar's eyes, and since Parlophone had a virtual monopoly of Scottish music he was *the* voice of Scotland, a position from which Kenneth was eventually to oust him. But Oscar was about to retire, and if I got his job I was really banking on having Kenneth. So I told him: 'I'm preparing a contract for you. We'll go great guns. I'm hoping to use you as a kind of pivot for the plans I have.'

Imagine my disappointment when he told me that he'd had an offer from Decca which he couldn't refuse, and that he didn't want to continue with Parlophone. It wasn't even a question of raising our offer. He had made up his mind. He'd had a firm offer from a very good and powerful label, Decca, whereas Parlophone was a tinpot little label, which in any case was about to lose its chief, with the prospect of being run by a man who was little more than a music student. So I couldn't blame him.

Then, in the spring of 1955, Oscar finally retired and went off with his encyclopaedia, and Sir Joseph Lockwood confirmed that

I was to be the new head of Parlophone. It was quite adventurous of him. I was a fairly brash young man, without much experience in the record business. But for me, it was an unbelievable chance. I was boss of a whole record label. I was on my own.

4

ALL YOU NEED IS EARS

WE ONCE went on holiday to Portugal, where we rented a villa that was straight out of *House and Garden*. Absolutely beautiful. It was built in concrete, with lovely curving walls and all the rest of it. Most dramatic of all was the dining-room. It was about sixteen feet across, and was built in a circle—like a drum, but in more ways than one. The floor was tiled, the walls were painted white, the ceiling was hard, and there were no curtains or soft coverings of any kind.

To eat in that room was sheer agony. Every word reverberated and met in the middle, where the table stood. The slightest clatter of a knife and fork immediately destroyed all the consonants of the people talking to you, and you couldn't make out a thing they were saying. From an acoustic point of view it was the worst possible design that could have been dreamed up, but it wasn't unique. I am continually amazed at how architects still put up buildings without any thought about the acoustics, which, after all, are just as important a factor as pretty wallpaper in making a place habitable.

Nor are the architects alone. Many people in the recording industry, many would-be producers, have little idea about the principles which govern the commodity in which they are dealing, namely sound. So this chapter is devoted to a discussion of some of those basic principles, most of which are founded on common sense.

What is sound? It is the transmission of pressure waves. The human being receives those waves through his ears, organs specially adapted to interpreting them. The waves are comparatively low-frequency, compared with the electromagnetic waves of radio and light, and unlike them cannot travel through a void. Sound waves require a medium, whether it be air, water, metal or whatever.

The human ear can respond to sound waves ranging from roughly twenty hertz (that is, vibrations per second) up to about 20,000 hertz if the hearer is young and very fit. A dog can go up to 25,000 or 30,000 hertz, which is why you can call a dog on a high-pitched whistle whose sound the human ear can't detect. The pitch of a note in music is determined by the number of times per second that the instrument is vibrating. For example, a tuning fork vibrating 440 times a second will give you a note equivalent to middle A on the piano. What's more, all the notes we use have a sympathetic relationship with one another, which is why our music is so gloriously mathematical. The A one octave above middle A will vibrate at 880 hertz or cycles per second, and the A below it at 220.

Of course, those notes that we select for musical use are not the only ones. Any one cycle can be broken down into fractions, so that there are in theory an infinite number of notes. But for convenience we use only a few of them, and our normal scale divides the octave—that is, the range between any one note and the note that is exactly twice, or exactly half, its frequency—into twelve equal divisions. On a piano, those are the seven white keys and the five black keys.

Curiously, that division of the octave into twelve equal semitones is not a natural division, because the difference between the notes is not an equal one in real terms, but a percentage difference. In other words, the relationship of A to A sharp should be the same as the relationship of A sharp to B, of B to C and so on.

Today's scale is the way it is because we have made it so. Before Bach's time, we followed our hearts, and the natural laws of music, and music was comparatively simple. It rarely went outside the natural keys. Violins and keyboard instruments were always tuned in a proper harmonic fashion. The limitation to that was that you couldn't roam outside your nearby keys, because—while the instrument sounded right in a particular key—the moment you moved away from that into a strange key, it sounded out of tune, since the relationship of one note to another had changed.

So they dreamed up the idea of making all the semitones equal. That meant altering the natural harmonic sense, but it did have the virtue of enabling musicians to work in all sorts of keys. That was why Bach wrote *The Well-tempered Klavier*, which was a series of piano works written specifically to demonstrate how the new system allowed you to play in every key available—twelve minor and twelve major. It was also a demonstration of Bach's genius.

All this musical knowledge is not just abstruse and irrelevant. It can be absolutely vital in modern recording. For example, a recording machine has to travel at a certain speed in order to work. If that speed varies at all, the pitch of the music changes, according to the natural laws that link the frequency to the note. A record-player that has an uneven speed will vary the pitch and produce a nasty 'wow', and in the same way the tape in a tape machine has to run very, very steadily.

Today, professional tapes run at either fifteen or thirty inches a second, and there's only a tiny percentage of tolerance in those speeds if the notes are not to vary noticeably. But sometimes we have deliberately to alter that speed in order to alter the pitch of something we have recorded. On the *Sgt. Pepper* film I recorded one particular piece of music which caused a bit of a problem. When I listened to it, I realised the key was a bit unsuitable for the singer, and in addition the music sounded a bit slow. So I wanted to speed it up. But I've got a bit of a thing about keys. I hate music that is 'in the cracks'—in other words, not in any particular key. So I said: 'O.K., if we're going to speed it up, we'll speed it up by an exact semitone.'

Now fortunately we had in the studio a device that gave us

a digital read-out of the speed of the tape machine. We had been running at thirty inches a second, so the tape operator asked me, 'If you want a semitone up, what speed do I play the machine in order to get that?'

Whipping out my little pocket calculator I was able to tell him to increase the speed from thirty inches a second to 31.78, which was an increase of 5.9463%. That was the speed at which to play the machine in order to be precisely, statistically and logically a semitone up, without even listening to it. In some astonishment he asked: 'How on earth did you work that out?' The answer was that anyone can do it, because the percentage increase in each semitone is the same. It's like compound interest at the bank: 6% on £100 gives you £106. But 6% on *that* gives you something more than £112.

It's all part of the basic laws of harmonics. For instance, each scale on the piano has what we call a 'dominant'. In the scale of C, it's G that is the dominant. In lay terms, it's the chord that is preparatory for the final tonic chord—or, put simpler still, it's the note, having sung which, there is only one final note you *can* follow with. In any scale, that dominant is one and a half times the frequency of the bottom note. The dominant in the scale of A is E. So, as middle A is 440 hertz, the E above it must be 660. And these musical truths are linked to straightforward mechanical laws. (But, in the even-tempered scale, that E is 659.25 hertz.)

This is what happens. Take a violin or guitar string, and pluck it, and it will utter a certain note. Now put your finger halfway along it; instead of vibrating like a bowstring it will vibrate on either side of your finger. In fact, if you touch it very lightly, it will vibrate in the form of an S—the bottom bit will be going out as the top bit is going in. The note you hear will be precisely an octave above the note you heard the first time.

If you now put your finger a third of the way up the string, and pluck it, the vibration will be snake-like, and you will hear three times the original note. It will vibrate three times faster simply because it is three times shorter. So, if the original note was, say, the A below middle A, which is 220 hertz, then the second note would be 440, which is middle A, and the third would be 660. That note, you will find, is the dominant, in this case the E that I was talking about before: and that relationship works for any note you choose. It's a matter of natural harmonics.

Everything has its own resonant frequency. For example, if you take a reed, such as you use in an oboe, it will vibrate in its own unique way. And the logical, mathematical laws that apply to the lengths of strings also apply to all instruments. A wind instrument is just a length of tubing. You have a mouthpiece at one end in order to make it resonate, and the longer the horn, the lower the note. That's why an organ pipe has to be sixty-four feet long in order to produce the bottom octave. There's no way of getting round it. Similarly, that's why a contrabassoon has such a lot of tubing. The tubes go up, down and all round, and it's twice the length of an ordinary bassoon, as it has to be in order to reach the bottom range. Again, the French horn, if you unravelled all its tubing like spaghetti and stretched it out, would be about sixteen feet long. That would obviously be much too difficult to handle, which is why they wrap it up the way it is. Trumpets, too, are curled round, and are really quite long. The exception is the piccolo trumpet, which I used on the Beatles' 'Penny Lane' recording. It plays an octave above an ordinary trumpet, and is therefore half the length, almost like a toy trumpet—about ten inches long. In all these cases, it is the length of the horn which determines the frequencies the instrument will give.

But now comes the question of whether those frequencies will be tuneful or not. What is 'being tuneful'? Since all sounds are vibrations, you can draw a picture of them expressed in terms of waves, and tuneful sounds are those which are fairly regular in their frequencies. Noises are irregular sounds. But the perfect wave, which is absolutely regular, is boring. That's why pure synthesiser sound is the most boring in the world. It's a pure note, always in tune, and completely harmonious. My feelings about that may have a lot to do with the fact that I'm not a great stickler for being in tune. I think that people who are tend sometimes to overdo it. It may sound an Irishism, but I think that being out of tune, provided it's tuneful, is in itself an attraction.

Unlike the synthesiser, no human voice is ever perfectly in tune. No one ever sings an exact note that is completely the right frequency for as long as it lasts. The voice bends on either side of the correct frequency, and that's what is called 'vibrato'. Some singers have a very wide vibrato, so that, if they're trying to sing middle A, instead of hitting a pure 440 hertz they will fluctuate between about 430 and 450, occasionally hitting 440. They are going through it, straddling it, firing their guns on both sides of the target but rarely hitting it. To me, a really wide vibrato is extremely offensive to hear; but a good vibrato, which doesn't veer off the proper frequency too much, is fine. Besides, as I said, it's not possible to sing without some vibrato. Humans are not mathematically accurate beings—we can never draw an exactly straight line.

Nor is the vibrato always equally balanced on either side of the note. Some people in straddling the note favour one emphasis or the other, a little above, or a little below. That means they always sing slightly sharp or slightly flat, and it's that slight variation which determines whether a person is singing in tune or not.

I believe that it all depends upon the kind of voice a person has. I've known singers whose voices will still sound good, no matter how out of tune they are. Equally, there are people, myself included, who sound awful no matter how much in tune they sing.

Mind you, I've had artists who are great sticklers for being in tune. I record them, and then say: 'That's great. Come in and listen to it.' They come to the control room and listen, and then look at me in amazement and say: 'But I'm not singing that in tune.' Perhaps it doesn't square with what they expect from my reputation—I don't know; but I tell them, 'Well, I know it's a little bit under the note, but it sounds good. If you want to sing it a little more on the note, it won't make any difference to me; but I quite like it as it is.' Then they become astounded, and worry that I'm not being too particular about being dead in tune. But I don't think it's that important. What matters is whether the sound is offensive or good. After all, in jazz there are many notes, blue notes, which sound great simply because they are out of tune. So 'being in tune' is a matter of degree, and a matter of taste.

Today, in recording, it's possible to alter the pitch of a person's voice in relation to the backing. This can be done with an instrument called an Eventide Harmoniser, with which you can jack the recording up or down to make the singer sing at a different pitch all the way through. Of course, if he varies his pitch, so that one note is in tune and the next is not, you have a problem! But if, for example, he sings consistently flat, you can make him more in tune, a technique unheard of in the earlier days of recording.

The fact remains, however, that being in tune is not a scientific achievement, but a human one. Every instrument has a degree of tuning which depends upon the human ear—even the oboe, the instrument to which the rest of the orchestra tunes itself. It depends on the quality of the reed which the player puts into the instrument, and the length of the reed in the instrument itself. After that, the player's intonation will vary, but it's his ear which tells him whether he's playing in tune or not. Stringed instruments, of course, have to be tuned before a concert, and that, too, depends on the players' ears. The worst of all is the harp, because every string has to be tuned individually before it can be played, which is why the harp player comes in about an hour before a performance to tune up.

The only time the orchestra doesn't tune to the oboe is when there is a piano. Then it generally tunes to that, because tuning it is obviously even more of a chore than tuning the harp. Sometimes the string players will come in to me and say: 'That piano sounds sharp.' But they still have to tune to it. Quite often, too, the piano-tuners sharpen the notes a little as they go up the octaves, sacrificing absolute accuracy in order to make the piano sound 'brilliant' on the top.

What all this emphasises is that the important thing is for instruments, whether individually or as a whole orchestra, to be in tune with themselves. For example, it doesn't matter if middle A, which should ideally be tuned at 440, is actually tuned at 443. It will just be slightly sharper, but that's all right as long as everything else fits (in other words, the A above it must now be 886). A note is neither good nor bad in itself. What matters is the relationship between one note and another, which determines our harmonic sense.

But then another factor comes into play: the conditions in which you are hearing the sound. When someone talks to you, his voice is coming through the air (unless you're having an underwater conversation!) and being picked up by two receivers, your ears, one on each side; the fact that you can move your head around to balance the two inputs gives you a directional sense, rather like a range-finder. But in normal conditions you don't only hear the voice coming directly at you. It is also reflected off the walls, the windows, and the table or whatever other hard objects are in the room. If the room had no reflective surfaces, the voice would sound very different. Indeed, if you were ten thousand feet up, in still air, and the speaker turned his head away, you wouldn't hear the voice at all.

In fact, for sound-measuring tests, they have built what are called anechoic chambers, in which all the reflective surfaces have been eliminated, and the walls and ceiling covered in absorptive material. The only sound you can hear is the direct sound from one source to a receiver. I have been in one, and it's most uncanny. It would quickly drive you mad. Nothing is more terrifying than a totally silent room.

Without reflective surfaces, the voice is very directional, particularly in the higher frequencies. It's the same with a hi-fi player. Most loudspeakers have inside them a second, small loudspeaker called a 'tweeter', which responds to the high frequencies. If you move away from the direct beam of that tweeter, the torchlight beam, as it were, you won't hear, for instance, the real crispness of a cymbal. Bass sounds, on the other hand, are very diffuse, and come from all directions.

What this all adds up to is that the sound you hear will vary considerably according to the quality of the surfaces in the room you are listening in. Imagine sound being like a ray of light. Then imagine being in a room whose walls were covered with mirrors, and switching on a searchlight. It would dazzle you. In exactly the same way, the ear is dazzled by too many reflections. This 'reverberation' is what children delight in when they go into a tunnel, or under the arch of a bridge, and shout. The voice bounces back and forth around the hard surfaces until it gradually loses impetus and dies. The difference between that and echo is that echo is a repeat of a voice or sound, whereas reverberation is a continuation of that sound by means of its energy rebounding and rebounding.

In a studio, you're going to get unfortunate results if those reflections keep coming back in the same way. You get a nasty build-up of frequencies which changes the characteristic of the sound, making it messy, diffuse and very difficult to record. The ideal way of building reflective surfaces for acoustic purposes in recording is to make them refract the sound. You make the sound waves bounce off in a new direction rather than return the way they came. The ideal studio, therefore, is one in which the walls are never parallel. It's also preferable for them never to be straight. With continuous convex surfaces, the sound will hit one part of the surface and return in a particular way, but if it hits another part of the surface it will take an entirely new direction.

The other way to get round the build-up of sound is to have walls which absorb it rather than reflect it at all. You can have curtains and carpets, which kill off some of the high frequencies, and bass absorbers which take care of the heavy, low frequencies. For some of today's heavy rock groups you really need studios where the walls will absorb some of the aural energy. For instance, in our Number Two studio at AIR we have around the walls a number of boxes, all of different shapes and dimensions; each has a little lead weight, fitted in the centre of the front of the box. The boxes are tuned so that their fronts vibrate in sympathy with the bass frequencies, absorbing the impact. It's rather like a boxer taking a punch. They don't resonate and make any noise themselves, but they do move, and in doing so absorb the sound. There are other ways of achieving this, too. In America, they have what are called 'bass traps'—chimney-like affairs filled with hanging absorbent material, which again is tuned to absorb the bass frequencies.

The trouble is, the ideal studio doesn't exist, because different kinds of sound require different reverberation periods. Voices, for example, need a certain amount of natural reverberation, and in recording you usually add artificially what is known as 'echo', although it isn't really echo at all. Then again, a string ensemble needs a longer reverberation period than a rhythm section, which normally needs a very short period. We refer to this as the difference between a 'live' sound and a 'dead' or 'dry' sound.

A very large studio, like Number One at Abbey Road, which had a very long reverberation period of about two and half seconds, was great for recording an orchestra. It gave a beautiful sound to the strings. But put a rhythm section in there, and not only would you muck up the sound of the rhythm section itself, but also the sound of it would make its way on to the violin microphones, where you could never get rid of it. If you have too much reverberation on drums, they swim all over the place and become very muddy. In a live recording studio, all the sounds merge, and you can't discern one from the other.

To counteract this, people have built studios whose walls absorb all the sound. But they are uncomfortable to play in. The reason why people like singing in the bath, and reckon that they are the next thing to Gigli while so doing, is that their voices come back at them nicely off the reflective surfaces. In the same way, a violin player likes to hear himself coming back off the walls, and also to hear what the other players are doing. He likes to be able to hear that he is playing in tune with the rest, so that they are a team. In a studio where all the sounds are being absorbed he won't be able to hear himself or his friends, so that he might as well be playing alone among eighty other people who just happen to be there. That is not an orchestra.

So a studio has to be a compromise. At AIR, we generally have a hard floor and a fairly reflective ceiling at the string end of the studios. We keep one end of the studio live, and the other, where I normally put the rhythm section, dead. The studios which we have built in Montserrat aren't really for strings, but for the kind of instruments a rock group uses. On the other hand, although these tend to be electric, there are still many acoustic instruments used, such as guitars, piano and drums. Therefore, since I like a moderately live drum sound as long as it doesn't affect the other instruments, we will still keep a live end in the studio.

This awareness of acoustics is by no means something rarefied or only for the record producer. If only more people would listen to what rooms are doing to sounds, and therefore be aware that they are not hearing them properly, I'm certain that the pressure would make architects pay more attention to acoustics in the design of houses, restaurants, cinemas and auditoriums. In fact, if people were generally more aware of the quality of sound, they might make designers of television sets take more trouble with their sound—which is, frankly, abysmal. After all, I think even the men who built our old cathedrals benefited from their own experience. I don't think they knew anything about the technicalities of it, but having built one that sounded good they probably said: 'That sounds fine. Let's build another one like it.'

Cathedrals, of course, have enormous reverberation times, sometimes as long as four or five seconds. That's because of the huge volume of air and the distance between surfaces—most of which, stonework and glass, are highly reflective. Of course, that would be hopeless for a pop group, but it's marvellous for choral work. The reason is that it has the effect of sustaining the voice and its overtones. If you have a choir with a lot of voices, everyone won't be singing at the same frequency. If they did, it would sound like one voice. It's the same with a violin section. Twenty violins are not playing exactly the same, either in intonation or vibrato. Each is varying his vibrato slightly, both in pitch and duration, and the little frequencies beat against each other to produce a nice liquid sound. Likewise, the members of a choir will be singing slightly different intonations all the way through, and even the few bum notes will become merged and smoothed out. That's part of the delight of a good choir.

Of course, in a place like a cathedral you do get a multiplication of sounds, because of the long reverberation period, and if you were singing a very fast, bitty piece which required a great deal of articulation, like some of the Gilbert and Sullivan songs, it would sound awful. But for something like Gregorian chant it's marvellous, because it's a gradual diminution of sound. The walls nearest you reflect the sound first, and are louder; those from the far surfaces are weaker. The result is a progressive decay of sound.

The reverse happens if, at home, you take your hi-fi into a small room with a lot of resonant material, without much in the way of curtains, carpets or upholstery. You won't have any breathing space between the original sound and the kick-back off the walls, and the effect is going to be very unpleasant. A good rule of thumb is that the smaller the room, the deader it should be.

So next time you listen to a record, think about that. Think about the way you're listening, and think what you're listening to—not just the original sound, but what it's doing within the room. Not just the original sound on the record itself, either, but what has been added to it by means of studio acoustics and artificial reverberation. That way you will start to understand sound.

The real hi-fi buff, of course, does know a lot about acoustics. He will study recordings in great depth, far more than I do—but then, I am not a hi-fi buff. He will have special speakers in his living-room, and make everything subservient to that. He'll put the chairs in special positions, and he'll make sure the carpet is the right size and depth and so on. I'm sure his wife has a terrible time. You'll go into his room one evening, and he'll play you a record and say: 'Listen to that triangle. Isn't it fantastic?' Well, it will be fantastic, but as far as I'm concerned, life's too short for all that. If he is concentrating too much on listening for the triangle, he may be missing out on the piece of music as a whole. The technical may take over from the artistic.

On the other hand, if people get their kicks that way, it's fine by me, and as a producer I have to cater for them. It's easy to sneer at them, but in a way they are our pioneers. We have to think of them when we're making records, and thank goodness we do, because without them we would still have rotten sound. Pick up a copy of the *Gramophone* and look at the reviews of the latest recordings. Today, standards generally have become so high that if the critic is to differentiate between one record and another he must go into these technical factors. He may have been listening to two different performances of Rachmaninov's Second Piano Concerto, and he'll write something like: 'This one has a lovely gradation of tone from the pianist. The orchestra is finely balanced, and I love the conductor's reading because he takes the tempo exactly right. However, the recording is muddy.' Or he might write: 'The sound quality was superb. The living presence came over on this recording. You could hear the third flute player coughing in the pause.'

That leads to the whole question of what you are aiming to produce when you make a record. The trouble is that there have always been so many floating standards in music. When I started in the business, certainly in the making of classical records, the aim was to recreate on record the exact sound that you would get in a good auditorium, listening to a live performance. But then you have to ask who is listening? And in which concert hall? There is no standard,

although in the early days we went to tremendous lengths in search
of whatever standard it was, even to the extent of using just one microphone and arranging the players around it in such a way that it
was completely natural.

That leads to another problem. In real life, we have two ears, not
one; so you really ought to have two microphones. Try listening to
something with just one ear, and you'll hear what an enormous difference it makes. That's the effect of having only one mike. When
people go into a studio for the first time, they tend to put their head
down and listen to what the mike's listening to. They forget that they
have two ears, whereas the mike only has one. So when I want to
listen to what a mike's doing, I shut off one ear, and that gives me
much more accurate information.

Since the early days attitudes have changed. Now we tend to
say: 'The standard in the concert hall is one thing, but there's no
final arbiter of what makes good sound. We have to make up our
own minds about it.' In pop music, certainly, the sky's the limit,
which is the great thing about it. We have an infinite palette of
musical colours. We don't have to say: 'This has got to sound like
a section of violins in the studio,' or, 'We have to hear the fifth
French horn from the back clearly.' We're dealing with abstract
sounds. We can do exactly as we want in trying to achieve the most
pleasant effect. A lot of the sounds on records like *Sgt. Pepper* are
made by legitimate instruments, but the use of them doesn't necessarily correspond to what you would hear in a concert hall. You
can create your own sounds, and do it more effectively than if you
were performing live.

When I say that, one argument that is frequently levelled at me
is: 'You're not being very honest.' I say, to hell with that. We have
a different art form here, and I don't feel in any way inhibited. It's
like criticising a film maker for making a film based on a book,
which the critics do not feel is sufficiently true to the original. But
then, he's not writing a book, he's making a film. In the same way,
the recording of a concert performance at the Albert Hall may be

the same as a recording of a live stage play, but making a record in a studio is much more like making a film.

After all, if Roger Moore plunges through a plate-glass window in a James Bond film, you don't believe that it really is plate-glass. You see him just before he does it, and you hear the breaking of glass, and you see him immediately afterwards, and clever cutting gives you the illusion that he has done it. But you know in your heart of hearts that he hasn't. In the same way, it shouldn't be expected that people are necessarily doing what they appear to be doing on records.

That's not to say that I think we can replace the genius of the great performer. The human quality is something for which we should always strive, and I would be very sad if we ever lost it. But technically, we can help.

There was a famous case when I was still at EMI, in which the celebrated soprano Kirsten Flagstad was making a recording. When the day came for her to sing her top C, she was below par and just couldn't make it. So they brought in Elisabeth Schwarzkopf to dub in the high C for her, since they were pressed for time and the rest of the performance was magnificent. Schwarzkopf was duly paid, and was asked to keep quiet about the incident. Unfortunately the story leaked out and was reported in the papers, causing a minor scandal and fury at EMI. But I never really understood the fuss. Everyone has his off days, and if you're going to make a great record, why not dub in the one note? After all, it wasn't as if it was something the main singer couldn't do at all. On any other day she could have done it perfectly well.

People have ideas about what is ethical in recording and what is not, which they don't really think out properly. For example, there was even one time when I asked Paul McCartney to dub in a note on a record, and he said he didn't want to because he thought it was cheating. I told him: 'We've all been cheating all the time.' And he did it.

Again, some people expect to go to a live performance and hear what they heard on the record. Why should they? Those are two separate things. For that reason the Beatles never gave live performances of songs like 'Strawberry Fields'. But nowadays, there are other ways of doing it. 'Live and Let Die', for example, had a complicated score which I had written for a large orchestra. When I saw Paul McCartney and Wings perform it in Los Angeles in 1977, I was enormously impressed by the way he put it over. To back up the music he had a fantastic laser light show, explosions and so on, and the whole performance kept you enthralled. It didn't sound anything like the record, but you thought it did because you were seeing the whole performance as well as hearing it. There was no cheating about that.

On the other hand, there are some things I would describe as cheating. There was a big fuss about a group who had a number-one record, although none of them had played on it. It was a totally manufactured product, and that was undoubtedly cheating. It's perfectly possible to get a lot of session musicians into a studio, make a record, and call them Fred Nerks and his Oojahs. Then, if the record does well, everyone wants to see Fred N, only there isn't any Fred N. So you get a group to pretend to be Fred N and the Os, and you put them on at the Palladium and get them to reproduce as accurately as possible what you've done in the studios. But that's commercial deception, and I don't hold with it at all.

I believe that a certain amount of artifice is necessary in making a record, but by that I mean help, not deception. After all, nobody tries to hide the fact that a lot of rock groups have string synthesisers as a regular part of their make-up.

I have never liked the sound myself, though, because I find it artificial. Another argument against synthesisers is that while all sorts of computerised sounds are fine for a single note, they are no good when you want a bank of sound. You need individual effort, the cancelling out of one person's vibrato by another, and the dynamics that only a human performance can give. To create that artificially is a long and tedious process—and in any case, why deny the work to the people who are capable of doing it for real? You could argue for synthesisers on the grounds of absolute accuracy, but then, as I've said, I'm not a stickler for accuracy. If that was the be-all and end-all, we might as well give up and let computers do all the work. I happen to like a little bit of inaccuracy, a little bit of humanity. Even on a classical record I'd rather have a slight blur on one note, provided it's a great performance, than have a rendition that was perfect but soulless. I'd always prefer a great classical pianist with a few imperfections to Wendy Carlos giving a perfect performance on her synthesiser. Perfect beauty, whether in a woman or anything else, tends to be a bore, and I think that holds true for music.

Another of the things we can do to help the artist in recording is to play around with the frequencies. Within the audible frequency range, different frequencies have different effects. For example, if you're on holiday, it may be that you hear from your bedroom a disco booming away in the basement, and you simply can't escape the thumping of the bass guitar and bass drum. Because those are the most diffuse frequencies, they will go through anything, whereas the high frequencies are much more directional. Now, everyone who has a record-player knows about boosting bass, or treble, or middle, and of course we can also do that in recording. The question is what the effect will be. One example would be if you were to boost around 3000 hertz. That would emphasise all the sibilants and the clear-speech characteristics in the human voice. Equally, if you were to cut off everything above about 3000 hertz, you would be losing all the clarity of speech.

That is what takes place when people start to go deaf. They don't suddenly lose volume across the whole range; they start by losing the top frequencies. That starts to happen to most people comparatively early in life. Something not generally known is that women have a wider frequency range than men—though not as good as dogs! An eighteen-year-old girl will probably hear between 20 and 20,000 hertz, whereas a fifty-year-old man, depending on his physical state, will probably hear from 100 to 8,000 and nothing on either side of that range. Anyone can test his or her range by listening to a record with test tones on it. I, for example, can't hear 15,000 hertz any more, though I could once. You might think that could be very damaging to someone like a record producer. But the brain makes allowances for it: the sense of values remains the same. In fact the curious thing is that, if anything, the perception of differences in volume is sharpened.

However, I should end with a note of warning. Everyone suffers a progressive loss of hearing with age, but that can be greatly accelerated by damage to the ears. And with today's rock bands bashing out sounds at very high levels in discos and so on, it's all too easy to suffer that damage. If you listen to music at these high levels, there will be a limited amount of time before deterioration sets in, and that deterioration is irreparable, because it is the nerve endings of the ears which are affected.

That is very much a function of how long you listen to loud sounds. For example, you can listen to 130 decibels, which is the threshold of pain, for a second, and it won't harm you. Listen to it for ten seconds, and it will. You can listen to 120 decibels, which is still very noisy indeed, for half an hour without damage, but an hour would be too long. And so on down the scale of loudness.

The danger in recording, and for people playing in or listening to rock groups, is that the ear acts as its own limiter. After a period of heavy noise, everything gradually becomes normal to you and it's only too easy to step up the volume to impress yourself a bit more. Then, after a while at that level, you step it up again, without realising the damage you're doing to your ears. There have been occasions when, if I had suddenly gone into the studios at five in the morning, instead of having worked there all night, I would have been astonished at the levels I had been putting into my ears. But of course they had been increased gradually since nine the previous night. That is something the producer *must* guard against.

And don't be fooled into thinking that you've got away with it, because the worst factor in ear damage is that it is not immediate. If you harm your ears by listening to a very high level for too long, you'll just feel out of sorts for a day or two. You might hear some ringing, or feel a bit deaf, but you'll soon feel all right again. What you won't realise is that in four or five years' time your hearing will start to go, and that can be traced back and attributed directly to the earlier traumatic shock. The nerve endings wither, and although it takes a long time for them finally to decay, there's no going back once they have done so.

This applies to everyone, of course, not only musicians, engineers and producers. I know that people are becoming more aware of environmental pollution by noise, but they think in terms of things like Concorde flying overhead, which is nonsense. That won't affect your ears at all. You are much more at risk with the record-player turned up too loud at home, or in a disco.

To get the best enjoyment out of sound, all you need is ears. Make sure they stay in good shape.

5

COMIC CUTS

WHEN Oscar retired, they did manage to bring themselves to give him a farewell dinner as well as his encyclopaedia. It was still not clear who was to succeed him. I think the general feeling about me was: This young upstart is not experienced enough yet. They'll have to move in an experienced man to take over Parlophone. Besides, I had been something of a maverick during those first five years—an attitude which Oscar himself had encouraged, since he was quite a rebel himself in spite of his age.

So it was more than a pleasant surprise when C. H. Thomas approached me at the dinner and told me that I would continue in Oscar's job—as I had, in effect, been doing for some time without official recognition. Later, Sir Joseph Lockwood gave me the job officially, and told me that I was the youngest person to be put in charge of a label.

It was a challenge, and I wanted to do something with the label; but the nature of the first problem was quite unexpected. One day Judy came to me and offered her resignation. 'Now that you're setting up your own organisation and your own department,' she said, 'you'll want to make a clean sweep of it.'

She told me much later that she had felt sorry for me being lumbered with her without any choice in the matter. As far as I was concerned, it would have been disastrous to get rid of the one person who knew more about Parlophone's business than I did, and I said so. I asked her to think about it, and she decided to stay, which was an enormous relief. Apart from Judy and myself, the staff consisted of Shirley Spence, who had joined three years earlier as Judy's assistant, and Oscar's son-in-law Alan Tulloch, who acted as plugger, promotion man, and general run-around. Later, when Judy and I married and she retired to raise human beings, Shirley became my secretary, and has been ever since.

I was still married to Sheena then, and had two children. The first was Bundy, who is now an expert linguist and works as a court stenographer at the Old Bailey. Then there was Gregory, known as Poggy, who is an actor, God help him! It was their arrival, as much as anything else, which made us leave Acton and move to Hatfield, the only place where I could afford a house. It cost £2400, and having managed to get a 90% mortgage I was just able to scrape together the remaining £250 to attain the exalted rank of householder.

I wasn't the only one to move. The office space at Abbey Road was needed for other things, and we all moved to Great Castle Street, in the middle of the rag-trade district. Ironically, the AIR studios now look down on those offices, of which Parlophone were given half the top floor. But the fact that all the labels made the physical move together didn't prevent the continuing rivalry between them, a rivalry in which Parlophone suffered great disadvantages.

Wally Ridley on HMV and Norman Newell on Columbia both had tie-ups with American labels. Norman was a lyric writer as well as a record man. He always wanted to be a Stephen Sondheim. He wrote good enough lyrics, certainly, but his main strength came from his ability to handle big showbiz entertainers. He specialised in making original-cast recordings, especially of English shows, for Columbia. Columbia was an English company, but was tied up with the American Columbia Records and exchanged catalogues with them, so that they were able to put out over here such huge names as Mitch Miller, Guy Mitchell, Frankie Laine, Doris Day and Johnny Ray. Then, around 1952, the axe fell. American Columbia broke off the contract with EMI, cutting off the supply of these great artists. The contract was given to Philips of Holland, who at that time didn't have a label in England. But they knew what they wanted, and so did American Columbia, who had wooed the services of Norman and his colleague Leonard Smith; it was they who left to set up the new label. It was a stunning blow. EMI were not happy.

In an attempt to answer the challenge, EMI engaged Norrie Paramor, the bandleader, and Ray Martin to be joint heads of production for Columbia England. Ray was an English artist whom Norman Newell had brought to the fore, and who had had a big hit with 'Blue Tango'. Unfortunately neither he nor Norrie had any previous direct experience of record production.

Soon after this, matters were made worse when HMV similarly lost their contract with the RCA-Victor label; that meant that, apart from a lot of other fine talent, they lost the King—Elvis. At least none of EMI's key people left this time, but the revenue loss was tremendous. When you buy a recording label, you are buying people. You are buying the contracts of artists, and the talent to handle them, and you just hope that they will all stay with you. But of course you can never be sure they will.

So it was with considerable courage that Sir Joseph Lockwood decided on his response. He went looking for an American label to buy. And buy he did. For nine million dollars he acquired a brash young label named Capitol Records, of Los Angeles, founded by Glen Wallichs and the lyric writer Johnny Mercer. Johnny Mercer had a number of friends who recorded for him—some quite well-known names, you might say: Frank Sinatra, Dean Martin, Peggy Lee, Stan Kenton. At the time we thought nine million dollars was a high price. In retrospect, it was dirt cheap.

Watching from the sidelines at Parlophone, I must admit that I derived a certain amusement, tempered with sympathy, from this confusion among my rivals. But meanwhile I had to do something with my own label. Exactly what that would be, I wasn't sure, except that I was obviously going to try to improve it. For a start I had to maintain allegiance to the artists we already had—Jimmy Shand, who was our biggest seller, Eve Boswell, Ron Goodwin, Jack Parnell, Johnny Dankworth, Humphrey Lyttelton. At the same time, I had already started trying to get 'between the cracks' of the other labels, by doing things that nobody else had tried, or dared to try, like the original Peter Ustinov record.

My chance came when I went to a little theatre in Notting Hill Gate, where there was a new two-man show called *At the Drop of a Hat*, with Michael Flanders and Donald Swann. I loved the show, and managed to persuade them to let me have the rights to record it. In those days, the way to do an original-cast album was to get the cast on a day off, usually Sunday, bring them to Abbey Road studios and record them properly. But with Flanders and Swann I decided that would be silly, because one would lose all the audience atmosphere. So in early 1956, when they had moved to the Fortune Theatre, just behind Drury Lane, I recorded them there on five consecutive nights, using our mobile location unit. Then I was able to edit the best of the performances to make them flow as if they were one complete show. That record is still sold today, and was the start of a very long friendship with the pair of them. I was to make all their subsequent records, including *At the Drop of Another Hat*, *The Bestiary of Flanders and Swann*, and *More out of a Hat*.

After Flanders and Swann, my next excursion into recording theatrical humour came when some friends in the business told me there was a show up at the Edinburgh Festival which was being put on by university undergraduates but which was very funny. So I took myself up to see it. It was called *Beyond the Fringe*. I immediately decided to record it, and took the mobile van up to meet the group when they came back to Cambridge.

The record was a huge success, and we got to know its perpetrators very well. Jonathan Miller, for instance, often came into the office to talk about ideas, and I remember him telling me the silliest story there.

It seemed that, having been brought up in a very 'U' kind of family, his father didn't approve of his slopping around in jeans, or whatever the equivalent was in those days. He insisted that the youthful Jonathan should be clad in the hairiest and itchiest tweeds ever created in the Isle of Harris. So Jonathan was escorted to his father's tailor in Savile Row.

This worthy measured him up, and then enquired, 'Which side do you dress, sir?'

Jonathan, perplexed, considered this apparently absurd question, and then replied, 'Well, I generally get out of bed on the left-hand side in the morning, if I start thinking about it.'

Eventually the tailor managed to convey the delicate nature of his enquiry, and Jonathan suffered an immediate and terrible sense of inadequacy, realising with horror not only that he had never given the matter a moment's thought, but also that it simply made no difference.

Dudley Moore, on the other hand, was the lady-killer of the group, sweetly attractive, the image of Tyrone Power—Cuddly Dudley. He did have an advantage, it's true, in that he played the piano, and he was the ultimate proof of the adage that 'If you can play the piano, you get the birds'.

While they were at the Fortune Theatre there was always a gaggle of really lovely girls waiting to see him. In fact, one evening, after chatting to Jonathan, Alan Bennett and Peter Cook, I went in to see Dudley and he was in the process of saying goodbye to the most gorgeous blonde. When this lady had said her farewells we sat down, and had hardly been chatting for three minutes when there was a knock at the door and the commissionaire ushered in another female. In an aside to Dudley he murmured, 'That was just in time, wasn't it?' And that was *before* the show! Jonathan always said that the girls walked past his dressing-room to get to Dudley, and that this heightened his sense of inferiority.

It was a bit like that in the early days with Peter Sellers and Spike Milligan, too. In spite of Peter's glamour, it was always Spike who got the birds, for which talent Peter used to call him 'Goldenballs'. I guess Peter made up for it later!

I had made my first record with Peter back at the end of 1953. It was called 'Jakka', and was probably the worst-selling record Parlophone had ever made. It was a musical space fantasy, dreamed up by Ron Goodwin and his lyric writer, Ken Hare, and needed a lot of different voices, for which Peter was ideal—a sort of successor to Peter 'The Voice of Them All' Kavanagh. In retrospect, it seems a ridiculously primitive little piece. Jakka was a space-boy, whatever that might be, and he wandered around the sky on a space-scooter, accompanied by his five-legged dog. From time to time some god-like creature addressed him from the firmament, for which Peter opted to use a Churchillian voice. The whole thing was frightful, and in spite of sending copies to every contact I had, I might just as well have tried selling it on Mars. It didn't do a thing.

Now, three years later, I suggested to Peter that we start making singles, and we started off with 'Any Old Iron?', an old Harry Champion song. Peter loved it. His father had been in music hall, and he was steeped in that tradition. The record didn't do badly. Having seen what he could do, I decided that Peter was really an artist for a long-player.

As head of Parlophone I had a certain degree of autonomy, but for a big decision of that sort I had to go and persuade the monthly supplement meeting that it was a good idea, and get approval from the managing director of the EMI record division. They wouldn't let me do a full album, but after a lot of argy-bargy it was agreed that I could do a ten-inch album, which only cost about 25s as opposed to about 32s for a full twelve-inch. I thought it was a crazy decision, but they were adamant, so I went ahead. The record was called *The Best of Sellers,* and that's exactly what it turned out to be. Then, of course, they realised their mistake, and we reissued it as a twelve-inch record.

Working with Peter was terrific fun. He would 'corpse', because there was no audience: we frequently dissolved into giggles, which was fine, because we recorded them too. The only danger about it was that we enjoyed ourselves so much making these records that we sometimes thought we were much funnier than we actually were; it was easy to forget that we had to amuse people who were listening on record and didn't have the benefit of the atmosphere in the studio.

This, at times, was total uproar. For example, there's the track called 'A Drop of the Hard Stuff', in which a Ludwig Koch type of character goes out to make a field recording with an Irish band. 'Ah, watch this fellow, he'll look after us,' whispers a member of the band, before chaos breaks out. One player accuses another of playing 'a bum note', and a fight begins. Now in those days we didn't have the sound-effects tapes you can buy today. The BBC had a certain amount in their library, but we couldn't get at it. So we had to invent our own effects. For the fight we piled a heap of chairs and tables and music-stands in the middle of the studio and put mikes round them. Then, as Peter was doing his Irish bit, a chair was kicked away, and a music-stand was sent hurtling across the floor. Bedlam ensued.

Since there weren't enough people around to make a real madness of it, I joined them in the studio. At this point Peter shouted, 'Ah, mind me harp,' and gave a chair a tremendous kick, sending it flying across the room and into my unsuspecting shins, extracting from me a shriek of genuine pain. That's on the record. So my bruises did achieve something, because I don't think even Olivier could have acted that shriek!

A lot of the material was concocted in this ad-lib sort of way. Another track on that record was called 'Shadows in the Grass'. The idea was that a silly old lady in the park is picked up by a Frenchman. The old girl was played by Irene Handl, whose idea it was, and we just sat her and Peter down in the studio in front of a couple of mikes and let them go. Go they did, for about eleven and a half minutes. I guess it took about 150 editing cuts by Stuart Eltham, my engineer, to get out all the coughs and bumps and prune it down to five minutes. But it was worth it, especially as Irene was such a lovely lady. On the second day, by which time she had met all the studio engineers, she came in with an enormous and delicious cake which she had specially baked for the staff, and went round handing out slices of it.

Some of the tracks had proper scripts, of course, many of them culled from the current radio talent. Bob Monk house and Denis Goodwin did one. Frank Muir and Denis Norden wrote 'Balham, Gateway to the South'. Putting it all together involved writing special music, and the addition of sound-effects. This was something that no one else in the country was doing. After *The Best of Sellers* had proved such a success—to the private chagrin of the EMI people who had said it would be a waste of time—those same people now asked me to do another record. It was a kind of accolade, which recognised Parlophone as the label for humorous people.

But it was only as a result of personal friendship that it had happened at all. Soon after I had made the first singles with Peter, he and Spike Milligan came into the studios to make a Goon record. Harry Secombe couldn't be on it since he was already signed to Philips as a singer. One of the tracks was the Sellers–Milligan version of 'Unchained Melody', a hilarious send-up which ended with Peter singing, 'I played my ukulele as the ship went down', accompanying himself on the said instrument as he did so. At the next monthly supplement meeting I played the track to the assembled EMIcrats, one of whom said: 'Well, of course, if we're going to put out that particular version of "Unchained Melody", we'll have to get permission from the copyright owners, because you are distorting the song a bit.'

That was an understatement, but I couldn't see the problem. 'We're playing the song,' I said, 'and we're paying them copyright, so what are they going to be worried about?'

'Oh, no, it's not that simple,' he said, 'because you're making it sound worse than the original.'

My view was 'Issue first, and ask questions afterwards', but the stuffy fellow insisted that we send it to Chappells and get their permission. Chappells in turn sent it to its American writer, Frank Loesser, the man whose wife was once introduced at a cocktail party as 'the evil of two Loessers'. He listened to it and promptly threw something akin to a fit. 'No way is this record of my gorgeous opus going to be issued,' he declared, or words to that effect. He relayed this decision to Teddy Holmes of Chappells, and then, like the king telling the queen and the queen telling the parlourmaid, Teddy told me and I had to tell Peter and Spike.

Understandably, they were very bitter. So was I. We all thought the record was a knock-out. But I think in a way they blamed me at the time, and the next thing I heard was that they were recording for Decca, for whom Spike made his hugely successful 'I'm Walking Backwards for Christmas'. The ill-fated 'Unchained Melody' was never issued, and to this day remains somewhere in the archives of EMI.

Happily we all soon got together again, and I made my first record with Spike, a work of minor importance called 'You've Gotta Go Ow'. It was a resounding failure. It has always been a standing joke between us that we've never actually made anything together that has had the slightest success. Everything we ever turned our hands to seemed to end in disaster. Perhaps that's why we became such good friends—so much so, that when he got married for the second time, which was during this period, he asked me to be his best man.

Since he was a Roman Catholic, and his first wife wasn't, they had married in a registry office, so with typically crazy Goon logic he had decided that, since his new bride was a Catholic, they would have a full nuptial mass. His children would be the bridesmaids. Paddy, the lady in question, was a nun in the stage version of *The*

Sound of Music. She came from a very strait-laced Yorkshire family, and Spike, being Spike, was terrified at the thought of meeting the family, especially as he hadn't even met her father: an event which, coupled with the wedding, was to take place in Yorkshire.

He fretted greatly at the prospect. 'I've got to get up there in good time' was a fairly repetitious element in his conversation. 'Don't worry, Spike, I'll get you there' was my standard, and equally repetitious, response.

I had everything organised. We got our morning dress from Moss Bros, and set off for King's Cross station in the little Mini of which I was now the proud possessor. I knew exactly what time the Pullman train was due to leave, and we arrived well in time. I parked the car and left Spike to get out the luggage while I went to see about the tickets. With these safely in my pocket I walked to the barrier to check how full the train was. Horror upon horror! There was to be no getting on that train. I had forgotten to reserve the special Pullman seats. And there was no other train that would get us to Leeds by 9.30 that night, the time arranged for Spike to meet his future father-in-law.

Spike's jaunty prospective-son-in-law smile soon disappeared when I returned. 'Get back into the car,' I said.

'What's happening?' he demanded, not unreasonably.

'Well . . . I've changed our plans.'

'What on earth are you on about?' he enquired.

'We're going to drive there.'

'What in?'

'This.'

'This?!! We're driving all the way to Yorkshire in *this*?!!! We'll never do it. We've got to be there by half past nine.'

'Don't worry,' I said, trying to convey a confidence I certainly didn't feel.

It was just an ordinary Mini, with no specially tuned engine or any other refinement, but we piled into it and set off, with me doing my Stirling Moss bit and trying to beat the train. Poor Spike sat in the front passenger seat, gripping the fascia like grim death while I threw the machine round corners and hairpin bends. During the whole trip he didn't utter a word. He couldn't. He was paralysed with fear.

The nightmare lasted three hours, but we just made it in time. I switched off the justifiably protesting engine, got out, and walked around the car to open Spike's door for him. At last he spoke: 'Don't ever, ever ask me to drive with you again.'

The following day, after some tricky moments spent in trying to assess how morning dress worked and which stud went where, we made our way to the church, which was in the country outside Leeds. As we walked down the aisle, the left-hand side was absolutely packed with Paddy's friends and relations. On the right-hand side—not a soul. We were completely alone, just the two of us, with this vast crowd of Yorkshire folk staring at the strange idiot from London. Neither of us had ever felt so isolated.

Suddenly, there came the sound of heavy footsteps entering the church door. They came towards us down the aisle, clip-clop, clip-clop, accompanied by some light whistling. I looked round, and there was Harry Secombe striding along with a big, silly grin on his face.

We heard later that he'd had to make a great effort to get there, because he was in summer season somewhere like Llandudno, and had had to get a helicopter to take him to the nearest airport and then fly to Leeds. But then, Harry's that kind of person. He wouldn't have missed Spike's wedding for the world.

He knelt down in the pew behind us to say his prayers. Before getting up, he whispered: 'I've just recorded a new number.'

'What's this?' said Spike.

'It's called "Leather Thong".'

'What do you mean, "Leather Thong"?'

Behind us, Harry started to sing softly, 'Leather thong in my heart.' Suddenly, we didn't feel quite so alone.

Like many comedians, Spike is a sad person, enormously funny when he's on stage, but very serious in repose. He gets very worried about the state of the world. One week it will be whales, the next week baby food, or jazz or whatever. He gets very upset about things, and this tends to put a strain on his personal life.

On one occasion, when he was having a row with his first wife, he locked himself in the bedroom and got on to the telephone. Soon afterwards, his wife opened the door to find a messenger with a telegram from Spike. It read: I'D LIKE BACON AND EGGS AND TWO ROUNDS OF TOAST FOR BREAKFAST PLEASE.

The mad Goon humour could erupt anywhere, whether there was an audience or not. One day, Harry and Spike had lunch down at Shepherd's Bush Green, where Spike had his first office. It was a good lunch, heavily reinforced with quantities of wine. As they staggered out, Spike noticed the establishment next door: William Nodes, Funeral Directors. He whispered something to Harry, and the pair of them dived through the door and into the front parlour, which was empty. Grabbing a purple sheet, Spike lay flat on the floor and covered himself with it.

Harry put on an air of great seriousness and shouted, 'Shop!' Sadly, nobody came.

My history of failure with Spike was continued when we made an album which was a send-up of *Bridge on the River Kwai*. It was typical Spike humour, managing to make something very funny out of Japanese atrocities against British prisoners of war. To do this, we had to convey the impression of a jungle camp, with the noises of crickets and other beasts. Among the more terrible things we had to get over was the sound of a man's head being chopped off. 'How on earth are we going to do that?' asked Spike.

I pondered the problem for a bit, realising that whatever else we had, we certainly didn't have a recording of decapitation. Then I hit on it. I told Stuart Eltham, our recording engineer: 'Go round to that greengrocer's in Alma Square, and buy half a dozen of the largest cabbages you can find.' Stuart came back laden with the said vegetables, and putting them in front of the mike we chopped through them with a really sharp chopper. The result was totally blood-curdling—a most effective sound, helped of course by the imagination.

All in all I thought we had made a brilliant album. I finished editing it and was all ready to issue it. It was only then that I was told that if we did issue it under the title *Bridge on the River Kwai*, EMI would be sued for thousands of pounds, even though it was a typical Goon script and nothing to do with the film.

Somehow I had to salvage all our work, not least the cabbage trick. Then one night it came to me. We should simply call it something different. I got on the phone to Spike straight away. 'I've got the answer,' I said. 'We're going to call it *Bridge on the River Wye*.'

'But it's *Bridge on the River Kwai*,' said Spike. 'We've said "Kwai" everywhere on the record.'

'O.K.,' I said. 'So we cut off the K on every bit of the record.'

That's just what we did. We got out the scissors and went through all the tapes, cutting out the K whenever the word 'Kwai' appeared. It took ages to do, but at least we were then able to issue the record, and no one could sue us. Unfortunately, not many people bought it either.

Sound-effects were always a key ingredient in these humorous records, and we were forever having to improvise. For instance, there was a record I made with Michael Bentine, the former Goon, on one track of which he did a send-up of a horse show, a skit on the jingoism of English commentators. Obviously we needed horse noises, and we had a couple of horse whinnies on tape which we put in from time to time. But most of the sound-effects consisted of me patting my hand on a piano stool. In fact, you generally never use the real thing for a sound-effect, unless it's a frightfully good recording—and in any case, people have their own ideas of what things should sound like.

At that time I had no sound-effects library, and whenever I wanted a special effect I would ring up the chief effects man at the BBC, who liked to do a bit of moonlighting. He was a real craftsman, and after I had told him what I needed he would turn up with an extraordinary variety of impedimenta—roller-skates, maracas, bits of tin, pieces of metal to simulate breaking glass, and goodness knows what else. If there wasn't a stock answer to a problem, he would soon work one out. For a burning house, for example, he would crumple up tissue-paper in front of a mike. It certainly sounds as a burning house would—though, to be fair, I've never burned one down to make the comparison. Besides, tissue-paper is cheaper. For the sounds of sea and wind we had a pail of water in the studio, accompanied by someone blowing through the mike—though if a real thunderstorm broke we would always rush out and grab it on tape while it was there. For the sound of marching soldiers we had a large cardboard box with a few lumps of fine-grade coke in it. If you shook the box from side to side you had an instant regiment. The snag was that after a while the box got a bit worn and began to leak, and the operator would be covered in coke dust and emerge black at the end of the session. With somewhat obvious cunning I always got my assistant Ron Richards to do that effect.

It wasn't until ten years later, in the late sixties, that sound-effect tapes started becoming usable. Today, you can get a tape of literally anything, from Evel Knievel jumping into a river, to the birth of a baby. So life for the producer has become easier: but even now, one who wants effects will still try to gather his own. When I was in Hawaii I put up a stereo microphone by the seashore, simply because the sound of the waves and the surf there was so good. I've used that tape on a couple of records. Because recording now is so faithful, a tape like that would be better than anything you could manufacture, provided you took care not to get wind noise on the mike.

There were special musical effects to be found as well. On one occasion I decided that I needed four bugle players. I wanted the authentic sound of bugles, and didn't want to use trumpets, so I rang up the Guards.

I got hold of one of their band sergeants and told him: 'I need

four buglers for this recording. Can you provide me with four buglers who can read?' The point was that they had to be able to play
the exact notes I needed. A bugle is like a trumpet without valves,
so it can't play every note, only its own basic harmonics: it's essential, therefore, to write the proper music for it.

'No problem, sir, we'll get them along to you,' said the sergeant.
On the appointed day, along came four buglers from the Irish
Guards, together with their sergeant, who didn't play but who was
in charge of them. I ushered them into the studio, fetched music-
stands, put the music in front of them, and said: 'O.K., that's what
we're going to do. Just have a few goes at it by yourselves, then I'll
play you the track that we're going to fit you on to.'

The sergeant looked distinctly uncomfortable, and started to
wriggle in a quite unmilitary way. Finally he stepped over to me and
cleared his throat. 'Excuse me, sir. I'm afraid my buglers cannot read
your music.'

'But I specifically asked for four men who could read,' I said
testily.

'Oh, sure they can read, sir,' declared the sergeant proudly. 'They
can read all right, but they can't read music.'

In the end, I had to teach them the part by singing it to them.

I needed a different kind of effect for the second album I
did with Peter Sellers—the human voice. At that time, Frank
Sinatra's *Songs for Swinging Lovers* was the big hit, and we decided
to do *Songs for Swinging Sellers*. For the opening track, a song I
had written, I thought that Peter should sing with a voice as near
as possible to Sinatra's. Now Peter can sing, though not terribly
well, and I thought he could use his great powers of mimicry so
that it would actually sound like someone doing an impression of
Sinatra, which was the whole point of the record. I played him a
tape of Matt Monro singing the song, and said, 'All you've got to
do is sing like this.'

'I can't do that,' said Peter. 'It's great as it is. Let's use that.'

'We can't. That's another person,' I said.

'O.K., then let's call him Fred Flange,' said Peter, using a Goon-ish name always readily available.

So I approached Matt, who had just lost his contract with his recording company and was at a pretty low ebb, and asked: 'Is it all right if we don't use your name?' I think he was a bit disappointed, and maybe was hoping for stardom to come from the song, but I paid him £25, and the record was issued with a credit to Fred Flange as having sung that track.

It did very well. Peter sang all the other tracks, and the differ-ence between his voice and Matt's is quite apparent. They include the classic called 'Peter Sellers Sings George Gershwin', which is precisely what he did. He sang 'George . . . Gershwin.' Another of my favourites among his tracks was his rendering of 'Wouldn't It Be Lovely' in an Indian voice, so that it emerged as 'Wouldn't It Be Lubberly', with sitars and other weird instruments in the back-ground.

That was typical of the attitude I had to humorous records. The technique with Peter, and other artists I worked with, was to make amusing records which the public would like to listen to time and time again. I tried very hard not to make the side-splitting kind of funny record including a lot of heavy jokes, because they tend not to last for more than a couple of hearings. Once you know the joke, you know what's coming. But you can go on enjoying the way Irene Handl says 'a bottle of Borjolais' instead of 'Beaujolais', and you can always find something new to chuckle about in the little noises and gurgles she makes while being goosed by Peter. The humour would bear repetition simply because there were combinations of words that stuck in the mind. This was especially true of *Be-yond the Fringe*. If I'm a bit disappointed about something, I still say, quoting from them: 'Well, it wasn't quite the conflagration I was banking on.' And when we leave the house there is a family recitation of: 'Have you got the key? Got the tinned food? Got the tin-opener?'

In this world of catch-phrases, I suppose nothing became more universal than 'Goodness Gracious Me'. We made the record while Peter was working with Sophia Loren on *The Millionairess*; Herbie Kretzmer and Dave Lee had written it specifically with Peter in mind, and for the character he was playing. We recorded it in the Number One studio at Abbey Road, and since I had just been recording Rolf Harris, I got Ron Richards (he of the coke box) to play the wobble-board on the record.

It had 'Bangers and Mash' on the reverse side; we reckoned it was a knock-out and naturally wanted to tie it up with the film. So I took it along to the producer, Dimitri de Grunwald, and played it to him. 'Look,' he said, 'the film's still in the shooting stage. But I think this will be helpful to the film, and the film will be helpful to the record, so for both reasons I'll try and get it into the film.'

However, the director, Anthony Asquith, wouldn't have it. He took the view: 'No, this is a serious film. This is George Bernard Shaw. Your record is very amusing, but it's not in the same kind of class as our film.'

I couldn't wait, because I wanted to catch the Christmas season, and I went ahead and issued the record, which was a huge success. Some months later the film came out, and of course everyone went to it expecting to hear the recording. They didn't, and they felt cheated. De Grunwald told me later what a big mistake they had made, and of the tremendous number of complaints they had had. Exactly the same thing was to happen later with the film *Alfie* and Cilla Black's recording of the song 'Alfie'.

Following the success of 'Goodness Gracious Me', I thought it would be a good idea to make an album with Peter and Sophia—though by now it had become rather more difficult, with Peter a rising international film star: hard to get hold of, more choosy about the material he used, and more reluctant to commit himself to records. But we finally got the project on the road. Peter would do a few solos, Sophia a few, and they would do a few songs together. However, by the time Peter had done his parts Sophia was back in Rome, and obviously wasn't going to come to England just to record a couple of songs. So I said that I would prepare backing tracks for her numbers, guessing the keys that she would sing in so that I could write the accompaniment, and that we would go to Rome with the tracks and dub her voice on there. Then I could come back and mix the whole thing. Peter wasn't at all averse to coming out with me, since he and Sophia were, as they say, extremely good friends.

We were due to fly in one of the early Comets, and took our seats in the first-class compartment at the front of the plane. Unfortunately, as we taxied before take-off the nose-wheel broke; the front of the aircraft dropped about fifteen feet with a bump, and slewed along the runway. It was a nasty moment, and Peter was petrified and went green to prove it.

Luckily no one was hurt, and we were taken back to the airport buildings where, of course, newspaper reporters had gathered at the news that Peter Sellers was involved in a near-disaster. Poor Peter didn't want to talk about it at all, and just wanted to be left alone to recover from the shock, so they asked me if I had any comments. I said, 'Spike Milligan must have sawn it half-through before we took off.' The papers promptly reported 'Peter Sellers jokes . . .', ascribing the quote to him when he hadn't said a word.

Eventually we got to Rome. There was Sophia to meet us with her Rolls-Royce Phantom limousine, in which she took us to the villa she was having built on the Appian Way. She sat between us in the back, and I could hardly believe that I was actually there. Belief deserted me totally the following day, when we went to her flat in Rome to talk about the project. It was a marvellous place, entered through a courtyard where fountains were playing surrounded by sixteenth-century masonry. We must have been a little early, because when we got up to her flat we were invited to see her in her bedroom, where she was still in her negligee. This rather threw me, unaccustomed as I was to seeing film stars in their bedrooms at all, let alone in negligees. Peter, however, was clearly much more at home with the situation, and did his best to put me at my ease.

Sophia was incredibly charming, fun to be with and easy to work with. In no way did she play the big star in her private life. After we had finished the album I never met her again. However, years later she won an Oscar for her part in the film *Two Women*. I thought she was extremely good in it, and sent her a note of congratulation. In return I received a handwritten postcard saying: 'Dear George, It was so sweet of you to send me the note of congratulation. Thank you very much.' In itself that isn't very important, but the fact is that few people take the trouble or, if they do, they dictate a note to their secretary. I was even surprised that she'd remembered me, but it's always good to be reassured that there are still some superstars who don't forget, and who don't become inflated by their own ego, as so often happens.

If Sellers and Milligan were eccentric, they were nothing compared to the Alberts, who were quite mad. They used to deliver newspapers—perhaps they still do—and consisted of two brothers and Bruce Lacey. We were to make an LP called *An Evening of British Rubbish*, but we couldn't know how apt a title that was. I was very keen on audience reaction at that time, and we recorded them in front of an invited audience of five hundred people in Number Two studio, where they were ready to enjoy such delicacies as one of Bruce's robots complete with bubble-blowing machine. But before they came in, we had a test to do. The Alberts intended to fire a gun right in the middle of the performance, and we had to make sure that the loudness of the sound didn't ruin the recording.

There we were in the studio, with the five hundred chairs all laid out in neat rows, and everything spick and span. Just before the audience came in we did our test. The gun went off like the proverbial crack of thunder and brought down about a quarter of a ton of soot from the ceiling. It was a fairly dramatic sight to see all this stuff floating down, but it put the recording back by the time it took to clear the mess up.

On other occasions the audience themselves could be a problem. We did a live recording with Rolf Harris of 'Tie Me Kangaroo

Down, Sport' and 'Sun Arise', and to make him feel at home I got a load of Australians along for the audience. To make *them* feel at home I had cases of Swan lager specially brought in. That did it. We couldn't get them out of the canteen, and those who did make their way to the studio were trying to put cans of the liquid in the echo-chamber or anywhere else they could find. In the end I appealed: 'Come on, chaps, we've got to get on with the recording.'

To this I received the typically Antipodean reply: 'Oh, stuff yer bloody recording. Is there any more of that Swan?'

Most musicians enjoy a drink or two, and one band that was no exception was called, with due logic, The Temperance Seven (there were nine of them). They played in a very authentic style of the 1920s, and their musical mainstay was Alan Cooper, known affectionately as 'Hooter'. He was a genuine eccentric, who played various kinds of woodwind and was a master of the idiom. The vocalist was Paul McDowell, who sang through a megaphone, and in order to help the realistic feel of the recording I grouped them all round one mike and recorded in mono, even though stereo was with us by then.

The record was greeted with a great deal of scepticism at EMI, and they obviously thought I was becoming infected by its title— 'You're Driving Me Crazy'. But it wasn't so crazy; it was on the night I was recording *Beyond the Fringe* up in Cambridge that I received a phone call to say the record had reached number one in the hit parade. It was my first number one, and Judy, Shirley, Ron Richards and I promptly took ourselves out to a celebratory dinner.

Up till then, the highest I had made was number two with 'Be My Girl'. It was sung by Jim Dale—now a tremendously successful actor, but in those days my answer to Tommy Steele. Unfortunately, the association didn't last too long. His manager, Stanley Dale (no relation), exerted a Svengali-like influence over him. He had him tied up in more knots than I could count, and poor Jim never had the vaguest idea what his financial state was. After we had made a few records, including 'Be My Girl', it looked as though he had a big career in the making. But one day he came to me and said: 'I'm sorry, but we're not going to make any more records.'

'Why on earth not?' I asked.

'Stanley and I have talked about it, and I'm going to become a comedian,' he announced.

'You're crazy. You've got a good career going for you.'

But he wouldn't be shaken, and that was the end of our contract. After all, you can't force someone to make records, even if you do have a contract. He wouldn't have been allowed to record for anyone else for a period, but then he didn't want to. He wanted to be a comedian, for which he had always had a natural bent, and at least we parted good friends.

If he had been my answer to Tommy Steele, at least I kept my answer to the skiffle of Lonnie Donegan, which was the Vipers. They had a guy who played a bass made out of a tea-chest, and another who worked on a newspaper and played the washboard. They were amateurs, but they used to jangle away on the acoustic guitars and make the most enormous sound. The style was really the forerunner of the electric guitars which came later—in a way the precursor of the Beatles. They used to sing songs like 'John B Sails', 'Cumberland Gap' and 'Rock Island Line'.

One of the group was called Johnny Booker, a little guy with a limp, who was mad about animals. He had a flat in the basement of a very expensive block in Eaton Square, where he kept a pet marmoset monkey which he would often bring to the studios. It was quite a sweet little thing, but not exactly what you would call house-trained. One day he went out, leaving the monkey in the flat, but forgetting to close the window. While he was gone, it accepted this open invitation and shinned up the drainpipe to the top floor, where Lady Something-or-Other had a luxury flat. She too had gone out, locking her bedroom door and leaving its window open. That invitation, too, the monkey accepted. It then proceeded to do a tour of the bedroom, unearthing such delightful treats as face creams and hand lotions, which it ate. What it couldn't eat it plastered all over itself. It then decided the time had come to jump about, spreading the said lotions all over her silk cushions and bedspread—during the course of which frivolity it was, not unforeseeably, violently sick and seized with diarrhoea.

Tiring of this rampage, it then made its way home down the drainpipe. The wretched lady returned home, unlocked the flat door, unlocked the bedroom door and practically fainted at the scene of devastation. To this day, she has had no idea how the vandalism was achieved. She will have now.

But of all the mad incidents, the one I have most cause to remember is that which nearly cost me my job; because, if the demon drink seems to have played an overly important part in my early recording experiences, the exception was the case of Mr McRoberts. James McRoberts ran an outfit called The Scottish Festival of Male Voice Praise, a Bible-thumping hallelujah-chanting assembly which we used to record. McRoberts, not averse to the occasional joys of Mammon, used to do his own arrangements of things like 'Eternal Father, Strong to Save' and make sure he got the copyright on them.

I had been invited to appear on Scottish television with an interviewer named Larry Marshall, and hearing that I was going up there, the moguls at EMI's head office at Hayes asked to see me. 'We've made rather an unfortunate slip-up with Mr McRoberts,' they said. 'We've overpaid him on his royalties. In fact we've paid him much more than we should have done. Now, we don't expect you to get the money back, though it would be rather nice if you could. But at least you must make him aware of the fact that we've been making erroneous royalty statements, otherwise there'll be an awful lot of trouble.' The buck had been passed firmly to me.

The first obstacle to be negotiated was the television interview, which was for a chit-chat magazine sort of show. Being hospitable, the television people plied me with several drams before I went on. I have no doubt they also considered that moistening the tongue would loosen it a bit as well. I got on extremely well with Larry Marshall, and thus came to be plied with several more drams afterwards.

Luckily the Festival of Male Voice Praise was at the tabernacle just up the street. I say 'luckily' because, by the time I stepped out of the television studios and felt the cold wind biting into my lungs, it dawned on me that I had done severe damage to a bottle of best malt. Never mind, I thought, it would help me in what I had to tell poor Mr McRoberts.

I entered the tabernacle, its austere hall painted green and brown, redolent of Dettol, Lysol and piety, and hearing singing in the background went in to find the choir in rehearsal. Mr McRoberts, with his protruding teeth, bald head, and spectacles a-dangle on the end of his nose, was conducting the orchestra. Seeing me, he stopped the rehearsal, and came over and greeted me quite affably. I in turn greeted him quite affably, since I was in a highly affable mood.

'Hallo, Mishter McRobertsh. It'sh lovely to shee you again,' I declared. An extremely temperate man, to whom alcohol was the nectar of Satan, never to be tolerated in the tabernacle, he reeled back from the fumes. Not to be put off, and still flushed with the success (and the scotch) of the TV programme, I didn't hesitate but went straight for the poor man's financial jugular. 'We've got shome unfortunate newsh for you, Misther McRobertsh.'

'Oh, tsch, tsch, what's that?' he asked irritably.

'I'm afraid that EMI have overpaid you to the tune of shome-thing like four hundred poundsh. And ash you only get about twenny quid a quarter in royaltiesh, I'm afraid you're not going to get any more royaltiesh for about the necsht five yearsh.'

At that, I was seized of the most profound and uncontrollable fit of the giggles. Mr McRoberts was mortally offended. The sad tidings could hardly have been delivered with less tact. Fortunately his choir were not the most important of our artists. Had they been, I think it doubtful that I would have remained long with EMI.

And I might never have signed up the Beatles.

6

TWO HEADS ARE BETTER THAN ONE

DURING that whole period—before and even after the Beatles arrived—the record producer was basically an organiser. Of course, he could make decisions about what should be on a record, and he could advise artists on how best to put over their performances. But it was the advent of stereo recording which first truly made him what he has become today—a creative person in his own right. It allowed him to stamp his own unique impression on the recording. To understand just how great that impact was, it is useful to hark back to the scene which met my eyes when I first entered Abbey Road studios in the autumn of 1950: a scene which typified the state of the recording industry then.

The control room was not large, by any standards. Its décor did a poor job of concealing its factory origins—walls painted with green and cream gloss, and a thin rug on the linoleum floor which probably did more for the acoustics than it achieved in cushioning the feet. On the left, as one entered, stood a bulbous green monster of a metal cabinet, with a glass-topped lid through which one could see spools spinning. This was the BTR 1, the first production studio tape recorder that EMI had brought out. The studio staff regarded it with a great deal of scepticism. In the opposite corner, dominating the room, stood the recording lathe. It was an impressive piece of machinery, surmounted by a turntable and cutter, which gleamed in the light of a naked bulb hanging above it.

Between these two great machines was the control panel, if one could dignify it with that name. It resembled the dashboard of a vintage car. It had four large, black rotary knobs which controlled the volume coming in from the microphones in the studio, and numerous toggle switches. Above this panel was a tiny window, about two feet square; this connected with the studio by means of two small doors, which the engineer could open in order to speak to the musicians or singers. There was a desk on which the recording information book sat. And finally there was a glass-fronted cabinet, about the size of a wardrobe, within which thermostatically controlled lamps would glow from time to time, revealing racks lined with translucent amber discs. These were the blank waxes, kept at a constant temperature of 100° F, ready for cutting.

Standing by the lathe, as I first beheld this scene, were two men, both engrossed in the appearance of a wax disc on the lathe. The shorter of the two, clad in a white overall, was using a small, high-powered magnifying glass to examine the lines on the disc. The second, tall, and wearing a severe dark suit which accentuated his upright bearing, stood waiting for the engineer's verdict. Then he picked up the disc from the turntable, holding it at an angle so that the light showed up the pattern of the groove. 'Mm,' he murmured, 'looks a bit tricky there. What do you think, Charles? Will it hold?'

Charlie Anderson pursed his lips and smiled. 'Well, we've had louder ones than that before now. I think it's a good one, apart from that heavy spot just there. Look.' He pointed at a mark on the disc caused by a loud sound during the recording.

'All right, Charles,' said Oscar Preuss, 'let's mark it as a master. But we'll do one more take, just in case it goes down at the factory.'

The routine of another recording take began again. Charlie Anderson, the engineer, began winding a large crank, and a heavy weight rose slowly to the ceiling. As he did so, Oscar walked through to tell the musicians that he wanted another performance, murmuring a few words of encouragement to them. In the control room a fresh warm wax disc was taken from the cabinet and placed on the turntable, and the engineer checked his settings. Then he shut his little window, released a brake, and spun the turntable.

Slowly the weight began to fall. A buzzer was pressed to warn the musicians to get ready; then, as the needle was lowered on to the wax and a suction device began to devour the off-cuts as it bit into the surface, the buzzer was sounded a second time to tell the players that recording was imminent. Finally, a second or two later, the engineer turned a knob which tracked the needle into the right position to start its journey towards the centre of the wax; in the studio a red light was switched on, at which the musicians began to play. And play they had to, starting immediately on cue, for otherwise the piece, which would have been scored to fit exactly the playing time of the record, would overrun.

There could be no editing. There was tape, but it was still mistrusted. The dubs from tape were never considered to be as good as those from the direct wax recording, and the tape was used only as a standby, in case the waxes were destroyed in the factory process. It was also useful for letting the artists hear an instant playback of what they had done, which was especially helpful if they were going to have to do another take. Only a short time before I arrived there had been no tape recorder, and the unfortunate artist would have to wait a week before he could hear the results of his work on the test pressings which were sent up from the factory after the wax 'master' had been processed.

As for the wax discs, we went through them like the proverbial hot cakes. If someone made a mistake, or the recording was below the standard you expected, the wax was simply thrown away, later to be melted down and recoated. During an average recording session one would probably get through about fifteen waxes.

To my new and untutored eyes, the whole set-up seemed incredibly crude. I had thought, for instance, that the use of falling weights for motive power had gone out with Galileo. The answer, it seemed, was that electric motors in those days were not reliable enough to guarantee a completely steady and 'wow-free' 78 revolutions a minute. Gravity, on the other hand, knew no hiccups.

But if I thought that recording conditions and techniques were crude, they were nothing compared with the actual manufacture of the end product. Before I visited the works where the records were pressed, I expected immaculate, white-coated operatives standing by stainless steel, plastic-topped counters, pressing buttons and watching the automatic moulding of the discs. How wrong I was. Reality was a hot and dirty factory, with men stripped to the waist, bathed in sweat and forever grimy with the black carbon dust which hung in the air.

The carbon was mixed with shellac for the raw material of the records, then was rolled into sheets, which were cut into rectangular 'biscuits' about 18" by 10". The pressers, each of whom operated two machines, rolled these biscuits around on very hot steel plates until they formed solid 'doughnuts'. Next, a label was taken from a rack and placed face-down on the press, the black doughnut went on top of the label, and the second label, for the reverse side, was placed atop the doughnut. Then the top of the press would be pulled down, squeezing the material into the thin disc, whose grooves were shaped by matrices in the top and bottom of the press. As it cooled, the presser made ready the material for his second press.

And so it went on, day in, day out, a Dickensian process in the middle of the twentieth century. After seeing it, I realised how fortunate I was to be on the originating side of the business.

The 'sharp end' of that side, of course, was and is the microphone, and as such it deserves some discussion in a book of this sort.

The first point is that when I started we were only recording in mono, so that the input, from however many mikes were used, all went on to one track. I also mentioned that the control panel had just the four rotary controls. That effectively limited the number of mikes used to four, though on occasion it was possible to feed the input from two mikes into one control. There were times when we would only use one mike, in order to achieve a particular sort of sound, but in the main it was a multi-mike technique. For example, if you were recording people like Ivor Moreton and Dave Kaye, or Rawicz and Landauer, there would be two pianos and you would use one mike for each piano. By today's standards it was pretty crude.

The microphones themselves were pretty crude, too. The moving coil mikes which we used to use picked up almost as much from behind them as from the front—and the sides as well! They were in no way discreet about what they heard and what they didn't. This meant that the way to make good records was to use as few mikes as possible, because the interaction of one with another presented awful problems. It also meant that there was great skill in the relative placing of the mikes, because that, and the placing of the instruments, was much more critical than it is today. Apart from anything else, the mikes couldn't pick up the wide range of frequencies that is possible with their modern counterparts.

As they improved, not only did that wider range of frequencies become available, but the mikes became more discriminating. That refers to the fact that different mikes have different patterns of pick-up, or what are called 'polar diagrams'. If you place a modern mike in a room, you can actually draw a picture of the area from which it receives sound most favourably. In television studios, for example, you often see gun mikes used. These are extremely directional, but probably too much so. They are fine for speech, but not adequate for music.

For recording in the studio, you may use a variety of mikes. It's largely a matter of taste, and engineers and producers have their own particular favourites. But although mikes have improved greatly over the past ten years, the most recent have not, in my opinion, kept up with the previous quality. One reason may be that a lot of the earlier condenser mikes were valve-operated. In recent years there has been a tendency to get rid of the old valves—or 'tubes' as they call them in America—and replace them with transistors; and in trying to bring the same basic mike up to modern standards in that way, they lost something. For example, the old U47 Neumann mike was super, but you can't buy it any more. We still have some, but they are like gold-dust. The modern replacement is simply not quite as good. Again, the C12, a valve-operated condenser, was a marvellous mike. It was very sensitive, and could pick up things with great clarity from quite a distance away—a very 'hot' mike as the Americans would say. But they don't make that any more, either, and you just can't buy one. I believe that microphone manufacturers aren't really alive to the needs of the recording industry. Their research departments design things that look better, and whose theoretical graphs of performance look great on the walls; but they don't do any research in commercial studios themselves, which is where it matters.

After all, we are experimenting all the time. Just because I use one mike for strings on one recording, it doesn't mean that I'll always use the same one for all strings. Equally, there are some things you just can't do. You couldn't use the C12 on a bass drum or an electric guitar because, although it's very good, it's so sensitive that it would blow very quickly.

With the enormous volumes of sound we use in studios today, the tolerance of a microphone is of critical importance. In the old days mikes were very intolerant. They were roughly the same as the human ear in that they couldn't stand a huge amount of sound. But today you can get mikes which will. If you go into a studio where a rock group are playing guitars, the sound may be so loud that you will be on the threshold of physical pain twenty feet away. But the mike will be only three or four inches from the diaphragm of the loudspeaker, so that the poor electronic ear is withstanding an amazing volume.

Again, that means the other mikes have to be extremely directional in order not to pick up the edges of that sound. Simply in terms of decibels it's a very different technique from recording a string quartet. This was never more in evidence than when I recorded the Mahavishnu Orchestra for Columbia. The album was called *Apocalypse,* and was, I think, one of the best records I have ever made. Mahavishnu was a rock-jazz group led by John McLaughlin, and they were backed by the London Symphony Orchestra, conducted by Michael Tilson Thomas. Since it was what I would call a very live sort of work, I said at the start: 'Let's try and record this live. It's very extreme, but let's see if our techniques can cope with it.' So I got the LSO into our big studio at AIR and put the Mahavishnu group in the corner. It was all fairly cramped.

I got a good sound balance on the orchestra. I got a good sound balance on the group. But when they started playing together, *Apocalypse* wasn't the word for it. It was impossible. I was standing beside Michael Tilson Thomas on the rostrum and, after three or four bars, he flung down his baton, and said in desperation, 'George, I can't even hear the first violin down here.' Although the group were way over in the corner, you could hear nothing else; the difference in sound level must have been about sixty decibels. I just had to put them in a different studio altogether—it would have been no use asking them to play more quietly, because then they wouldn't have been playing what they were used to playing. The drummer wouldn't have been able to get the right sounds out of his instruments, nor would the electric-guitar player.

That is just an indication of the different sorts of jobs you have to ask different microphones to do. And they are very delicate instruments: if you overload a mike by putting too much volume into it, you will simply break it. We use the U47s for vocals, but if you put them in front of the drums the diaphragms will simply stop working.

In spite of knowing that, we do still break mikes. The reason is that we are always pushing equipment to its limits, trying to see just how far we can go. Because it's just a fact that the nearer the limits you go, the better your overall sound will be. It's like driving a racing car. You know perfectly well that if you hit it with 6000 revs, the gearbox will fold up. So you hit it with 5900 revs, hoping it will tolerate that. Do that sixteen times in a row, and the chances are that on the sixteenth time it *will* go. At AIR studios, we have to replace about a dozen mikes a week. That means either replacing the cartridge, or sending them back to the manufacturers for a replacement mike.

What the microphone is doing, of course, is to convert the sound frequencies it hears into a series of electrical impulses which are recorded on the tape, and thence translated on to the record. But how are they translated?

We all know there are grooves on a record, but I wonder how many know what one looks like. On a mono record, it's a V-shaped channel which, when magnified many times, looks like a watercourse with a rounded bottom. The needle going along that groove is rather like a car driving along a motorway. If you imagine the disc as standing still and the needle as moving, instead of the other way round, then the needle becomes the car. But the road isn't straight like a motorway; it's more like a winding English lane. As it follows this road, the needle wiggles from side to side. The sharper the bend, the higher the frequency generated through the medium of the needle.

In a mono record, that groove is a constant depth. The needle only moves laterally, rather like a wave turned on its side, following the bends in the 'road'. So if you were to generate, say, a constant frequency of 3000 hertz, there would be 3000 such 'bends' in every second of playing time, and the needle would therefore vibrate 3000 times a second. The volume of the note is determined by the depth of the 'bends', so that if it's very quiet, the needle will move almost imperceptibly.

But just as a car on a road will turn over if it tries to take a sharp bend too fast, so too is the needle limited in what it can take. If the frequency is too high, and if the modulation—the swing—is too wide, the curve that the needle has to follow becomes too sharp, and it will jump and be thrown off the record, rather like a toboggan going over the edge of the Cresta Run. So the cutting of a record becomes a very fine art, a matter of getting the maximum possible sound out of it without throwing the needle off. As with microphones, the possibilities in disc-cutting are pushed to the limits, because everyone wants a louder record than the man next door, and only an expert disc-cutter can achieve the maximum amount of sound without overdoing it and getting a lot of rejects which jump the grooves. I always go along to the cutting sessions on my records to make sure the cutter is getting a good sound out of them. But equally, the producer has some responsibility, in making a record that will cut easily.

That explains how we get one frequency out of a record's groove. But a piece of music, of course, has a myriad frequencies in it. In fact, no sound we ever hear, apart from a computer sound, consists of just one frequency. For instance, if you play a middle A on the piano, the most distinguishable frequency you will hear is 440 hertz. But you will also be hearing 880, and probably 660 and 330 as well, which are the natural harmonics. Moreover, if you stopped an orchestra playing at any one moment, you could say: 'What we're hearing now are violins, violas, cellos, double basses, bassoons, trombones, oboes, French horns, woodwind, harp, glockenspiel, and whatever.' But you could also analyse the frequency spectrum at that moment with the help of a computer, and it would give you a complete break-down in frequency terms. In effect it would tell you: 'I am hearing 120 hertz at an amplitude of 32 decibels, 121 hertz at an amplitude of 37 decibels . . .' and so on. What the groove in the record does is to reflect that complicated combination of frequencies, rather than follow an orderly series of curves. A pure note of 440 hertz will have its own particular swing, but if you add a note of 880 hertz the curve will be a combination of those two swings, and so on as more frequencies are added.

The question then arises as to why a particular frequency played on one instrument sounds different from the same frequency played on another. The answer is that the harmonics within the note are different for each instrument. If you looked at the groove where a piano was playing A, and then where a trumpet was playing A, you would see in both the overall swing of the 440 hertz. But within that you would also see all the little decorations, the extra frequencies peculiar to each instrument.

There is also another difference—the 'envelope' of the note, which roughly means its shape. Take the trumpet. In its first few milliseconds, the note will be comparatively quiet, almost nothing. Then it will be quite loud, after which it will reduce in volume, settling to a steady note which rises and falls according to the vibrato. On the piano, on the other hand, the first thing you hear will be a very high impact noise as the key strikes the string. Then it will diminish very quickly, fall below its normal level, rise, fall, and finally settle down to a fairly sustained but decaying sound. Every instrument has its own unique 'envelope' of this kind, together with its unique set of harmonics. Each of those harmonics is a frequency which forms part of the complicated set of curves interpreted by the needle.

That's how a mono record works. But now we have stereo. In fact, it came in soon after I entered the record business. They issued stereo tapes before stereo discs, and could have put stereo on the old 78 r.p.m. shellac discs. But they never did, and it wasn't until LPs came in that stereo really gained acceptance.

The bases of stereo lie in hearing more than one recording at a time, and in the fact that we hear with two ears. Some years ago there was a vogue for stereo pictures (they always seemed to turn up in dentists' waiting-rooms) which went into 3D when you looked at them through a special pair of spectacles. That worked by using the relationship of one eye to the other. Just as we have two eyes, so we have two ears, and it's natural to want to build space into recordings as well.

The original way of putting the two separate sounds into the groove of the record was by making the needle move not only laterally, but also up and down: the 'road' had not only its curves, but also a lot of bumps. The information was interpreted mechanically, with one part of the pick-up reading the lateral movements, the other the up-and-down movements. This last movement was known as 'hill-and-dale' recording. It soon proved not to be a very good system. In the first place, it was very difficult to press good records, because now there were two different directions in which too loud a sound could make the needle jump. It seemed to be flung off more often than it stayed on! Secondly, there was a certain amount of feedback between the two movements, which interacted so that you got distortion in the middle.

The answer came from a man called Blumlein who worked for EMI at Hayes. He came up with the idea of a groove combining two different motions, running side by side at forty-five degrees from one another. Now the needle was analysing two sets of lateral information, by means of a much more sophisticated type of pick-up. There were two sets of information, each going to a different loudspeaker. But the amazing thing was that to our ears, functioning as they do, there *weren't* only two sets, but an almost limitless variety.

This was proved at the first demonstrations of stereo records. The two speakers were placed behind thick gauze curtains. Then demonstration discs were played, all designed to emphasise the stereo effect. There were recordings of ping-pong matches, the click-clack of railway trucks going through a siding, trains hurtling through stations, jet planes roaring overhead, and so on. You could hear not only the sounds coming from the speakers on the left and right, but all those from the centre too. I well remember the excited feeling of participation one got from first hearing it. Then, the demonstration over, the gauze curtains were drawn aside—to the accompaniment of oohs and aahs from the audience, because of course there was no speaker in the centre; yet you could have sworn you heard things coming from there. And so, in a sense, you did.

It was the human ear which did it for us. If you play a mono record on two speakers, the ears will automatically balance those sounds and hear them as if they were coming from the middle. But, unlike mono, stereo had two different sources of sound, and all the producer needed was a perfect spatial approach. Where a sound came only from the left-hand speaker, you would hear it only as coming from the left. The same with the right. Where a sound was identical on both speakers, it would appear, as with mono, in the middle. But it didn't stop there. You could place a sound at any point you wanted between the two speakers, simply by the proportion of that sound you put into one speaker compared with the other.

This was achieved partly by the placing of the microphones during the recording, but mainly by where you decided to place that information during the mixing of the record. For instance, when I did a record with Peter Sellers in which he played all five characters in a sort of Brains Trust spoof, I only recorded him in mono, as five separate tracks, one for each voice. Then I mixed those tracks on to stereo. The interviewer, or chairman, obviously had to be in the middle, so that voice went equally on to each track. The voices who were supposed to be sitting at the ends went one on the left-hand track alone, and one on the right. Then, to get half-left and half-right, I put each of those voices three-quarters on one track, and a quarter on the other. It had the desired effect. In fact, the variety of positions where the sound can be placed is limited solely by the fineness of the balance you can achieve between the two tracks.

A physicist will tell you that space is allied to time, but a record producer will assure you that it is closely allied to sound as well. However, stereo gave us more than just the ability to hear things coming from different places laterally. There was a bonus. It gave us perspective. Exactly as the stereo photograph allowed us to see things as being in the background and the foreground, so stereo recording gave us depth. We could hear things to the front and things to the back, and the ambience of our recordings became much more lifelike. Listen to a good stereo recording and try to 'see' with your ears, and you will hear how the sounds do vary in depth.

With quadraphonic recording, of course, you could go even farther: you could place sounds all over the place. But it hasn't really caught on yet, and I doubt whether it ever will. It's too complicated and too cumbersome for the average person. Mum didn't like it much when two speakers appeared in the living-room, and she likes it even less when threatened with four.

For all practical purposes, I believe that stereo is perfectly adequate. And although quadraphonic tapes are fine, the process of making quad discs is terribly complicated. You have to have a decoder and two stereo amplifiers, and if you want to make quad records that can be played on stereo machines it becomes worse still: you tend to get a lot of 'cross-talk' between the tracks, making the sound more impure than on a straightforward stereo record. In fact, I'm so convinced that quad has come and gone, that in the design of our new studios out in Montserrat we have not included quad recording equipment.

Stereo, however, is a different matter altogether. When it arrived, one of our first problems was how best to place the microphones. In the early days, we had two ways. One was to have two microphones, each in a corner of the studio, facing along the two diagonals. That way you got two different kinds of information out of the same source. The other way was to use what we call a stereo pair. This is when two microphones, of either the 'cardioid' or 'ribbon' type, are placed together at the centre of the recording, but facing at ninety degrees away from each other. Because of their particular pattern of pick-up, as in the 'polar diagrams' I was mentioning earlier, not only will the mike facing left pick up the left-hand side of the orchestra and the other the right-hand, but each will also pick up a little of the other's area. The result is that the sound will be spread over the whole stereo picture; when it is put on to stereo tape in the form of two signals, one from each mike, it will have the same spread as the pair of microphones received in the first place.

That was the simple way of making a stereo recording. Today, with both classical and rock music, it has become a very complicated affair. We use not only stereo pairs, but also mono mikes whose output is fed into the stereo picture wherever the producer wants. All this is purely a matter of taste. For example, when using the Fender electric piano, many producers give that a stereo effect of its own, making it oscillate between one speaker and the other. Stereo took the producer into the realm of 'anything goes'. He no longer had to think in terms of making a record sound as the original would have sounded on the stage or in the concert hall. He could make any artificial sound he wanted, provided it was pleasing to the ear.

On the *Sgt. Pepper* album we did all sorts of things with the stereo effect. We had things in absurd positions. We had movement, with an instrument floating from one side to the other, giving the listener the impression that it was almost flying over his head. On the other hand, taste would prevent you from trying something like that if you were recording Rachmaninov's Piano Concerto. People do like to listen to their favourite works recorded in a way that evokes the concert hall. They don't want the piano, in the middle of its cadenza, floating through the roof and travelling across to the other side of the platform. Equally important, Rachmaninov didn't have that in mind, either. But if I'm going to write an electronic work called 'Space Odyssey', I can do whatever I please, and my only regret will be that I won't be able to reproduce my recorded sound in the auditorium.

But then again, you have to remember that an auditorium isn't just one seat. There are seats right at the front and others right at the back. So where do you place your sound? As I said, it's a matter of taste, but if I'm recording a piano concerto, I will want it to sound as if you're standing right in front of the orchestra, a little behind the conductor. I will have the piano in the centre, first and second violins on the left, violas and cellos on the right. The harp would probably go left, trumpets and trombones possibly on the right, horns and woodwind in the centre. Something like that.

What I would never do is to make it sound as though you were listening to it from the back of the auditorium, for one very good reason. When the record is played at home, the room becomes the auditorium, and the farther you get from your speakers, the more mono the sound is going to become. To take it to the absurd, if you stand a mile away from a pair of stereo speakers four feet apart, you won't hear any stereo effect at all. But if you go within the magic triangle, the equilateral triangle of which you are the apex and the two speakers the other two corners, that is the ideal position. Some people, including quite a few engineers, actually prefer to sit just outside that triangle; my preference is to sit just inside it. If, however, you had made the original recording with the idea of re-producing the sound from the back of the auditorium, you wouldn't get much stereo effect wherever you sat, because you wouldn't in real life either.

The danger in stereo recording comes with the greater number of mikes we use. The more we use, of course, the more flexibility we have in placing on our stereo picture the particular sound each mike is recording. But that leads to the risk of picking up too much of what other mikes are recording, which can lead to 'ghost images'. In a live recording you're bound to get a certain amount of pick-up between mikes. You're bound to get a certain amount of trumpet on the string mike, for instance—though the other way around, strings on the trumpet mike, is not so likely, since the trumpets are much louder. In Abbey Road Number One studio, large, live, and highly reverberant, we got a glorious string sound, but the bane of our lives was the tremendous amount of 'dirt' we picked up on the string mikes from the other instruments—the bass guitar, the drums, the heavy brass.

Not that I want to eliminate that altogether. To my taste, a certain amount of it does help to colour the sound. Sometimes I set out to do it deliberately. In recording drums, I sometimes put a mike in the distance in order to get the sound space around them. The reason is that today's technique of close-miking means you tend to lose a lot of the natural overtones. So I actually encourage a certain amount of spillage between one mike and another.

It's true that close-miking is often necessary in order to achieve separation of sounds. Again, it's a matter of placing. If you have a cardioid mike ten feet away from one instrument, and another instrument ten feet behind the first one, you'll pick up more of the second instrument than if you put the mike four inches from the first and had the second twenty feet behind. But certain instruments don't work well with close-miking. A violin sounds awful if you put a mike four inches away from it. You lose all the beautiful resonance of the body which is generating the tones, and instead you pick up all the scratch and scrape that you would hear if you put your ear next to a violin while it was being played. I remember the John Barry Seven—before John became a film composer—recording a piece in which he used four violins with the mikes about four inches from them, and lots of echo. The *pizzicati* sounded like machine-guns going off! It was an effective sound, all right, but it was a gimmick, and it doesn't happen to be how I like to hear violins. Apart from anything else, you're losing the benefit of Stradivarius and his colleagues!

A bass drum, on the other hand, will sound flabby and boomy if you record it from a distance. But put a mike two inches away from it and you get a nice crisp sound, which is what you need for rock instruments. It's a question of horses for courses, and it's the producer's job to know the characteristics of each instrument as much as the technical qualities of different microphones.

When stereo arrived, it was with techniques like this that the producer could make the best use of the new tool he had been given. But at first stereo had one great limitation. It was effectively two separate recordings, on two separate tracks—and only two. There was no such thing as re-mixing. We made the recording as we went along, and apart from a certain amount of equalisation—cutting a bit off the top or bottom frequencies, or compressing them—that was the final product. You couldn't alter the balance between the instruments on the tape. The relationships of voice to rhythm, of drums to bass, were fixed once they had been recorded.

It was pretty obvious that it would be a great luxury if we could delay the moment of truth, the moment of combining all those sounds as a final product, as long as possible.

For that, there was only one possible answer: more tracks. Luckily, they were on their way. We were going to need them.

7

HARD DAYS AND NIGHTS

IT WAS in April 1962 that I got the phone call from Syd Coleman, a friend and one of the music industry's nice guys, who was head of Ardmore & Beechwood, the EMI publishing company with offices above the HMV shop in Oxford Street.

'George,' he said, 'I don't know if you'd be interested, but there's a chap who's come in with a tape of a group he runs. They haven't got a recording contract, and I wonder if you'd like to see him and listen to what he's got?'

'Certainly,' I said. 'I'm willing to listen to anything. Ask him to come and see me.'

'O.K., I will. His name's Brian Epstein.'

When I said that I was willing to listen to anything, it was absolutely true. The comedy records had been fine, and had begun to put Parlophone on the map. But I was looking, with something close to desperation, for an act from the pop world. I was frankly jealous of the seemingly easy success other people were having with such acts, in particular Norrie Paramor, my opposite number on Columbia, whose artist Cliff Richard was on an apparently automatic ride to stardom.

It seemed to me that all that was needed, in producing someone like that, was a good song—whereas, with the comedy records, every one was a major production. For instance, I recorded 'Hole in the Ground' with Bernard Cribbins; but there was no automatic follow-up to a record like that. I had to search until we found 'Right Said Fred'. To maintain that sort of standard meant a completely new set of ideas each time, because Bernard Cribbins didn't sell just because he was Bernard Cribbins. It was the combination of Bernard Cribbins and a very amusing song which sold, while to a certain extent someone like Cliff Richard would sell whatever he recorded. What I wanted was a 'fireproof' act like that.

The day after Syd's call, Brian Epstein came to see me—a well-spoken, smartly turned out, engagingly amiable, 'clean' young man. What I didn't realise at the time was that he was in London for his final, desperate attempt to get someone interested in his group, the Beatles.

Decca had turned them down, after at least giving them two auditions. Pye, Philips and everyone else had turned them down out of hand. He had even been to EMI, through the good offices of Ron White of the EMI sales team, whom Brian and his father knew through NEMS, the large music shop they ran in Liverpool. Ron White says that two of the four EMI heads of label heard Beatles tapes before I did. The other three producers and A&R men who heard them were Norman Newell, Walter Ridley, and Norrie Paramor. Two out of those three must have been at least as guilty as poor old Dick Rowe of Decca, who got all the public 'stick'.

For his final effort, Brian had decided that he should have some discs cut from the tape he had with him, because they would be easier to play to people. That was what took him to the HMV shop in Oxford Street, in one of whose departments, for a fee of something like £1 10s, anyone could get a disc cut privately. The engineer who cut the discs for him was Ted Huntley, who used to work at EMI studios, and who I believe is now successfully retired and running a hotel in Jersey. Ted thought that the sound he was hearing was rather good, and while Brian was still with him he rang

Syd Coleman on the floor above. 'I think you might be interested in this group,' he said, 'because I don't think they have a publisher at the moment.'

So upstairs went Brian with his newly cut discs. But he told Syd: 'I don't think I want a publisher until I get a record deal.'

Syd asked: 'Well, what kind of dealings have you had with the record people?'

Brian had to confess that he had already been to most of the record companies.

'Why don't you go round and see George Martin at Parlophone?' said Syd. 'He deals in unusual things. He's had a big success with the most unlikely recording acts. I'll give him a ring and make an appointment, if you like.'

That was how Brian came to arrive in my new office in Manchester Square, to which we had moved from Great Castle Street. To start with, he gave me a big 'hype' about this marvellous group who were doing such great things in Liverpool. He told me how everybody up there thought they were the bee's knees. He even expressed surprise that I hadn't heard of them—which, in the circumstances, was pretty bold. I almost asked him in reply where Liverpool was. The thought of anything coming out of the provinces was extraordinary at that time. Then he played me his disc, and I first heard the sound of the Beatles.

The recording, to put it kindly, was by no means a knock-out. I could well understand that people had turned it down. The material was either old stuff, like Fats Waller's 'Your Feet's Too Big', or very mediocre songs they had written themselves. But . . . there was an unusual quality of sound, a certain roughness that I hadn't encountered before. There was also the fact that more than one person was singing, which in itself was unusual. There was something tangible that made me want to hear more, meet them and see what they could do. I thought as I listened: Well, there just might be something here. At least it's worth following up. I did not do handstands against the wall and say: 'This is the greatest thing ever!' I simply thought it was worth a shot.

I suggested to Brian that he should bring the boys, who at that time were performing at the Star Club in Hamburg, to Abbey Road studios for a recording test. Unknown to me at the time, he groaned inwardly. It seemed to him that he had heard that sort of song before. But we went ahead and fixed a date for 6 June.

It was love at first sight. That may seem exaggerated, but the fact is that we hit it off straight away. I met them at Abbey Road's Number Three studio, where we were to do the test—John, Paul, George, and Pete Best, their drummer, with all their gear. My first impression was that they were all quite clean. That was obviously Brian's influence. Their haircuts were fairly shocking for that time, of course, though compared with today's styles they were almost short-back-and-sides. But the most impressive thing was their engaging personalities. They were just great people to be with.

From their point of view, I suppose I was fairly famous. They were great fans of Peter Sellers, and knew that I had been making his and the other comedy records, and they were obviously prepared to like me from knowing what I'd done.

I remember George Harrison being the most talkative at that first meeting, and Pete Best not saying a word throughout the whole afternoon. But he did have the advantage of being the handsomest of the group, very sullen, and rather like James Dean. His drumming, on the other hand, was not good. At the end of the test I took Brian to one side and said, 'I don't know what you're going to do with the group as such, but this drumming isn't good enough for what I want. It isn't regular enough. It doesn't give the right kind of sound. If we do make a record, I'd much prefer to have my own drummer—which won't make any difference to you, because no one will know who's on the record anyway.' What I didn't realise at the time was that the group already wanted Pete Best out and Ringo

Starr in, and that my remarks were something in the nature of a last straw.

The group as a whole confirmed by their playing my earlier feeling that we might be able to do something together. But what that something would be was the big question. At the test they played a few of their own numbers, like 'Love Me Do', 'Hello Little Girl', 'P.S. I Love You' and 'Ask Me Why'. The rest was mostly old stuff, like 'Besame Mucho', as it had been on the discs Brian had played me. Frankly, the material didn't impress me, least of all their own songs. I felt that I was going to have to find suitable material for them, and was quite certain that their songwriting ability had no saleable future!

By July, I had made up my mind, and told Brian that I wanted to sign a contract with the Beatles. It was a tough contract. It lasted for a year in the first instance, during which I guaranteed to record four titles. In return, they, the four of them and Brian, would receive a total of one penny per double-sided record sold—a grand sum to share between the five of them! Then there were four further options of a year each, and with extreme generosity I included a yearly rise in royalties in stages of one farthing. In the second year they would get a penny farthing, and so on up to the princely sum of twopence in the fifth year. What that meant, if I chose to exercise those options, was that they were bound to EMI for five years, during which I was not forced to record more than two singles per year. In retrospect, it was a good indication of the EMI training/brainwashing to which I had been subjected.

But at least they had been given a recording contract. There's no doubt that as things had worked out for them, I was the last chance. At that time I was very much the joker in the music-business pack, and if I, too, had turned them down, it's very hard to guess what would have happened. Possibly they would just have broken up, and never have been heard of again.

And even I hadn't got it right to start with. When I first met them, there was no obvious leader. They all spoke in turn, and I went home wondering which one of them was going to be the star. My thinking was so coloured by the success of people like Tommy Steele and Cliff Richard that I couldn't imagine a group being successful as a group. I felt that one of them was bound to come out as having a better voice than the others. Whoever that was would be the one, and the rest would become like Cliff Richard's backing group, the Shadows. I was quite wrong.

I put them all on test individually, getting them to sing numbers in turn, and my original feeling was that Paul had a sweeter voice, John's had more character, and George was generally not so good. I was thinking, on balance, that I should make Paul the leader. Then, after some thought, I realised that if I did so I would be changing the nature of the group. Why do that? Why not keep them as they were? It hadn't been done before—but then, I'd made a lot of records that hadn't been 'done before'. Why not experiment in pop as I had in comedy?

The idea was reinforced when I decided, before we made a record, to go up to Liverpool with Judy to see 'on the ground' what all the fuss was about. The Cavern was a sweaty little railway-arch kind of place. It was literally like a dungeon. There were arched brick walls, and the boys were playing in one of the caverns. Some of the audience were in the adjoining arches, so that they couldn't even see the group. But they could hear them. How they could hear them! A lot of people could hear them from Liverpool docks.

The place was crammed full of teenagers sitting on bare benches, with no room to dance. The story has often been put around that as we came into the place, our hats and coats were taken by a hat-check girl named Cilla Black—but she hotly denies it, and I certainly don't remember it. But I do remember that they tried to make room for us, which was impossible, since there wasn't any, and that meant that some of the kids had to be removed. In one case it was an involuntary removal, when a girl fainted and had to be brought out in the only possible way, passed from arm to outstretched arm, supine above the heads of all the others.

The walls were streaming with condensation. It was amazing that the boys didn't get electrocuted, because there was water everywhere—a combination of general dampness and sweat, evaporated and re-condensed upon the walls. The atmosphere too was what is frequently, though often inaccurately, known as 'electric'. They sang all the rock-and-roll numbers that they'd copied from American records, and it was very raucous, and the kids loved every minute of it. Up till then there had been nothing to involve young people to quite the same extent. The rock-and-roll gyrations of Tommy Steele and Cliff Richard were clinical, anaemic, even anaesthetic, compared with the total commitment of the Beatles, which somehow got down to the very roots of what the kids wanted.

A group they were, and a group they had to stay, and on 11 September 1962 we finally got together to make their first record. Since they were obviously very keen on their own songs, I asked them to give me a selection. From that selection we decided on 'Love Me Do', backed by 'P.S. I Love You'.

I wanted to get them involved from the start in the techniques of recording, so after the first run-through I called them out to the control room to hear a playback. 'This is what you've been doing,' I said. 'You must listen to it, and if there's anything you don't like, tell me, and we'll try and do something about it.'

That was when George Harrison, the smart-ass, replied, 'Well, for a start, I don't like your tie.' Everyone fell about with hoots of laughter, and the others were hitting him playfully, as schoolboys do when one of them has been cheeky to teacher. I learned later that when they were out of my hearing they got on to him about it again and told him: 'You mustn't say things like that to him. He's very touchy.' The fact is that I too thought it was funny. As I was to learn, it was typical Beatle humour.

But there was a problem to go with the humour of that first session. They had told me that they had found a great drummer from another group, whose name was Ringo Starr and who would be replacing Pete Best. I had said, 'Fine. Bring him along and let him see what we're doing, and next time he'll have a go.' When they turned up, however, Ringo and all, they were fully expecting him to participate straight away. I wouldn't have it, especially since I had engaged a very experienced and good session musician named Andy White to play the drums. So I told them: 'This is nonsense. I've been bitten once. I'm giving you a very good drummer, who's probably better than Ringo Starr, and that's who's going to play the drums.' Ringo was obviously very upset. I learned later that he was very depressed about it, and thought I was trying to put him down. But I wasn't. I simply didn't know what he was like, and wasn't prepared to take risks.

In the end we worked out a compromise. We made two versions of 'Love Me Do'. On one of them Andy played drums and Ringo played the tambourine. On the other, Ringo played drums. I think that in the end we issued the one with Ringo playing drums, but what happened to the version with him on tambourine I just don't know. It didn't matter to me then, and it doesn't now, though I know that all the Beatle maniacs will scream: 'God! Such an important historical fact. You should have made a note of it!'

But I did quickly realise that Ringo was an excellent drummer for what was required. He's not a 'technical' drummer. Men like Buddy Rich and Gene Krupa would run rings round him. But he's a good solid rock drummer with a super steady beat, and he knows how to get the right sound out of his drums. Above all, he does have an individual sound. You can tell Ringo's drums from anyone else's, and that character was a definite asset to the Beatles' early recordings.

We released 'Love Me Do' on 4 October, and I began the process of trying to get it plugged. Not that EMI were much help. I was already treated with some scepticism because of the oddball recordings I had made, and when I announced that I was issuing a record by a group called the Beatles, everyone at the monthly supplement meeting fell about laughing. 'Is this another of George's gimmicks?' someone asked. 'Is it really Spike Milligan disguised?'

I told them: 'I'm serious. This is a great group, and we're going to hear a lot more from them.' But no one took much notice. They were too busy laughing. And Ardmore & Beechwood, the EMI publishers, whose Syd Coleman had first put Brian Epstein on to me, did virtually nothing about getting the record played.

But I was determined. I was by now absolutely convinced that I had a hit group on my hands—though I knew that I hadn't got it with the first record, feeling the quality of the song wasn't really up to it. In the end it only got to number seventeen in the charts, in spite of Brian Epstein's efforts to push it through his family's store. I remember Brian phoning me up to tell me he couldn't get fresh supplies of the record—which was sad, since I suppose that most of the sales which pushed it even as far as seventeen were in Liverpool. 'What on earth is happening with EMI?' Brian demanded. I knew damn well what was happening, or rather what wasn't. The people down south simply didn't have confidence in the record, although at least number seventeen was a start. Brian wasn't happy. 'Ardmore and Beechwood didn't help us very much over that record. When the next one comes out I don't want to give the publishing to them.'

'That may be so,' I said, 'but the first priority is to find a hit song for the boys to sing.' I set about the task. I knew I had it when Dick James brought me a number written by Mitch Murray called 'How Do You Do It?' After he'd played it to me I jumped up and said, 'That's it. We've got it. This is the song that's going to make the Beatles a household name, like Harpic.'

Brian pressed on with his search for a new publisher. Finally he came to me and said that he was going to give the publishing to an American company called Hill & Range.

'Why an American company?' I asked.

'Because they're jolly good publishers, and besides, they do all the Elvis Presley stuff.'

'Well, it doesn't really make sense, Brian,' I said, 'because what you really want is someone who's going to work flat out for you, someone who's going to give us that extra push I need to plug the records. In other words, someone who's hungry.'

'So, who shall I go to?' he asked.

'As I said, someone who's hungry, and above all someone who's very straight.'

I gave him the names of three very good friends, all of whom I knew to be honest people, all very hard-working publishers—David Platz, Alan Holmes, and Dick James. The only problem with David and Alan was that, like Hill & Range, they were American-owned. Nor were they as hungry as Dick, who had just left Sidney Bron to set up his own publishing company. He needed work, he needed money, he badly needed a hit. So I suggested that Brian see him first of all.

Dick had been the first person I had recorded on my own initiative in the early days of working under Oscar Preuss. Isobel Burdett, a contact of mine at the BBC, had told me: 'Dick's unhappy with his present recording arrangements. Why don't you meet up with him? You'd get on well together.' And so it proved. We made some fair records. One of them was 'Tenderly', on which I used for the first time a young arranger named Ron Goodwin who had been working with Petula Clark. That was the start of my long association with Ron.

Dick was delighted. Straight away he agreed to take the publishing, and in so doing made a very clever deal. He suggested to Brian that a new company, to be called Northern Songs, should be started, of which he would own 50%, and the Beatles and Brian the other 50%. It was clever because in offering as large a slice as 50% he ensured that they would sign a contract for a long period of time, during which all their works would go to that company, exclusively. He wouldn't have got a deal like that had he offered them a smaller share. In addition, as I later learned, he made it a condition that Northern Songs would be handled and managed by Dick James Music, which took a 10% handling fee off the top. In effect, of every £100 that came in royalties, Dick James Music took £10, and the remaining £90 was split 50–50.

Generously, he then came to me and offered me a share in the company. I couldn't accept. 'It's very kind of you to think of me like that,' I said. 'But on the other hand, it isn't ethical. I'm working for EMI. I'm an employee of EMI, and I'm engaging an act, and therefore, in a way, I'm engaging you. I think it would be wrong to split my interests.'

I couldn't know at the time that saying those few words was the equivalent of turning down millions of pounds. But that's neither here nor there. I'm certainly not a millionaire, but I can say with my hand on my heart that I have no regrets about turning down the offer. I've been very lucky with what I went on to do. And I sleep well at nights.

With the publishing arranged, the immediate job was to get the next record out, and when the Beatles and I next got together I played them 'How Do You Do It?' They were not very impressed. They said they wanted to record their own material, and I read the riot act. 'When you can write material as good as this, then I'll record it,' I told them. 'But right now we're going to record this.' And record it we did, with John doing the solo part. It was a very good record indeed, and is still in the archives of EMI. I heard it recently, and it sounds quite good even today. But it was never issued. The boys came back to me and said: 'We've nothing against that song, George, and you're probably right. But we want to record our own song.'

Somewhat testily I asked them: 'Have you got anything that's any good?'

'Well, listen to this, George. You've heard it before—"Please Please Me"—but we've revamped it, and we've done it this way . . .'

I listened. It was great. 'Yeah, that's good,' I said. 'Let's try that one.' I told them what beginning and what ending to put on it, and they went into Number Two studio to record. It went beautifully. The whole session was a joy. At the end of it, I pressed the intercom button in the control room and said, 'Gentlemen, you've just made your first number-one record.'

They had. Dick worked like a demon after the record was released in January 1963. He managed to get hold of Philip Jones, who was head of light entertainment for one of the commercial TV stations, and persuaded him to put the Beatles on 'Thank Your Lucky Stars'. It was a tremendous coup. On top of that, EMI finally got off their backsides, and realised that George wasn't quite so crazy and that this was something worth backing. They actually played the record on their Radio Luxembourg programme, which was jolly decent of them. It reached the number-one spot very quickly, and suddenly the whole thing snowballed and mushroomed and any other mixed metaphor you care to think of. From that moment, we simply never stood still.

After the success of 'Please Please Me' I realised that we had to act very fast to get a long-playing album on the market if we were to cash in on what we had already achieved. Because, while a single which sells half a million doesn't reap all that great a reward, half a million albums is big business. I knew their repertoire from the Cavern, and I called the boys down to the studio and said: 'Right, what you're going to do now, today, straight away, is play me this selection of things I've chosen from what you do in the Cavern.' There were fourteen songs in all, some by the Beatles, some by the American artists whom they liked to copy. We started at ten that morning, with Norman Smith as the balance engineer, and recorded straight on to twin-track mono. By eleven o'clock at night we had recorded the lot, thirteen new tracks, to which we added the existing recording of 'Please Please Me'.

All we did really was to reproduce the Cavern performance in the comparative calm of the studio. I say 'comparative', because there was one number which always caused a furore in the Cavern—'Twist and Shout'. John absolutely screamed it. God alone knows what he did to his larynx each time he performed it, because he made a sound rather like tearing flesh. That *had* to be right on the first take, because I knew perfectly well that if we had to do it a second time it would never be as good.

Like its namesake single, the album rapidly went to number one, and because of the popularity of 'Twist and Shout' (which was not actually a Beatles song) we issued an EP with that and three other titles. It too went to number one in the singles charts, the first time an EP had done so. The boys were elated with their success. I asked them for another song as good as 'Please Please Me', and they brought me one—'From Me to You'. I said, 'I want more.' Along came 'She Loves You'.

There seemed to be a bottomless well of songs, and people have often asked me where that well was dug. Who knows? To begin with, they'd been playing about at writing songs since they were kids, and had a large amount of raw material which simply needed shaping. A lot of the songs we made into hits started life as not very good embryos. When they had first played me 'Please Please Me', it had been in a very different form.

The way that Lennon and McCartney worked together wasn't the Rodgers-and-Hart kind of collaboration. It was more a question of one of them trying to write a song, getting stuck, and asking the other: 'I need a middle eight. What have you got?' They were both tunesmiths in their own right, and would help each other out as the need arose. In the early days, that was a matter of necessity. But as they developed their art, each moved on to writing songs entirely on his own. Collaboration became rare, apart from the odd word or line: it was either a John Lennon song or a Paul McCartney song. We established the working format that whoever wrote the song generally sang it, and the others would join in. If it were John's song, he would sing it, and when we came to the middle eight— the section in the middle of a song where the tune changes—Paul would sing thirds above or below, or whatever; if a third part were needed, George would join in. It was a very simple formula.

I would meet them in the studio to hear a new number. I would perch myself on a high stool, and John and Paul would stand around me with their acoustic guitars and play and sing it—usually without Ringo or George, unless George joined in the harmony. Then I would make suggestions to improve it, and we'd try it again. That's what is known in the business as a 'head arrangement', and we didn't move out of that pattern until the end of what I call the first era. That was the era which lasted through 'Love Me Do', 'Please Please Me', 'From Me to You', 'She Loves You', and 'I Want to Hold Your Hand', which were the first batch of recordings.

At that point there wasn't much arranging to do. My function as producer was not what it is today. After all, I was a mixture of many things. I was an executive running a record label. I was organising the artists and the repertoire. And on top of that, I actually supervised the recording sessions, looking after what both the engineer and the artist were doing. Certainly I would manipulate the record to the way I wanted it, but there was no arrangement in the sense of orchestration. They were four musicians—three guitarists and a drummer—and my role was to make sure that they made a concise, commercial statement. I would make sure that the song ran for approximately two and a half minutes, that it was in the right key for their voices, and that it was tidy, with the right proportion and form.

At the beginning, my speciality was the introductions and the endings, and any instrumental passages in the middle. I might say, for instance: '"Please Please Me" only lasts a minute and ten seconds, so you'll have to do two choruses, and in the second chorus we'll have to do such-and-such.' That was the extent of the arranging. Again, the way they first sang 'Can't Buy Me Love' was by starting on the verse, but I said: 'We've got to have an introduction, something that catches the ear immediately, a hook. So let's start off with the chorus.' It was all really a matter of tidying things up. But that record was the point of departure for something rather more sophisticated.

With 'Yesterday' we used orchestration for the first time; and from then on, we moved into whole new areas. The curious thing is that our relationship moved in two different directions at once. On the one hand, the increasing sophistication of the records meant that I was having a greater and greater influence on the music. But the personal relationship moved in the other direction. At the start, I was like a master with his pupils, and they did what I said. They knew nothing about recording, but heaven knows they learned quickly: and by the end, of course, I was to be the servant while they were the masters. They would say, 'Right, we're starting tonight at eight o'clock,' and I would be there. It was a gradual change of power, and of responsibility in a way, because although at the end I still clung to putting in my two cents' worth, all I could do was influence. I couldn't direct.

But that was later. Now we were in 1963, surely the busiest year of my life. I was totally caught up in the excitement of it all, and Brian Epstein was working round the clock. Naturally we had to spend a lot of time together, and we became very firm friends. I remember his telling me, 'We're going to have a tremendous partnership, George. With you recording my acts, we're unbeatable. And with Dick publishing them, we're an unbeatable trio.'

It certainly seemed that way. The next group he brought me was Gerry and the Pacemakers. For them, I dipped into my song-bag and once more produced 'How Do You Do It?', the song that the Beatles hadn't wanted to issue. Gerry recorded it, and it went to number one. But if that was a little personal vindication of my faith in the song, a more interesting recording Gerry made was of 'You'll Never Walk Alone', the old American standard. He always got a great reaction from audiences when he performed it, and it was Brian's idea to record it. For the first time, I backed Gerry with a large string orchestra, which was a great departure for him. He had been a very jolly rock-and-roll star, doing little two-beat songs, and suddenly here was this big ballad with which his voice could hardly cope. All the same, I think it was largely that record which was responsible for the song becoming the universal football-crowd song it is today.

Not content with two successful groups, Brian now brought me a third, Billy J. Kramer and the Dakotas. Billy was certainly a very good-looking boy, but when I listened to him I was forced to the conclusion that his was not the greatest voice in the world. 'I've got so much on my plate, Brian,' I said, 'and I don't think that Billy has really got the voice that will do what we need.'

But Brian had an enormously persuasive way about him. 'George, you know perfectly well that you and I and Dick can make it work. You can produce a record with Billy that will make the grade—I know you can.'

'That's all very well, Brian, but you can't make great things when the raw material isn't up to scratch.'

'You listen again,' he said. 'I'm sure you'll find Billy's voice isn't as bad as all that.'

It wasn't all that good, either; but Brian was so keen that I agreed. I decided the only way I could ever make a hit out of him was always to double-track his voice—in other words, to record the song once and then have him sing it a second time, following his own voice. There were places where even the double-tracking didn't work too well, and to cover these I invented what I called the windup piano. After I'd done my basic track, I overlaid piano, which I played myself—recording it at half speed and then doubling it to normal speed to give a kind of harpsichord effect. Where there was any offending phrase from the Kramer tonsils, I put in a bit of this piano and mixed it a bit louder. For the inquisitive, I may add that I didn't pay myself for these pieces of gratuitous musicianship, since I reckoned that if I did so, I would be getting money that a musician should be getting.

For Billy's first record we chose 'Do You Want to Know a Secret', a song from the Beatles' first album. In those days we had a policy that anything the Beatles recorded as an album title was not issued by them as a single, and vice versa. The song had been on the *Please Please Me* album (we'd obviously made an exception in the case of 'Please Please Me' itself, to cash in on their new popularity), and the Beatles didn't want to issue it as a single. In any case, they could already see the advantage of having their songs covered by other people, and since it suited Billy down to the ground, we decided to make it with him. It was issued on 26 April 1963. It went to number one. The process was starting to seem almost inevitable.

Then we had what appeared at first to be a setback. Brian brought me a girl singer named Priscilla White. All her friends called her Cilla, and Brian, for some reason best known to himself, didn't like the idea of Cilla White, so he'd gone to the other end of the spectrum and called her Cilla Black. For me, she was even more of a problem child than Billy had been. Although she had a good, if thin, voice, she was a rock-and-roll screecher in the true Cavern tradition, with a piercing nasal sound. That was all right in itself, but finding songs for her was clearly going to be very difficult.

On the other hand, the Beatles by this time were bubbling over with enthusiasm for their own works—and rightly so. We had opened the vent, the oil had started gushing up, and the well, which I had originally thought might soon dry up, simply kept on producing more and more. Cilla had been singing a song of theirs at the Cavern called 'Love of the Loved', and we decided to record that, with a special arrangement I had written for trumpets. It didn't sell well at all. It was not a number one.

Then Brian went to America, to try to get people over there interested in his stable of artists. When he returned he brought me a song he had heard over there by a young man named Burt Bacharach. It was called 'Anyone Who Had a Heart'. I absolutely flipped. I thought it was marvellous. 'Brian,' I said, 'what a lovely song. Thank you so much for bringing it over. It's absolutely ideal for Shirley.' By whom I meant Shirley Bassey, whom I was recording at this time.

Brian looked askance. 'I wasn't thinking of her, I was thinking of Cilla.'

'Really? Do you think Cilla could sing a song like this?' I asked, doubtfully.

'I know my Cilla. She can do it.'

'O.K., let's have a go, then,' I said, still not convinced.

By now I was so busy that I didn't have the time to score the song myself; besides, although I had done the trumpets on her first record, I wasn't then known as an orchestrator, and with others around who had big reputations it would have been cheeky of me to assert myself too much. So I brought in Johnny Pearson, who did a marvellous score for the song. Cilla recorded it, and it did go to number one, making her a star in the process.

I heard that Dionne Warwick, who recorded the song in America, was furious because we had pinched her version. Well, yes and no. Most songs have something inherent about the way they're done which is in itself an arrangement. What Johnny did was to retain that part, which was absolutely right for the song, and then orchestrate it. The two records sounded similar, but I am sure that ours was better than the American one. Certainly from an orchestral point of view we had a much better sound, and it deserved to be number one.

With all this talent on the move, Brian and I had to establish a working formula. For the Beatles, we agreed that if possible we would release a single every three months and a long-playing record every year. Having Gerry, and Billy, and Cilla as well, we had to stagger the issue of their singles too, so that as far as possible there was an overlap but no clash. It seemed to work. Out of the fifty-two weeks of 1963, we topped the charts no less than thirty-seven times.

Sleep was something of a luxury that year, because in addition to the Epstein stable I was still recording a lot of my earlier artists, like Ron Goodwin, Matt Monro, and dear old Jimmy Shand. But the year belonged to the Beatles, and the search for talent from the north became a kind of Klondike gold rush. Record companies are notorious for trying to hop on a bandwagon, and if there's a smell of anything new happening they all rush after it, even if it's something as tasteless as punk rock. After the Beatles had struck gold, every record company sent men up to Liverpool to find a group— and they all came back with one! Some made it, many didn't. Pye had the Searchers, who had a big hit with 'Needles and Pins'. Even my own assistant, Ron Richards, went north in search of musical nuggets, and found, not in Liverpool but in Manchester, a group called the Hollies. He came back and said: 'I've got this group. What shall I do with them?'

'Sign them up,' I said, wondering where this bonanza was going to stop. 'But I can't cope with them. You'll have to record them yourself.' Of course they proved to be immensely successful, with one of them, Graham Nash, going on to become an American superstar with Crosby, Stills & Nash.

The flood of adulation that greeted this music from the north broke open another dam. Northern became chic. Northern writers and comedians became the 'in' thing. It was the beginning of decentralisation from London, which had always been the Mecca of the entertainment business, monopolising television, radio and records. Suddenly we found that there were other people out there.

By the same token, I think it's rather sad that recently there has been a reaction from people in Liverpool who have almost rejected the Beatles because they 'deserted' their home town. There was a lot of hostility to a plan to erect a statue to them. The feeling was: 'Why the hell should we? They left us anyway, and they don't give a damn about Liverpool any more.' That's very unfair. They had to leave Liverpool; they couldn't stay there all their lives. Why should they be singled out as deserting the city, when there are almost no world entertainers who have stayed in their home towns? And they have never denied their background—a background that gave the world two tunesmiths of genius.

I have often been asked if I could have written any of the Beatles' tunes, and the answer is definitely no: for one basic reason. I didn't have their simple approach to music. Of the four, Paul was the one most likely to be a professional musician, in the sense of learning the trade, learning about notation and harmony and counterpoint. At that time he was friendly with Jane Asher, who came from a musical family. Her mother was a fine musician, a freelance teacher who by sheer coincidence had taught me the oboe when I was at the Guildhall. I think that that family must have had quite an influence on Paul.

Soon after we got together he started taking piano lessons. I, on the other hand, bought myself a guitar and started to teach myself that. There was good reason for both: in the early stages there was a certain lack of communication, and we had to find common ground in which to talk about music. If I suggested a particular complicated chord or harmony to them, and they didn't know it, I would go and play it on the piano and say: 'Look, this kind of thing.' Then they would get their guitars and start trying to find the same notes on them. But they wouldn't get it very readily, because although they could see my fingers on the piano, that didn't mean much to them. All they could try to work out was the sounds they were hearing. But if I played the chord on the guitar myself, they would be able to look at my fingers and say: 'Oh, yes. It's that kind of shape.' With both the guitar and the piano you can learn a great deal from the shape of the player's fingers. But the two instruments are very different, and there's no way of extrapolating from one to the other—which is why I started the guitar. John and Paul, however, learned the piano far more quickly than I could master their instrument. So I dropped the guitar.

But at least we now had a rapport, and could talk to each other about particular notes. There's no doubt that Lennon and McCartney were good musicians. They had good musical brains, and the brain is where music originates—it has nothing to do with your fingers. As it happened, they could also play their own instruments very well. And since those early days they've all improved, especially Paul. He's an excellent musical all 'rounder, probably the best bass-guitar player there is, a first-class drummer, brilliant guitarist and competent piano-player.

But those accomplishments didn't affect their extremely practical approach to music. They simply couldn't understand the need for complication. For example, John once came to me while I was working in the studio with a saxophone section, overdubbing one of his tunes. 'Look,' he said, 'I like what you've done there, but I think it would be a good idea if the saxes did such-and-such . . .', and with that he picked up his guitar and played me some notes.

'Yes, that's quite easy,' I said. 'It'll be a good idea for the saxes to reinforce that.' I quickly wrote out the notes, turned to the saxophone players and said, 'O.K., chaps, these are the notes you play.'

'No,' said John, 'they're not those notes. These are the notes they play—look . . .' and he proceeded to play them to me all over again.

'I know, John,' I explained. 'They're the notes that you're playing. But I'm giving them the notes for their instruments that will correspond to what you're playing.'

'But you've given them the wrong names of the notes!'

'No, I haven't,' I said. 'Because their instruments are in different keys. That's an E flat saxophone, and that's a B flat saxophone. When you play a C on that one, it sounds in B flat. When you play a C on the other saxophone it plays an E flat. So I've got to work out other notes to compensate for that. Do you see?'

'That's bloody silly, isn't it?' he said in disgust.

'Yes, I suppose it is.'

He turned and walked away and left me to it. He just couldn't understand one of those silly little facts of life. Equally, I think that if Paul, for instance, had learned music 'properly'—not just the piano, but correct notation for writing and reading music, all the harmony and counterpoint that I had to go through, and techniques of orchestration—it might well have inhibited him. He thought so too. (And after all, why should he bother, when he had someone around who could do it for him?) Once you start being taught things, your mind is channelled in a particular way. Paul didn't have that channelling, so he had freedom, and could think of things that I would have considered outrageous. I could admire them, but my musical training would have prevented me from thinking of them myself. I think, too, that the ability to write good tunes often comes when someone is not fettered by the rules and regulations of harmony and counterpoint. A tune is a one-fingered thing, something that you can whistle in the street; it doesn't depend upon great harmonies. The ability to create them is simply a gift.

There have been many great musicians who couldn't write a pop tune to save their lives. Equally, the pop world in particular has seen many who have known nothing of music but could write great tunes. Lionel Bart, for example, can't play an instrument. I believe he just whistles his tunes as he thinks of them. Irving Berlin couldn't read music, and could only play the piano in the key of G flat, which is all the black notes. He only played on the black notes. It was the only way he knew. Once he had some success, he could afford to have a special piano built for him. It had a lever at the side, like a fruit-machine, and if he wanted to change key while keeping his fingers on the same notes, he just pulled that.

Wherever the genius came from, the Beatles could certainly write great tunes. Of course, they were already idols in Liverpool, but that was a long way away. By the middle of the year we had screaming kids outside the Abbey Road studios from the moment they heard the Beatles were coming. Their information grapevine was amazing. We tried to keep the session times secret, because the kids became a real problem, and it became harder and harder just to get into the studios. Even so, it was still a fairly local phenomenon—a private English pleasure.

That was before America.

8

LAYERING THE CAKE

For me, making a record is like painting a picture in sound. If I have said that before, the reason is that I cannot over-emphasise it. That is exactly how I think of it, and I suppose the feeling started way back when I made those first records with Peter Sellers.

Not only are we painting sound pictures, but our palette is infinite. We can, if we wish, use any sound in the universe, from the sound of a whale mating to that of a Tibetan wood instrument, from the legitimate orchestra to synthesised sounds. That may be why, of all painters, my favourites are the Impressionists—Renoir, Degas, Cézanne, Monet, Van Gogh, Sisley. It's surely no coincidence that they seem to match so well, almost as visual counterparts, the music of my favourite composers, Debussy and Ravel.

The fascination of recording is that you really do have an unlimited range of musical colours to use. That's one of the main reasons why I enjoyed working with the Beatles so much, because our success won me artistic freedom. For so long I had been the maverick at EMI, always wanting to try new things but seldom given the proper backing to do it. Now, at last, I was able to say: 'Let's have a go at this. It doesn't matter about the cost—we'll just try it.' The bosses could always have stopped me, but by then they didn't want to kill the goose that was laying golden discs, and I was able to explore what were then the more curious corners of innovative recording: multi-speed techniques (like recording something and doubling it up in speed), lifting a tape off and recording it backwards, unusual sound-effects—every possible way of building up a picture in sound.

To do those things a record producer, like any craftsman, needs tools. As I indicated earlier, the first tool that turned him into a craftsman was the advent of stereo. The primary idea behind stereo was to give the *listener* a broader experience; true stereo is the use of two tracks to give a spatial dimension between two speakers. But I soon realised that even where we were not issuing the records in stereo, the stereo recording technique could still be very useful to the *producer* if he simply used its two tracks and mixed them to make a mono record.

That was the very beginning of multi-track recording. Its importance was absolutely fundamental to the producer, because now he could deliberate; he could change his mind. He didn't even have to record both tracks at the same time. What's more, he could record without loss of quality. With only one track, he either had to record the voice at the same time as the backing, or else dub one tape on to another, in which case he lost one generation of sound quality.

With two tracks, it became feasible for the first time to record the basic rhythm and to add the vocal track later, in sync with the previous recording. The advantages of this became evident when I started making hard rock records. Up to the time of the Beatles, most records had been fairly medium pop, for which Jim Dale was my answer to Cliff Richard and Tommy Steele. But, round about the end of the fifties, the beginnings of rock arrived in England, inspired by people like Elvis Presley, and our records were getting harder, our rhythm sounds more definite. This led to much experiment. John Burgess, for example, who today is my partner, was recording Adam Faith, accompanied by John Barry, and they tried ideas like close-miking the strings, resulting in the strange sound I described earlier. Strange or not, the records sold.

I found, starting with Jim Dale and moving through the Vipers skiffle group to the Beatles, that, if I recorded all the rhythm on one track and all the voices on the other, I needn't worry about losing the voices even if I recorded them at the same time. I could concentrate on getting a really loud rhythm sound, knowing that I could always bring it up or down afterwards to make sure the voices were coming through.

In addition, I was able to get an even harder sound, and still retain clarity, by the use of compressors. A compressor does just what its name suggests—it squeezes the sound. The loud sounds are pushed down a bit in volume and the quiet sounds up. This was especially necessary where records had a wide dynamic range, where the peaks and troughs of sounds were widely distributed, because of the problem of the needle jumping off.

The late fifties and early sixties were a great time for compressing everything. The compressor was a bit of a new toy, and often people would overcompress. I remember describing the effect of that as being able to hear things punching holes in the sound. If you had a very heavy drum track, for example, and a voice that had to go on top of it, you could compress the whole thing so much that the drums, the loudest thing on the record, would be regulating the volume. You could only hear the voice when the drums weren't impacting. A drum has a very high-impacting sound, one which decays rapidly, and as soon as it started to decay the voice would appear, as if by magic, rather like Pepper's Ghost in the old-time music hall.

Compressed or not, the advantages of being able to add more tracks to your original sound soon became very evident. You would be able to concentrate on the individual sound of each instrument at much greater length than you could afford to give it during the recording session. Musicians' time is money, and economics dictate that you try to record as many titles as you can in a short time. You can't afford to be too self-indulgent about getting perfection within that time. But obviously, if you can play around with the sounds *afterwards,* the whole situation is changed. It was clearly an inno-vation that had to come, but it would need capital investment, and EMI weren't too keen on that. I was forever saying: 'When are we going to get some more tracks in our studios? We're behind the times. Let's bring the studios up to date.' I got a bad reputation at EMI as being the guy who always wanted a bit more—and never got it!

So perhaps it was with some desperation that, amazingly, EMI sent me to America in 1958, to see what the opposition was like. The ostensible reason for going was that I had had a moderate success with Ron Goodwin's 'Skiffling Strings'. For reasons best known to themselves, the Americans retitled it 'Swinging Sweethearts'; it had some success there too, and Ron Goodwin was sent over to do a promotional tour. I was to accompany him.

Capitol Tower, on Hollywood and Vine in Los Angeles, is a thirteen-storey building shaped like a stack of gramophone records. I was hugely impressed. Capitol, who had been bought by EMI a couple of years earlier, were riding on the crest of waves as dramatic as those which thump on to Malibu Beach—Sinatra, Nat King Cole, Peggy Lee, Stan Kenton. Voyle Gilmore, one of the produc-ers, invited me to a Sinatra recording session in studio C at Capitol Tower. The songs were eventually to be issued on the album *Come Fly With Me,* and it was all to be done live. Sinatra was backed by Billy May's orchestra, normally a sound concocted from brass and slurpy saxes. But Nelson Riddle had just enjoyed a run of suc-cesses, and Sinatra liked the sound of Riddle's strings, so Billy May's set-up was augmented by a string section.

Sinatra, accompanied by Lauren Bacall, his current lady, was the complete, efficient professional. He came into the control room, listened to the tracks being run over, and hardly interfered with the engineer, the producer, or Billy May, except perhaps to say, 'Take it up a bit, Bill,' or something of that sort. Mostly he would come in and say, 'O.K., that's it for me.' He did very few takes, and they got through five titles in about four hours.

The only sour note came at the end of the session, when Voyle Gilmore showed Sinatra the design for the cover of the album. Sinatra exploded. He called Gilmore every name under the sun, and disappeared still fuming. I, the country cousin from England, couldn't for the life of me understand what all the fuss was about. Then I was shown the cover, and I did understand. It's the cover that was eventually issued, and it shows Sinatra in his broad-banded hat with a TWA airliner in the background. Sinatra's view was that Capitol were ripping him off by doing some private deal with TWA. The innuendo was that if the record went out like that the Capitol executives would get free publicity, free fares, or free something-or-other. Whatever the truth, Sinatra's attitude was plain—TWA were getting a free advertisement out of his face. Soon after that he left Capitol and set up his own Reprise label.

I returned to England with a head full of ideas. The first thing that had struck me had been that the monitor level in the Capitol control room was much louder than anything I had experienced in London—but in spite of that, the sound was much cleaner, much crisper. I had a careful look at the techniques they were using in their studios, at the kind of mikes, at the acoustics. I remember thinking: Gosh, we've got an awful lot to learn at Abbey Road.

The second great difference was that, compared with our two-track recording on quarter-inch tape, they were using half-inch tape to produce a three-track recording. The reasoning behind this stemmed from an inherent distrust of the 'sound from the middle', which was a development of film techniques and had so astonished people when they had first heard stereo. Their first thought was: Well, if we're going to have more than one track, let's have three, and be *sure* we're getting a good sound in the middle. That is something which you cannot do in stereo using only two tracks. The reason is that if you record your backing on one track and split it between the two stereo speakers, then the backing, being equally divided, will appear to come from the middle; and when you add the voice, splitting that also *in order* to make it come from the middle, the overall effect is mono. On the other hand, if they used two tracks out of their three to get a nice stereo sound from the orchestra, they could then use the third track for the vocal, splitting it between the two stereo channels to put it on its own in the middle, and raising its volume where necessary in relation to that of the stereo backing. It made a lot of sense at the time.

I may have returned to England full of enthusiasm for these new ideas, but it was to be five years before EMI did anything about it. When the Beatles arrived in 1963, I was still forced to record all their early songs using twin-track to produce a mono sound, with the rhythm on one track and the vocal on the other. It was a technique that was to rebound on me many years later.

Bhaskar Menon had become the president of Capitol Records in America. As a student and trainee he had spent a while with me at Parlophone, learning my end of the business. In 1976 he phoned me (I was living in Los Angeles at the time) to say that he was proposing to issue an album called *Rock and Roll Music,* using some of the early Beatles numbers. He asked me if I would approve the tapes before they went out, since they couldn't get hold of any of the Beatles, and I was the only other person of whom they could think who had been involved. So I went along to listen—and was appalled.

EMI were terrified of the Beatles, who had issued an edict that the tapes must not be touched in any way. No one was to 'mutilate' them, and if they were reissued it had to be exactly as they were recorded. EMI had taken this absolutely literally. They had put the tapes on a transfer machine and were going to issue them just as they were—but in stereo! The effect was disastrous. Where I had made the original recording using one track for rhythm and the other for voices, we had put the rhythm track down in volume in order to avoid distortion. The result was that the voices sounded terribly forward. Not only that, but when they stopped singing there was an awful lot of 'dirt' coming up on the vocal track, because when we recorded live we had left the mikes open—which of course hadn't mattered in mono. But in stereo—ugh! And, of course, all the voices were on one side, and all the backing was on the other.

'You can't let that go out!' I said.

'We daren't touch it,' they said, 'because the Beatles wouldn't like it.'

My response was: 'Stuff that for a lark. Let's do something about it.'

I spent two days re-dubbing the tapes, aided by the sophisticated new equipment which had never been available in those early days. I filtered out the sound of the bass from the rhythm track, and brought it into the centre. I brought the rhythm track as a whole away from the edges. I brought the voices to the centre, raised the volume of the rhythm, and compressed the whole lot so that it sounded more of an entity. With a bit of echo to bring them up to date, they really sounded quite tolerable.

Of course, it wasn't really my job. I'd long since left EMI, and I wasn't getting paid—since they were early records, I was not even receiving any royalties on them; I just wanted to make sure that our work didn't get mutilated. But that didn't prevent fierce rows breaking out with the people in England. Roy Featherstone, head of EMI records, said that I shouldn't do it, and that they would have terrible trouble with the Beatles. 'Well, get hold of the Beatles, and tell them I'm here at Capitol, and see what they say,' I told him. But they wouldn't, or they couldn't. The Beatles all had pretty heavy protective shields around themselves anyway. At least the record went out in America in its modified form, so that it was acceptable, but I have a nasty feeling that it went out in England in the original version, which is horrifying.

That was a boomerang from the twin-track days. But at last, towards the end of 1963, with the success of the Beatles adding weight to my continual demands, the EMI bosses decided to join the world of modern recording, and we got four-track. It had taken a long time, so perhaps it is ironic that Abbey Road was to become the best studio in the world—while Capitol had hardly changed.

I went back there a couple of years ago, and that same studio C, where I first saw Sinatra at work, now seemed antiquated. The sound emerging from it was so old-fashioned. I felt so strongly about it that I told Bhaskar Menon: 'For God's sake, why don't you do something about that studio? The studio I once thought was so great hasn't really changed in the last ten years!' It is now, I am happy to report, equipped with a new Neve desk and NECAM automation.

But for us, in 1963, four-track was a huge leap forward. It was on one-inch tape, which was the Continental standard, and we adopted it rather than the American system simply because we thought three-track was too limited. Four-track was to be our standard for many years. Naturally, once the advantages of extra tracks had been realised, we didn't limit our demands to four. We wanted all we could get. But the manufacturers couldn't provide us with the goods; the European manufacturers said, quite rightly, that tape quality at that time didn't allow them to reduce the width of each individual track, and that therefore four tracks were the maximum that one-inch tape would accept. Still, we were constantly pushing them. The record producers always provided the spur, and it was up to the manufacturers to try to satisfy their demands.

When we first got four-track, it was an enormous relief not to have the worries about how many generations of sound quality had been lost which we had suffered in twin-track. But even four tracks are very few. I still have the work-sheet of the recording of 'The Night Before' with the Beatles. It tells me the time I started the session, which was 2.30 in the afternoon, and the way we went about it. Drums, bass and rhythm guitar were on one track; George Harrison's lead guitar on another; the voices on a third. The fourth track was reserved for any little extras, like piano overdubs or backing voices. It was little enough to play with. After all, if you're dealing with a group, and you want some simple thing like having them sing little 'oohs' in the background, that requires an extra track. If you double-track it to make a nicer sound, you will need two extra tracks.

It doesn't take a mathematician to calculate that four-track was still terribly limited. The only way we could get round it was to dub from one four-track to a second four-track—and that, of course, meant losing sound quality. Still, it was a start, and it gave us two great advantages. Remember, four-track is simply a way of saying four individual mono recordings. The problem was how to mix one against another in perfect synchronisation. The film people had done it for years, but then they were using sprocketed tape, which was easy to sync. In the world of ordinary tape there were no such mechanical aids. What four-track gave us was simply four separate recordings which, being on the same tape, were locked together physically, so that when you mixed them to make your final product, they *had* to be in sync.

The second great advantage was that we could play with the sounds on each particular track regardless of what we might or might not subsequently do with the others. For instance we could equalise the sounds—that is, cut the bass, cut the top and boost the middle. We could introduce varying degrees and types of echo. It wasn't limited to the ordinary echo-chamber echo, but included tape-delay echo, and our own invention, which we called Steed, a mixture of tape-delay and echo-chamber. We could compress one track to give more punch to the sound. Later, there were techniques like artificial double-tracking, where the machine did the work, rather than our having to get the artist to sing against his own voice.

Perhaps most important of all, if we weren't satisfied with one track, we could replace it without having to do the whole performance again. We could hedge our bets. I suppose it was that ability to deal with the tracks one by one which first made me think of the process as being like making a layer cake. At the bottom you put a nice heavy layer of sponge as a base. Then you put a layer of jam. Then a layer of cream. Then you top it with more sponge, or icing, or whatever. Recording is like that. Your first track is always your rhythm track. Nowadays, the various components of the rhythm will be split into different tracks, but in the days of four-track the first one took the drums and the bass. To that you would add, on a second track, the harmonies, which might be played by guitars, piano or something else. The lead voice would go on a third. The fourth track would be for the extra little bits—what today we call the 'sweetening'.

So now you had your four layers, linked together physically on the tape, and you could play around with the volume and the dynamic range of each track to your heart's content in order to achieve the balance you wanted. What is more, when you came to the final stage—putting those four sets of sound on to a stereo record—you could place them wherever you wanted within the stereo picture, the sound picture that people who bought the record would ultimately hear. As I explained earlier, that was accomplished simply by the proportion of the sound you allotted to each side of the stereo picture from each of the four tracks—the proportion that would eventually emerge from each of the two loudspeakers at home.

Fired with enthusiasm for these new techniques, like children wanting more sweets, and more, and more, we soon found that the four-track system ran out of tracks all too quickly. We had to find ways of getting more, and the only means of doing that was to dub from one four-track tape to another. And we still wanted to retain our 'stereo picture'.

One technique was to mix your four original tracks down to what would normally be the finished two-track stereo product. You would then put those two tracks on to a fresh four-track machine, which would leave you two spare 'open' tracks to play with. What you couldn't escape was the loss of one generation of sound quality in the process. Again, if you were very courageous, and if you wanted a very heavy sound on one particular track, you could dub all four original tracks down to that one, provided you kept that sound in the centre of the stereo picture. Now you had three other tracks with which to sweeten it. But for the most part I would dub four tracks down to two, giving me two extra tracks. When it later came to the making of the *Sgt. Pepper* album, that technique was taken almost to absurdity. To accommodate all the gimmicks and weird sounds, I needed every track I could lay my hands on. And I didn't have them.

Nor was I to get them until 1967, well after *Sgt. Pepper*. That was the year when eight-track arrived. By that time, tape quality had vastly improved, and we were able to have all eight tracks on the same one-inch tape we had used before. But, and it is an important 'but', the width of each track was halved. Now you might think that since we had started off with two tracks on quarter-inch tape, there should be no reason why we should not have eight tracks on one-inch tape. There was a reason: noise.

As I explained earlier, when each track passes the recording head, not only does it receive the input from the microphone or microphones that are being fed on to it, it also receives the effect of the various imperfections in the tape itself. These imperfections set up magnetic impulses within the recording head, which are passed back on to the part of the tape which is being recorded. That is 'noise'—hiss, crackle, what you will—and is obviously undesirable. Two other things follow. The narrower the track, the more relative noise is induced in the recording head; and equally, the more tracks you have, the more noise you get in your final product. That is the price you pay for multi-track working. Because, don't forget, a stereo recording is all boiled down to two tracks in the end, whether you start with two or four or a thousand tracks. The noise, unfortunately, does not disappear in the wash, or in the mixing. If you start with four tracks, you are going to end up with the noise from four tracks. If you start with a thousand, you are going to end up with the aggregate noise from a thousand.

We haven't reached that stage yet! But when the transition came from eight tracks to sixteen, and subsequently to twenty-four, which is now pretty well the standard equipment, the noise problem could not be ignored. Something had to be done about it. The man who came up with the answer was an American named Dr Ray Dolby.

His invention was called the Dolby Noise Reduction Process. It was first marketed in this country, because although he was an American he found the British much more ready to listen to his ideas.

The technology for his process had probably existed for many years, but it hadn't been used for the simple reason that it wasn't needed. The European tape-machine manufacturers were always very conservative. They designed machines to cope with the existing tape technology. That is why, when they built the first four-track machines, they went straight from a quarter of an inch to one inch, rather than a half, in order to keep well within the tolerance limits of the tape then in use. But when we came to sixteen tracks, on two-inch tape, it became very evident that they could no longer cope with the problem. We were getting far higher background noise than we had come to expect.

One way round that was to load each track to its maximum sound level, 'drowning out' the background noise. But that caused problems in the studio. Imagine, for example, that you had a very quiet flute passage in a piece of music. You would put that on its own separate track. Then you might have a very heavy drum track, a very heavy bass guitar track and a very heavy vocal track. And perhaps a quiet track with a string ensemble on it. If you had recorded the piece naturally, then the bass, drums and voice would probably be fairly well balanced simply by playing them back at normal level. And if you wanted the right balance for the quiet flute, and the quiet strings, they would be way below that level.

But that would allow the noise to come through on those tracks. The answer would be to load each individual track up to the point at which it was saturated with sound, though still well recorded and free of distortion. But if you did that, the flute and strings would be uncomfortably loud in relation to all the other sounds. In cutting down your noise problem, you would meet a problem of balance. So, if possible, you should record fairly naturally.

The solution came from the good Dr Dolby. Put as simply as possible, this is how his process works. When the signal is taken from the recording studio and fed into the Dolby unit, the Dolby automatically raises the level of the quieter sounds, keeping the loud ones at their existing level. It also does something else: it splits up the audio range into three chunks.

Imagine the overall sound of an orchestra. The Dolby, listening to it, will say: 'I'm going to take the bottom end of the audible range, from about 20 cycles up to about 800 cycles.' That is the really low end of the audible spectrum. 'That,' says the Dolby, 'I will treat as one module of sound. Next, I'll take the middle bit, from about 800 to 4000 cycles. That I will call the middle sound. Thirdly, I'll take the range from about 4000 to about 20,000 cycles, and call it the top sound.

'I will treat these three bands of sound separately. Within each band, I will allow any loud sounds to go through as they are. Any really quiet sounds I will boost a lot—say by about fifteen decibels.' That, of course, was exactly what you didn't want in the studio. Don't worry, that was just the input. The Dolby unit had a second function. After all those signals had gone on to the tape, it reversed the process. Everything that had been boosted up was then taken down by the same degree. The result was that what you heard off the tape was identical to the sound you would have heard in the studio.

In effect, what it meant was that the quiet sounds that went on to the tape weren't quiet sounds at all. They were amplified, drowning out all the noise. And when they were reduced again, they reverted to pure, quiet sounds, and the noise was reduced that much more.

The critics of the system claimed that it tended to colour the sound, and that something was lost in the process, but frankly, I have rarely been able to hear the difference. What did worry me was the complication, and particularly the expense—especially when we went to twenty-four tracks—because each track needed its own Dolby unit. Dolby equipment also needs a lot of lining up, and constant adjustment and maintenance. In my own studios at AIR

I know that this is done. But I found that some American studios were apt not to take the same care, with the result that Dolby units there did colour the sound to a degree that even I could hear. So I stopped using them when I recorded in America.

There is also an important qualification to be made about them. They do not eliminate noise altogether; they don't claim to. What they do is, as their name implies, to reduce it. So the arrival of Dr Dolby's invention didn't mean that you could stick to, say, eight tracks and simply re-dub and re-dub. And the addition of more tracks always aggravates the problem, which is one reason why I am sceptical about the need to go to thirty-two tracks, as many people are advocating. Personally, I don't see the need for any more. Besides, the change means a whole new set of equipment. We would have to go from two-inch to three-inch tape—and we would certainly need different recording heads on all our machines.

If people really feel that they have to have more tracks, then the simplest way out, which we have already tried and which works beautifully, is to synchronise two twenty-four-track machines together. Allowing for the fact that you have to leave one track on each machine free to carry the pulse which synchronises them, that gives you forty-six tracks. Lord knows, no one should need more than that!

This technique has another advantage over building, say, a single forty-eight-track machine, and that stems from the actual way in which we tend to use multi-track recording. On the 'layer-cake' system that I was describing earlier, we usually put down the basic tracks first and then start adding other bits to them. Each time we do that we have to run the tape back and forth, and in the course of a few weeks of recording, with all the various alterations one may wish to make to each track, the tape may have to pass the recording heads thousands of times. Even with modern quality, there is an obvious danger of tape wear, and although we haven't had great problems so far, we are reaching the point where we could have. So if someone really wants more than twenty-four tracks, I think it is much more sensible to mix the first lot down to a rough twin-track, which you put on to a second machine for monitoring purposes while you start again with a virgin tape.

When you come to mix the whole thing, of course, you can go back to your original tape as well as the new one, since they are linked electronically by the pulse track which you have put on each. In the old days of four and eight tracks that was simply not possible; once you had dubbed your first tape down to two tracks and transferred them to a second tape, you were irrevocably fixing the balance on those two tracks. There was no going back—and even if there had been Dolby units to eliminate all the noise, that would still have been a major disadvantage.

There was another: the inability to do double-tracking, in most cases, because of the sheer lack of available tracks. I have mentioned double-tracking briefly already. It was something we found out ourselves, by experiment. We discovered that the double-tracking of voices or instruments gave them a different sound. In other words, if you record Fred Smith singing a song, and then re-record him singing the same song in the same way in time with his own first recording, it will be different from having two Fred Smiths, identical in every way, singing at the same time.

Why this is so is not absolutely clear. It may be partly to do with the cancelling-out of vibratos. It may be something to do with being in and out of tune, since nobody actually sings the same song twice in exactly the same way—a fact which can have odd implications. I was working with the Bee Gees recently, and Barry Gibb in particular was a great stickler for being dead in tune. I actually found myself telling him that by being so exactly in tune he was tending to spoil the nice parts of the double-tracking. He was so accurate it sounded almost like a single track.

Not all voices, though, are suitable for double-tracking. In fact, there is a kind of inverse law: the better the voice, the worse it sounds when double-tracked, and vice versa. Frank Sinatra, for example, doesn't sound very good when double-tracked. Billy J. Kramer, on the other hand, had to be double-tracked nearly all the time.

Nowadays it is done a great deal. Elton John quite often double-tracks. Paul McCartney's 'Live and Let Die' was basically double-tracked. Paul does it so accurately that it almost sounds like a single voice, though it still gives a stronger and better sound. Like all effects, it can easily be overdone, but handled properly it is a very useful tool.

Artificial double-tracking, or ADT, was the work of one of the backroom engineers at EMI studios. Ken Townsend, who is now head of Abbey Road studios, was on a lot of my sessions in the early sixties, and he saw how much time and effort was being spent on double-tracking voices and instruments. One night in 1964 he thought about it as he went home after a Beatles session. He had the idea that, if you could take the signal off the recording head of the tape machine as well as off the playback head (rather than off the playback head alone), and delay it until it almost coincided with the signal from the playback head, you might get two sound images instead of one. Moreover, by varying the relative distance of the two images, adjustments could be made until it sounded really good.

The original device was quite a lash-up. The process needed a couple of other tape machines as well as the multi-track one, and of course it could only be done at mixing time, since it involved manipulating an existing recording. But we found that varying the speed of the second image gave a bonus. It varied the frequency, thus making the second voice a little different from the first. The variation in distance could take us from a long echo effect, through ADT and into phasing, until the two images become one. ADT is like having two photographic slides overlapping and moving fractionally in relation to each other.

Unwittingly, I coined a new word in our technical language.

When I first tried ADT on John Lennon's voice, he was knocked out by it. What was it? How was it done? I replied in gobbledygook: 'Well, John,' I said very earnestly, 'it's a double-bifurcated sploshing flange.' He knew I was putting him on, but he always referred to it as 'flanging' the voice. Many years later I was in an American studio and heard someone using the term. I asked where he had got it from, and was given the explanation that it referred to varying the speed of the tape in the early days of recording by placing a thumb in the flange of the tape spool.

These days there are many sophisticated devices that do this kind of trick—ADT, flangers, phasers and others, besides Harmonisers and so on. And flanging now means something a little different from ADT.

Double-tracking is clearly an extravagant tool if you only have four or eight tracks with which to work. And although it was another reason for wanting—no, needing—multi-track recording facilities, even today's twenty-four tracks require a fair degree of discipline. Self-indulgence in one area may demand economies in another. For example, I tend to be quite extravagant in my use of tracks for rhythm. I usually have the bass drum on its own track, then two tracks for the stereo overhead sound of the drums, in order to get an ambient 'feel', and a fourth track for the snare drum. That's four tracks for drums alone. Bass guitar normally takes up just one track; but sometimes, if I'm a bit concerned about that sound, I also record it from the sounds of the studio coming out of the amplifier, while another track is recorded by direct injection from the instrument, without going through a loudspeaker. I usually record the piano in stereo, which takes two more tracks. It may not end up as stereo, because I may bring the two parts together later, but at least I know I have the option of spreading the sound of the piano, if I feel I need to fill out my 'stereo picture' with a 'wash'.

So that might be a total of eight tracks used up already, before even thinking about vocals, or brass, or strings, or any backing voices, or any other instruments. But we've still come a long way in the decade or so since the Beatles, Geoff Emerick and I made *Sgt. Pepper* on four-track. Sometimes, looking back, it seems hardly possible. We did though and how we did it is a story in itself.

9

AMERICA FALLS

AMERICA mattered. It mattered because, quite simply, it was the biggest record market in the world. In January 1964, when 'I Want to Hold Your Hand' reached number one in the American charts, it opened that market to us.

If our excitement seems over-dramatic in retrospect, it is important to remember that no British artist had got near breaking into that market in the same way. America had always been the El Dorado of the entertainment world. In the glory days of Hollywood we used to worship the British stars who went over there and managed to make it—Robert Donat, Madeleine Carroll, Ronald Colman, C. Aubrey Smith, Cary Grant, Ray Milland and, of course, Charlie Chaplin. To make it big in the world, you had to make it big in America.

In the record business, it seemed to be universally accepted that the Americans held sway. In England, certainly, imported American records dominated the market, and we could never break that stranglehold. If anyone thinks imported Japanese cars are a problem today, it's worth remembering that American records used to outsell the home product by five to one. It was hardly surprising. After all, the roll-call ran from Sinatra, Presley and Crosby to Mitch Miller, Guy Mitchell and Doris Day. There were scores of huge names, and of course most of the jazz players—Ellington, Armstrong, Basie and the rest.

Against that traditional background, any idea of reversing the trend had been almost unthinkable. Vera Lynn made some impact with her record 'Auf Wiedersehen', which went high in the charts in America. The only other English person to do that was Little Laurie London with 'He's Got the Whole World in His Hands'. But these were just one-off successes with single records. No one from the British recording world had achieved a lasting success on both singles and long-players. What the Beatles were about to do was unprecedented and, to us, almost unbelievable. To be there, and to see all those famed American stars queuing up to see the Beatles and pay homage to them, was an extraordinary experience.

It had not been easy, though. From the moment the Beatles broke in England in January 1963 we had tried terribly hard to sell them in America. Everything we attempted seemed to meet a resounding slap in the face. By then, of course, EMI had bought Capitol, so I was naturally enthusiastic about making use of our company in the States. Immediately following the success of 'Please Please Me' I had said: 'Right! Let's ship Beatle records over to the States and get them sold there.' I got a curt reply from Alan Livingston, the president of Capitol: 'We don't think the Beatles will do anything in this market.'

That was rebuff number one. But Brian Epstein and I refused to leave the matter there. We took the view that if Capitol didn't want them, we'd send them somewhere else. That somewhere else was VJ Records, a tiny label but the only one to accept the record we were offering, 'She Loves You'. It didn't sell well, but at least it did something, and at least we had a record on the American market. When we had a second record to offer, we went to Capitol again. Again they turned us down. The results with VJ having been less than spectacular, we went to a second tiny label, Swan Records, and waited to see what they could do. The answer was, not much.

But again, at least a small impression was made. Then came the third record. A third time we went to Capitol. 'For God's sake, do something about this,' we said. 'These boys are breaking it, and they're going to be fantastic throughout the world. So for heaven's sake, latch on to them.' For the third time Capitol refused.

But unlike St Peter, they were to get a fourth chance; finally, at the beginning of 1964, they said: 'We'll take one record and see how it goes.' The truth of the matter is that by then so much was happening in England, and so many people were pushing on so many fronts, that even Alan Livingston could see that he wouldn't be taking any great risk. Of course, anyone at EMI who had had the authority should simply have instructed Capitol to issue the earlier records. But no one did, and I was still a weak force, controlling my little empire at Parlophone but with no say at all in what happened in America.

So when the Beatles first arrived in America, and I with them, the Capitol people were embarrassed to a degree. They had already been implying that the Beatles were their product, and my appearance naturally cast doubt on that point of view. Their reaction was to keep me out of the way. At the Beatles' first press conference in New York, Alan Livingston ran the whole show. He kept me away from the press, which I must admit seemed a mite peculiar. To top it all, he introduced the Beatles as the Capitol recording artists—words which came ill from the lips of the man who had turned them down three times!

That was not the only crazy thing about the Beatles' first descent upon New York. There was a complete, collective madness, which it is hard for anyone who was not there to understand. Middle-aged men were walking down Fifth Avenue wearing Beatle wigs, to show how in tune they were. The boys were staying at the Plaza Hotel, at the top of Fifth Avenue on Central Park. There is a sort of pedestrian precinct outside the hotel, and, throughout the time the Beatles were there, this square was jammed solid with people, like Trafalgar Square on election night.

There were one or two exceptions to the general mania. Judy had paid her own way out to see it all happen. She was staying at the Vassar Women's Club, since a friend of hers had once attended that upper-crust American ladies' college. All the ladies staying there spent their time telling Judy the places of cultural interest she might visit while in New York. She didn't like to reply that she was really there for the Beatles' concerts.

But that was where most people seemed to want to go. If you switched on the radio at any time of day or night, on any station, you would hear a Beatles song, and New York is certainly not short of radio stations. By then a year of recording had passed, and we had an album out, an EP, and five singles. I had recorded about twenty titles, and they played them all, all the time.

Of course it wasn't the music alone which caused the hysteria, just as the music had not been the sole reason for my signing the Beatles in the first place. That enjoyable charisma came through to the world at large, which was seeing something it had not seen before. It was an expression of youth, a slight kicking-over of the traces, which found a ready response in young people. Curiously, it was a response that the parents, though they might not have liked the music themselves, did not seem to begrudge. At the first concert in Washington many of them came too. It was given in a boxing stadium, so that the boys were completely surrounded by the audience. After about every fourth number they would turn towards the next quarter of the audience and play to them in turn.

The audience, despite the various parental presences, was mostly teenage, and very hot. In the seat next to me, a little girl was bouncing up and down and saying, 'Aren't they just great? Aren't they just fabulous?'

'Yes, they are,' I said, somewhat inadequately for her, I suppose.

'Do you like them too, sir?' she asked.

'Yes, I do rather,' I said, all too aware that she couldn't understand what this old man was doing sitting next to her! But perhaps she was put more at ease when the boys played a song like 'I Want to Hold Your Hand', and everybody in the audience started singing with them, for then Judy and I just found ourselves standing up and screaming along with the rest.

That may sound daft, but it was exactly the same screaming that adults do at football matches. And for us especially, in the midst of sixty thousand people who were all enjoying themselves to the full, identifying completely with the people who were performing, people we knew intimately, people with whom we had made all the records and every little bit of music—in that situation it was all too easy to scream, to be swept up in that tremendous current of buoyant happiness and exhilaration.

Afterwards, it was not so good. It was snowing and, when Brian Epstein shepherded us outside to a theoretically waiting limousine, we simply couldn't find the said vehicle in all the pandemonium, and we had to walk in search of transport, trudging through what seemed like two feet of slush. Nor were the Beatles too happy with the ensuing party at the British Embassy, whose full quota of chinless wonders behaved abominably. They would approach the boys with an off-hand 'Oh, which one are you?', and one actually got a pair of scissors and snipped off a piece of Ringo's hair while he was talking to someone else. It almost created a diplomatic incident. It was worse when we finally got back to New York on the train. Grand Central Station was besieged by fans, and at first they had to lock us in the train. In the end they got us out in a lift which was supposed to be used only for parcels and heavy goods.

But the only time I was really frightened was in Denver. Where we had flown from, I forget. Indeed, I probably never knew. An American rock tour is a whistle-stop business, and you literally don't know which town you are in. You're whipped into a plane, you land somewhere, give a concert, go back to some hotel, fall into bed again, have a party—and then you're fed into another plane. The boys would ask, 'Are we in Oklahoma or Kansas? Are we in New York City or Cincinnati?' The only way to find out was by asking someone who knew, and such people were hard to find. But I do remember Denver. It lies about five thousand feet up, and to get into the airport the aeroplane has to do a fairly steep bank before it lands. George Harrison was not prepared for this, and he was scared out of his wits, alternately praying for deliverance and yelling 'We're going to crash!'

Five Cadillacs were drawn up on the runway to meet the plane, and we piled in. But instead of going straight to the hotel, the mayor asked us if we would do a tour of the airfield perimeter. The reason was soon obvious. All the way round, it was packed with fans, about ten deep, jammed up against the barbed-wire fence, like Stalag Luft III turned inside-out. We drove round for what seemed miles, about five feet from the fence, five feet from a sea of happy, screaming people all waving frantically.

Once this 'royal' procession was complete, we set off for Brown's Hotel in Denver, which was surrounded by so many people that we needed a diversion. This consisted of a number of people pretending to be Beatles and drawing up in limousines at the front of the hotel, while we went in at the back, through the kitchen entrance. The trouble was that all the photographers and newsmen had tumbled to what we were doing, and they piled in after us. A terrible melee in the kitchen resulted, with pots and pans flying in all directions. Brian, the four boys and I finally made it to a service lift, but before we could shut the doors the reporters, the most ruthless people on earth when it comes to getting a story, simply jammed themselves in with us.

Even before the doors shut it was like the Black Hole of Calcutta, all pressed tight up against one another. Someone pressed the button to take us to the top floor, but the wretched lift, overloaded beyond endurance, managed a mere two and a half floors before deciding to call it a day. It expired between floors. Since we had hardly room, or air, to breathe, it looked distinctly possible that we might go the same way.

Eventually they forced open the gates of the floor above us; we got the top of the lift up, and climbed up one by one. But I had really been quite frightened; and later that evening I was to experience a different kind of fear. The concert was at the Red Rock Stadium, a natural amphitheatre carved out of rock. It held about twenty thousand people. The seating was in the natural bowl of the rock, with the stage below it; two huge towers on either side of the stage housed all the amplifying equipment and spotlights.

During the concert, Brian and I decided that we would like a bird's-eye view of the proceedings. So we climbed one of the towers, whose summit was about level with the top of the crowd. Even beyond the amphitheatre we could see people perched on trees and so on, trying to see over. That was the moment when we realised just how vulnerable the boys were. We could see them below as little dots, but one sniper among all those people could have picked them off very simply. Nor is that some wild piece of over dramatisation. The whole thing was frenetic, fanatic, and slightly unreal, and Brian was already worried for their safety.

After all, President Kennedy had been shot in 1963, and the Denver concert came after John Lennon's celebrated remarks about the comparative popularity of Jesus Christ and the Beatles. Knowing the religious fanaticism one can find in the States, that didn't help matters. Of course, like so much that was said and reported at that time, the whole thing was blown up out of all proportion. I can't remember John's exact words, but I know his intention. He was slightly bemused by the effect the Beatles were having on the world, and his statement was factual. It was to the effect that 'When you look at it, we are actually more popular than Jesus'. That was true. Far fewer people went to church than listened to Beatles records and went to Beatles concerts. But he didn't mean that the Beatles were more important than Christ, which was how most people interpreted the remark. On the contrary, he was deploring the situation, regretting that it was the case.

With the constant over-exposure that they suffered—or enjoyed, depending on one's view of the matter—this sort of misunderstanding was inevitable. Every little snippet of information about what they ate, what they drank, how they slept, almost whether they breathed, was grist to the media mill. Interviews quickly became tedious, because they would be asked the same old questions again and again. On those rare occasions when a question was out of the ordinary, they would rise to it and try to score off it. For example, they might have been going through a stock run of questions like 'How do you write your music? Do you write the words as well as the music?' Then out of the blue some bright spark might suddenly ask, 'Well, now, do you think cornflakes are affecting the intelligence of the average American male?' Off the top of his head John Lennon might come straight back with something like, 'No, but I think cocaine might have done'. The next day the headlines would read JOHN LENNON ADVOCATES COCAINE. Every little thing they said became translated into Beatle instructions as to how we should behave—yet again.

After all, they simply didn't have the experience of a Jim Callaghan or Harold Wilson at parrying questions and spotting lurking dangers in their replies. So they were constantly being proclaimed as advocating things about which they knew little. Then, once attacked, they would be forced into a corner, and find themselves having to justify what they had said. For inexperienced people, it was a very tough ride.

Nor was it simply a problem with the media. The public were tough on them, too. Whenever the Beatles saw something happening, or someone coming towards them, that seemed a bit dubious, they would give each other a password they had developed among themselves: 'Cripples!' That meant they had to take cover. If that seems harsh, the fact is that they were constantly having cripples and others forced upon them. They might be doing a television performance, and during a break would be in their dressing-room having a quiet snack. Suddenly the door would open, and in would come the assistant director, wheeling a spastic who wanted to meet the Beatles. They would have to talk to this unfortunate, and try to be pleasant. This was happening all the time. It was almost like going to Lourdes. There were people who actually wanted to touch the hems of the clothes they were wearing. Royalty are trained from birth to cope with that sort of thing; the Beatles were not. They can hardly be blamed for wanting to put up a barrier against the world.

Of course, people may rightly say that the hysteria and the adulation in themselves helped to sell records, and that selling records was what we were trying to do. But somewhere a balance should have been struck—and it never was.

However, the music sold, and sold, and sold. Once the dam had been breached, the sales that first year in America were enormous, though only a drop in the ocean compared with what was to follow. To me, that brought great excitement and great pride. It wasn't a question of the glamour; after all, I had been used to dealing with the Peter Sellerses and Sophia Lorens of this world. It was more bound up with the idea that something one had made was being heard in millions and millions of homes throughout the world; that it was, literally, becoming a part of the language. That thrilled me enormously, and gave me great satisfaction—even if it didn't bring me any wealth: I was still earning less than £3000 a year with EMI.

In retrospect, I think it more than likely that the Beatles thought that, because of our success, I was doing frightfully well, and that they were responsible for it. But I never discussed it with them, or indeed with Brian. Besides, in those first two years even they weren't rolling in money. Royalties take a long time to flow in, and Brian certainly wasn't rushing around ordering Rolls-Royces. Nor was there really time to think about money. We were all simply working frantically hard to build the whole thing up.

In any case, the Beatles were never ones for showing concern about, or gratitude towards, anyone else. Although they obviously did appreciate what I was doing, they were never the kind of people who would go out of their way to say: 'What a great job you've done there, George! Take three weeks off.' But then, I never expected that of them. They had an independent, cussed streak about them, not giving a damn for anybody, which was one of the things I liked about them in the first place, and one of the factors which made me decide to sign them.

Nor was I really interested, to be truthful, in any gratitude or appreciation they might show towards me. All I wanted from them was good songs. And those they gave me. At the start I thought: God, this can't last forever. They've given me so much good stuff that I can't expect them to keep on doing it. But they did. They amazed me with their fertility. To begin with, the material was fairly crude, but they developed their writing ability very quickly; the harmonies, and the songs themselves, became cleverer throughout 1963. Although one obviously had to be a good producer to make the records commercially viable, there was certainly no genius attached to my role at that early stage. There were probably a number of producers who could have done it just as well. The turning point probably came with the song 'Yesterday', on the *Help!* album which we issued in 1965. That was when, as I can see in retrospect, I started to leave my hallmark on the music, when a style started to emerge which was partly of my making. It was on 'Yesterday' that I started to score their music. It was on 'Yesterday' that we first used instruments or musicians other than the Beatles and myself (I had often played the piano where it was necessary, as on *A Hard Day's Night*). On 'Yesterday' the added ingredient was no more nor less than a string quartet; and that, in the pop world of those days, was quite a step to take. It was with 'Yesterday' that we started breaking out of the phase of using just four instruments and went into something more experimental, though our initial experiments were severely limited by the fairly crude tools at our disposal, and had simply to be moulded out of my recording experience.

As I suggested earlier, a two-way swing developed in our relationship. On the one hand, as the style emerged and the recording techniques developed, so my control—over what the finished product sounded like—increased. Yet at the same time, my need for changing the pure music became less and less. As I could see their talent growing, I could recognise that an idea coming from them was better than an idea coming from me, though it would still be up to me to decide which was the better approach. In a sense, I made a sort of tactical withdrawal, recognising that theirs was the greater talent.

Great talent it was. They were the Cole Porters and George Gershwins of their generation, of that there is no doubt. Somebody compared them to Schubert, which sounds a bit pretentious, but I would go along with that to the extent that their music was perfectly representative of the period in which they were living. Of course there was a certain amount of rubbish, but then that was true of people like Cole Porter too. And while a lyric like 'A Day in the Life' may not be exactly Lorenz Hart, it is a very, very good lyric of a very strange nature. It is of its generation. It turned the kids on. It was right for its time.

Besides, of course, hundreds of artists have made cover versions of the Beatles' songs. Now, many people have felt that that was the criterion of their credibility as composers; that when someone like Ella Fitzgerald sang 'Can't Buy Me Love' it gave them an almost royal seal of approval. But I don't agree with that, because the fact is that an awful lot of people jumped on the bandwagon. Even the Ella Fitzgeralds of this world are not above that when it means increased sales. She didn't necessarily think it was the greatest song ever. She might well have preferred to record 'Moonlight in Vermont', but a Beatles song was a commercial certainty. Again, there is a lot of snobbery in music. Some people might have felt that Ella Fitzgerald was better than the Beatles, and that therefore she was doing them a favour. I don't think that was necessarily so. She is a great singer, but in terms of sheer artistry I wouldn't be too certain about the comparison.

What is certain is that their songs were great. Starting with 'Please Please Me' we had twelve successive number ones. It was a unique achievement, so perhaps it is worth listing them: 'From

Me to You', 'She Loves You', 'I Want to Hold Your Hand', 'Can't Buy Me Love', 'A Hard Day's Night', 'I Feel Fine', 'Ticket to Ride', 'Help!', 'Day Tripper', 'Paperback Writer', and 'Yellow Submarine'. It became almost an accepted fact of nature. The question was not whether a record would get to number one, but how quickly. In the end, it was happening in the first week, with advance sales around the million mark.

Then came number thirteen, unlucky number thirteen. That was quite extraordinary, because in my estimation it was the best record we ever made—'Penny Lane' and 'Strawberry Fields' (you can hardly use the phrase 'backed by' in this context, because it was really a double-A-side record—meaning that the record promoters should regard both sides as being equally important). It only got to number two in the week of issue. The record that kept it out was made by Peter Sullivan, who was to be my partner in later years. It was of a fellow named Engelbert Humperdinck singing 'Release Me'! With cold and unbiased hindsight I ask: 'Was that just?' I still find it absolutely astonishing. Happily, however, it was only a stutter in our progress, and the 'normal service' of immediate number ones was resumed immediately afterwards.

Meanwhile, of course, I still had all my other artists to attend to. It was inevitable that with the success of the Beatles, and to a lesser extent the other artists of Brian's stable, there should be a certain amount of frustration and jealousy, a feeling that some were getting more attention than others. Luckily, the only time that really came to a crunch was with Shirley Bassey.

Shirley had had a pretty chequered career. She was a very volatile person, and had already been with various recording companies including EMI, for whom Norman Newell had recorded her. Finally she came to me, because, I suppose, I was the 'hot' one at that time, with the Beatles and so on. She was very emotional, but I liked her very much. And of course she was a tremendous artist. 'I Who Have Nothing' was the first big hit I had with her, and later we did 'Goldfinger'.

We got on fine, until one day she came into my office to 'routine' some songs. Routining meant that I would collect a number of songs I thought would be suitable for the artist, in this case Shirley, and then she would come to the office and we would run through them on the piano. Having agreed on the numbers she would sing, we would work out which keys they would be sung in, what the shape of the recording would be, how many choruses they would have, what kind of orchestral backing, what kind of beginning and ending, and so on. She spent the whole afternoon routining these songs with me. When we had finished I said: 'There's only one problem, Shirley: we haven't actually fixed the date for the recording.'

'Oh, yes, I know when I want to record,' she said. 'I'm going away for a holiday, and I'll be back on the Sunday, so I'd like to record on the Monday, in the evening.'

'O.K.,' I said. Then I looked at my diary. 'Oh, no, I'm sorry, Shirley, I can't do that night. Any other night that week I can do, or during the Monday afternoon is fine. But I can't do that particular night.'

'But I want to record that night.'

'I'm sorry, Shirley, but I really can't. I can do Tuesday, Wednesday, Thursday or Friday, but not Monday.'

I'm as sure now as I was then that she knew why I couldn't do that night. Because she went on to say: 'If I mean anything to you at all, you will do it when I want to. I want to do it on the Monday night.'

'I'm sorry,' I repeated, 'but I'm not going to work that night, because I've got another engagement.'

At that she stalked out of the room, practically smashing the glass in the door, and saying, 'I've lived in the shadow of the Beatles and Cilla Black far too long now, George Martin.'

The fact was that, on the Monday night in question, Cilla was appearing in a Command Performance, and I had promised to be there. I am as sure as I can be that Shirley knew that, and that for her it was just another instance of taking, as she saw it, second place to other people.

In my book, she was just one of a very good roster of artists that I was handling. There's no doubt that if I had run down the corridor and said, 'Look, sorry, Shirley, I'm sure Monday will be O.K.,' she would have been quite happy and gone on recording with me. But I can be a stubborn old goat too. I thought: I like you, Shirley, but I don't need you that much.

I never recorded her again. It was no loss to either of us. She stayed with EMI, though, and I think Wally Ridley took her over. I'm glad to say that we've seen each other many times since, and remain good friends. But it was an example of the way in which the Liverpudlian triumphs could spread ripples to the edge of the Parlophone pond.

I, in turn, found ripples reaching me from quite another direction, the Apple organisation, which the Beatles set up around 1965. A great deal has been written about Apple, but in order to give an idea of what hopes they had for it, one can do no better than quote verbatim from the appendix to Hunter Davies' authorised biography of the Beatles, written a couple of years later. 'Apple. At the time of writing, this is still developing and expanding, but this will be the main Beatle business company in the years ahead. Already there is Apple Corps Ltd, Apple Films Ltd, the Apple Publishing Company, Apple Electronics, and Apple Records. These companies run various enterprises including the Apple Boutique in Baker Street, London, with a chain of other shops to come throughout the world. Eventually there will be recording and film studios. The Beatles see Apple one day as a giant corporation on the American lines, producing products of all kinds as well as backing other people and firms. It is owned completely by the Beatles, run by people they have personally chosen, and backed by their vast financial resources.'

Apple was a complete fiasco, and it cost them millions. From the start, and this is not speaking with hindsight, I took a jaundiced view of the whole proceedings, because I could see the awful way it was going, and that it was doomed from the outset. But it wasn't really my concern. It was Brian's concern, and he was able to cope with it less and less. The trouble was that it was being run by four idealists, with nobody really in control. Ostensibly Neil Aspinall, their road manager, was in charge. He was chairman, but each one of them would give orders in turn, sometimes conflicting. I remember meeting Sir Joseph Lockwood, head of EMI, and his telling me: 'You know, Neil Aspinall rang me today and said, "As one chairman to another, can you give me advice on such-and-such?"'!! Neil has quite a good brain, in fact, but he was out of his class in dealing with people like that.

The tragedy was that it was an extremely praiseworthy idea. They wanted to put to a good use all the monies which were coming in. The motivation was, roughly: With these resources we can do anything. We can employ people to build things for us, develop new arts and new sciences, encourage scientific people to develop new inventions, encourage new writers. . . . And so on. It was a marvellous Utopian idea. If it had been handled properly it would have been a great boon to the music business. However it attracted some unusual people and there was very little control over research and development.

Of all the army of hangers-on, the one I recall most vividly, because he impinged on my work and my musical relationship with the boys, was Magic Alex. I can never remember his real name, but he was a Greek who had ingratiated himself with John Lennon, and who was so preposterous that it would have been funny had he not caused so much embarrassment and difficulty with me in the recording studio.

He was one of a group of sycophants who were forever making mischief, telling the boys they weren't getting the best treatment, telling them they deserved better than the rotten old equipment that everyone else was using. I didn't need that. I knew better than anyone that we lacked certain facilities which were available in independent American studios. I was still working on four-track machines when I knew that eight-track was already common in America, and that sixteen-track was just around the corner. It annoyed me as much as it did the boys. But I could do without Magic Alex turning up one day and announcing in a supercilious voice: 'Well, of course, I'm designing a seventy-two-track machine.'

Alex was certainly clever, a good electronic technician; but the boys pandered to his wildest whims. He would bring little toys into the studio as throwaway gifts, which of course pleased the boys. One day he came in with a little machine about half the size of a cassette, powered by a microcell battery. When it was switched on, it made a series of random bleeps.

'Fantastic!' said John. 'You've made that?'

'Oh, just a little gadget I knocked up in ten minutes,' said Magic Alex. Then he would launch into the sales spiel. 'That's just to give an idea of the sort of thing we can do. Now, I've had an idea for a new invention. It's a paint that, when I spray it on the wall, and connect it up to two anodes, will make the whole wall glow. You won't need lights.'

'Fantastic!' said John.

'Mind you,' said Magic Alex. 'I'll need a little backing to set it up.'

'Fantastic!' said John.

On another occasion Paul came in to tell me about Magic Alex's idea for a telephone invention. 'You know, we're so out of date with our telephones in this country,' he said. 'But Alex is working on something. We won't even need telephone directories. I'll be in my drawing-room, and I'll just say, "Get me George Martin," and the phone will hear that and be computerised to understand the words. It'll automatically dial your number, and you'll be on the other end of the phone, and I won't have to do anything about it. It's so simple with computerisation, and Alex has got it all worked out.'

'Really?' I said.

I confess that I tended to laugh myself silly when they came and announced the latest brainchild of Alex's fertile imagination. Their reaction was always the same: 'You'll laugh on the other side of your face when Alex comes up with it.' But of course he never did.

I suppose his prize idea was his sonic screen. I was informed of this work of inventive genius by the boys one day. 'Why do you have to put Ringo with his drums behind all these terrible screens?' they asked. 'We can't see him. We know it makes a good drum sound, and it cuts out all the spill on to our guitars and things, but damn it, with those bloody great screens locking him in, it makes him feel claustrophobic.'

I waited silently, knowing that the problem would have been solved by a flash of Greek inspiration. And so it had.

'Alex has got a brilliant idea! He's come up with something really great: a sonic screen! He's going to place these ultra-high-frequency beams round Ringo, and when they're switched on he won't be able to hear anything, because the beams will form a wall of silence.'

Words, I fully admit, failed me.

The trouble was that Alex was always coming to the studios to see what we were doing and to learn from it, while at the same time saying 'These people are so out of date'. But I found it very difficult to chuck him out, because the boys liked him so much. Since it was very obvious that I didn't, a minor schism developed.

The final irony came when the boys decided that they were going to build their own studio in their building in Savile Row, and that it was going to be the best in the world. And who should they turn to for the design of this electronic Mecca? Why, Magic Alex, naturally. Once he had built it, the boys sat down to wait for the installation of the famous seventy-two-track machine. They waited. And waited. And finally, when we came to the recording of the album *Let it Be*, late in 1969, which they wanted to do in their own studio, they had to admit that Alex still hadn't quite worked his miracle.

'You'd better put some equipment in, then,' they told me.

'O.K., we'll use mobile equipment,' I said, and went back to EMI, whom I had left by then, to borrow some. With Keith Slaughter, and Dave Harries who eventually became my studio manager at AIR, I installed at Apple all the multi-track machines and other equipment necessary to make a proper recording—just for the one record. With that done, I examined the Alex-designed studio for its acoustic properties. For a start, there was very nasty 'twitter' in one corner. But our problems didn't end there. Alex had overlooked one small detail: there was no hole in the wall between the studio and the control rooms. The only way to get the cables through was to open the door and run them along the corridor.

Another thing—the heating plant for the entire building was situated in a little room just off the studio. And since the sound insulation was not exactly magical, every now and then in the middle of recording there came a sound like a diesel engine starting up.

Apart from these minor points, I suppose, it wasn't a bad attempt at studio design.

But that was Apple, and I suppose it is ironic that the man brought in to clear up the administrative mess, Allen Klein, who tightened up the control and put things on a proper basis, should also have been the man who because of Paul's dislike of him was a great factor in the final break-up of the Beatles.

He had come in, of course, because by then Brian Epstein was dead. In the five years that I knew Brian we came to be very good friends. He always did things with great flourish and style, and spent up to the hilt. It was always champagne and smoked salmon, rather than fish and chips.

There is no secret now about the fact that he was a homosexual. Because he rarely had any lady in tow he, Judy and I became a trio of close friends. He was very fond of Judy, and we all used to go racing together. One of the happiest times we had was at Portmeirion, to which he introduced us—knowing it well as he did, coming from Liverpool.

I know that he wasn't happy at school, and I know that he never managed to form any real relationship with a man or a woman. I think that for these and other reasons, like his unsuccessful desire to be an actor, he had suffered great frustration in life. That frustration was ended by the success of the Beatles, for which he was to a very large extent responsible. What he gave them was complete dedication. Many people would have given up long before he finally came to see me at Parlophone.

He also gave them style. He told them: 'If you're going to be successful, you're going to do it my way.' It was he who insisted on their hair being a uniform shape and size, and who put them into those collarless suits, which they hated. But of course he was right. The image became a part of the total package. You never saw middle-aged men queuing to buy Rolling Stones wigs!

Later, they broke away from that, and exerted their own taste in clothes and so on. They liked to see how far they could go, how much people would take. I must say that even I was disconcerted when John acquired his Rolls-Royce, only to paint it matt black all over, chrome and all. I don't think Rolls-Royce were too pleased, either! On the other hand, these were indulgences which they were entitled to have, and they hurt no one.

But a lot of Brian's influence rubbed off on them. Paul, for instance, went on a veritable bender of culture; the idea of Apple as their marketing symbol was taken from a Magritte painting he bought.

The fish and chips and jam butties gave way to more elegant foods, and good wines—though there were occasional hiccups: on one occasion we were in a restaurant and John was asked if he wanted any mange-touts. 'O.K.,' he said, 'but put them there on the side. Not near the food.'

Brian's Diaghilev style was never better illustrated than in June 1966. By then, my first wife and I had been divorced, and Judy and I had decided to get married—something I could never have foreseen from those first frosty encounters when I had joined EMI in 1950. Brian decided to give a special dinner for us to celebrate. As usual, the table at his house was set with lovely silver and glassware. The wine was excellent, as was the food, prepared by Lonnie Trimball, his black chef, who was first-class. There were eleven of us there: Paul and Jane, John and Cyn, George and Patti, Ringo and Maureen, Judy and I, and Brian, on his own. As we sat down and took our napkins from their silver holders, Brian said: 'I'd like you to look at your napkin-rings, because I'm afraid I shan't see them again after tonight.' They were solid silver, and each was inscribed with the letter M—a wedding present to Judy and me. Just eleven of them, to commemorate the fact that there were just the eleven of us at dinner. That was his style.

It was mirrored later, after his death, in the amazing fancy-dress party the boys gave to mark the opening of their film *Magical Mystery Tour*. Since the whole of London knew that a party was going to happen, and wanted to come, security had to be very tight, but the boys still insisted on fancy dress. That had some off-beat results. Cilla Black, for instance, came as a Cockney costermonger, in flat cap and trousers, and her husband, Bobby Willis, came as a nun.

Bobby has a very pale complexion, and in a nun's habit he looked incredibly authentic. He was in his outfit when he and Cilla drove in their Rolls-Royce Corniche convertible to pick up a friend at the Westbury Hotel en route to the party. He could see their friend waiting, and drove straight into the hotel entrance, where the taxis were piling up. In so doing he blocked the way for a moment. A commissionaire immediately pounced. 'Excuse me, sister,' he said, 'but I'm afraid we can't leave our car here. Would you mind putting it round the corner?'

Bobby looked him straight in the eye and replied: 'Why don't you piss off?' The look on the man's face is said to have been a study in sheer disbelief.

Judy and I went as the Queen and Prince Philip, which was an 'in' joke. The boys always thought she sounded just like the Monarch, and whenever they saw her would ask: 'How's your husband and you?' I acquired an Admiral of the Fleet's uniform from one of the naval outfitters; since they wouldn't let me have a sword I put my old observer's wings on the sleeve, out of sheer cussedness. Judy had a lovely tiara and silk ball dress, a blue sash with some star-and-garter type of apparatus draped across her bosom, and a handbag a-dangle from her left wrist. Paul told me afterwards: 'You know, your entrance was very striking.' People formed themselves into a line, bowing and curtseying, while Judy and I gave limp handshakes to one and all. In the background, someone said loudly: 'My God! I didn't think they'd get *them*!'

That was the fun. But for Brian, life was becoming very difficult. He had an ever-increasing stable of artists. Then he started to bring me acts in which I had little faith, and I had the embarrassing job of telling him that I didn't rate them. But, persuaded by his charm, I would record them as a favour to him. That was wrong, and I told him so.

He was tending to lose control. When Cilla opened at the Savoy, he upset her greatly by forgetting something or other, and had to make it up by sending her a little television set as a present. He was spreading himself too thinly, and his ever more complicated private life was beginning to intrude. He kept himself going by taking pills, uppers and then downers: sleeping pills at night and waking-up pills in the morning.

The Beatles started to be very critical of his handling of their contract—the one to which I had originally signed them, starting at a penny a record. That had not been his fault. He had been in no position to argue, and he knew it. But once they had tasted blood, they realised that they could get much higher royalties.

There were two sides to this. On the one hand, like many

people who eventually make it big, they were very pleased and grateful to get their first break, but ended up not wishing to be reminded of it. On the other hand, EMI were stupid about the whole thing. They were very mean with the Beatles' contract, and when it ran out, the boys had them over a barrel. EMI ended up having to pay through the nose for the privilege of having the greatest group ever, whereas, if they had been fairer in the first place, I don't think they would have been pushed that far. The truth was that the Beatles had no loyalty towards EMI, for the simple reason that they had been given no cause for loyalty.

The whole business led to a revolution in the recording industry. At the time the Beatles first signed, royalties were traditionally low. The highest we ever paid was 5%. When the breakthrough came as a result of what had happened with the Beatles, royalties became astronomical, and the record companies had completely to reverse their policies, charging much higher prices for records.

But that came after Brian's death. The irony was that even if he had lived he would, I think, have had a very hard time coping with life. Because it was inevitable that he would shortly have lost the Beatles, and to him that would have been like losing his children, his whole reason for living. He could never have parted from them, as I did, with great friendship but no sense of loss. If they had come to him and said, 'Brian, we don't want you to manage us any more,' it would have destroyed him. And they would have: there is absolutely no question about it.

On 9 August 1967 Judy had our first child, Lucy. After she came out of hospital, we went down to our cottage in the country. On Sunday, 20 August, we went for a drink at the little pub in the village, and the publican came straight over to us.

'I'm afraid I've got bad news for you. Your friend's died.'

'Who?' I asked, having no idea at all.

'Mr Epstein.'

I believe that what happened was pure accident. He had been drinking, had taken some pills to go to sleep, probably woke in the middle of the night, forgot how many he had taken, took some more and died of an accidental overdose.

Judy and I drove straight back to our house in London. There, waiting for us on our grand piano, was a marvellous bouquet of flowers from Brian, to congratulate Judy on Lucy's birth. They must have been sent some days before; they were very, very dead. And so was Brian.

10

CALLING MY OWN TUNE

FRUSTRATION has many fathers, but few children, among them bitterness, anger and resentment. Those had come to be the unhappy ingredients of my feelings towards EMI.

By 1959, I had been running Parlophone for four years. My recordings with Peter Sellers, Milligan, Flanders and Swann and the others had started to make the label mean something. Originally a poor cousin, it had become a force to be reckoned with. But I was still only earning something like £2700 a year. There wasn't even a car thrown in; fifty-odd pounds a week was not very much for being boss of a record label—especially when you compare it with the £25,000 a year I was offered ten years later to rejoin EMI!

But it was not simply a straightforward question of my wanting more cash. I wanted participation, profit-sharing. I reckoned that, if I was going to devote my life to building up something which wasn't mine, I deserved some form of commission. After all, the sales people got it, so why shouldn't I?

In 1959 I signed a new contract for three years, which gave me a munificent rise of £75 a year. When that expired in April 1962, they offered me another contract which would eventually take me to about £3000 a year. 'That's all very well,' I said, 'but I'd much rather stay at my present level and have a commission on sales.'

They wouldn't hear of it.

'I'll have to leave, then,' I said.

Their generous response was: 'If you feel like that, be our guest. Goodbye.'

I didn't leave. Against my better judgement I signed, because I couldn't afford to be out of work. But I had been sorely tempted, because I could see a new generation of young entrepreneurs, like Mickie Most, and Andrew Oldham who had the Rolling Stones, getting better deals from the companies for the same sort of work. Then, in 1962, along came Brian Epstein with the Beatles. If I thought that I had worked hard before, it was as nothing compared with the furious, frantic activity that was about to begin. I was working every evening and almost every weekend. It was very tough, but still great fun, because at least I had successful records coming out of my ears. That was my only reward. Apart from fun, I got—nothing.

In fact, I got less than nothing. It was usual for EMI employees to get a bonus at Christmas, geared to each person's salary and generally equivalent to a week's earnings. So at least I was looking forward to my Christmas bonus at the end of 1963. That year, the first full year of the Beatles, the directors of EMI announced with supreme generosity that everyone would receive four days' pay as their Christmas bonus. Four days' pay at the end of a year in which I had had the number-one record in the charts for thirty-seven weeks! But I didn't even get that. When it failed to arrive, I phoned the accountants down at Hayes. 'There must be some mistake,' I said. 'My secretary has had her four days' pay, but I haven't had any myself.'

'Oh, no,' they said, 'there's no mistake. You don't get it now, you know.'

'What do you mean, I don't get it now?'

'Well, it's one of the rules of the company that people earning more than £3000 a year are on a different salary scale to the others, and they're not entitled to a Christmas bonus. You're earning just over £3000 a year.'

So that was it. What I got for that incredible year's work was a polite note saying, roughly, 'What a marvellous job you've done, George. Absolutely super. Do better next year.' That made up my mind, in no uncertain way. Blow this for a lark, I thought. I'm leaving. At that time I was halfway through my new contract, which stipulated that I had to give a year's notice in writing if I wanted to leave, failing which the contract automatically renewed itself. So six months later, in the middle of 1964, I wrote to tell them: 'Please take notice that in a year's time I shall no longer be working here.'

That really set the cat among the executive pigeons. 'What do you mean by it?' I was asked. 'After all, you've been with us for fourteen years, and suddenly you do this. . . .'

'It's very simple. I've had EMI right up to here.'

They wanted to know who was after me. I told them that no one was, and they clearly didn't believe it. When I told them I was going out on my own, I got remarks like 'Oh-oh, you won't last long'. Then the tack changed. Throughout the following twelve months, at regular three- or four-week intervals, I was treated to lunches and drinks, and blandishments like 'Come on now, old chap, I think you're being a little silly about this. I mean, you should have more money, you're quite right.'

The man I was dealing with mostly was the man who was now managing director of EMI Records, Len Wood. 'I don't want more money, Len,' I told him. 'I just want commission. I want tangible results from my efforts, that's all. I want to see something off each record that is mine. I don't care how small it is, but that's what I want.'

Eventually the crunch meeting came. Len Wood called me up to his office and said: 'Look. I know you're being very stubborn about this. But I'm determined to keep you on. You're a good producer, and a good chap, and too good to lose. You're definitely going to stay with us. I'll tell you that right now.'

'O.K., what have you got to offer?' I asked him.

'Well, you're definitely going to get a commission on sales. What I propose is that you get 3% of our profits, minus your overheads.'

'Well, that's a bit vague,' I said. 'Can you tell me what it amounts to?'

'Yes, yes, hold on,' he said, like some angler convinced that the fish is about to take the bait. 'Let's take last year, for example. If this had been operating last year, 1963, you'd have ended up with a bonus of £11,000. How does that sound to you?' he asked, triumphantly.

'It sounds very good,' I said. 'But how do you arrive at that?'

'Well, take your salary, and your secretary's salary, and your assistant, and his typist, and for the sake of argument we'll double that, to allow for overheads. To that we add the musicians' fees that you paid during the year for session work. I've worked out that on that basis, your department cost us roughly £55,000 last year.'

'I know what I did last year, and how hard I worked, but I think I've been jolly economical!'

'Yes, you were very good,' he said. 'You always are. No problem about that. Now, on the other side of the sum, you'd have had 3% commission on our profits. O.K.? Last year, that would have amounted to £66,000. From that we take away the £55,000, which leaves you with £11,000.'

There was a pause, while I pondered. He watched me, obviously thinking I was a bit overwhelmed at his generosity. The truth was that the sheer horror of what he had just said was slowly beginning to seep into my brain.

Then I spoke. 'Wait a minute. I think I must have misunderstood you. That must be turnover you're talking about, not profits. Because £66,000 is 3% of *two million two hundred thousand*!'

'That's right,' he said, calmly.

'But that *must* be turnover,' I exclaimed.

'No, no,' he said. 'That's profit. That's the profit we made from the sales of your records last year.'

With that simple sentence he cut straight through whatever vestige of an umbilical cord still bound me to EMI.

But I had one final check to make, to ensure that what I was hearing was really true and make certain that the combination of my frustration and their meanness wasn't making a paranoiac of me. 'There's one other thing, Len. You seem to be putting net against gross—the net of your profits against the gross of my costs. If, for example, the profits had been only one and a half million, then 3% of that would be fifty thousand. So with costs of fifty-five thousand, the theory would be that I'd pay you back five thousand!'

'That's the general idea,' he said, with equanimity. 'I'm sorry. Perhaps the first example wasn't very clear-cut.'

I was flabbergasted. First, the meanness of the whole thing was so transparent. Second, I could hardly believe the stupidity of the man in letting me know what I was worth. 'Thank you, very much,' I said. 'I haven't changed my mind at all. I'm leaving.'

It is difficult, looking back, to describe the depths of my bitterness. I really had been devoted to the company, and always valued loyalty in other people. But there comes a moment when you realise that your idea of being a good, loyal worker without complications is being misconstrued, and you are being taken for a ride. I was bitter; I was sad—sad for the company that I knew I had to leave.

At that time, there was a pool of about eight people who did the creative work on the pop side for EMI. Apart from myself, there were Norman Newell, head of Columbia, Wally Ridley on HMV, and Norrie Paramor, together with our assistants. I decided to offer the young people the chance to go with me: my own assistant Ron Richards, Norman Newell's assistant John Burgess, and in addition Peter Sullivan, who had been Wally Ridley's assistant although he had left for Decca a year before, and whom I knew to be friendly with Ron and John. We had our fiercely devoted ladies, too. Carol Weston, John's secretary, volunteered to come with us. Shirley Spence (now Mrs Burns) and my own Judy came with Ron Richards and myself. Seven of us were to start a new company. We left in August 1965, and with our going EMI was stripped of all its young blood. Only the old remained. In a sense, it was Martin's Revenge.

But it didn't stop there. The artists whom we were producing made up a formidable list. John had Adam Faith, Manfred Mann, and Peter and Gordon. Ron Richards was producing P. J. Proby and the Hollies. I had the Beatles, Cilla Black, Gerry and the Pacemakers, Billy J. Kramer and the Dakotas, and the Fourmost. When we set up on our own, most of them chose to stay with us to produce their records. It was a great loss to EMI.

The way we set up AIR—Associated Independent Recording— was along the lines of a commune. The blueprint was based on the way Spike Milligan had worked when he had set up Associated London Scripts with Eric Sykes, and later Galton and Simpson, Frankie Howerd and others. What I proposed to my partners was this: 'Let's start a producers' organisation. It will be four for all, and all for one. We will pool our income, and we will distribute it according to the way we are earning. I'm still very keen on incentives, but to start off with we'll have equal shares in the company, 25% each.' I did add the rider that 'I reckon I'm equal to you, but on the other hand, as George Orwell would have put it, I reckon I'm a bit more equal. All the same, we'll have 25% each.'

I went on: 'Income is another matter. If we're making individual records, we'll run the company on a levy from each person. We'll each contribute 25% of our income to running the company. If I earn £10,000 from making records, I'm going to put £2500 into the company to run it. If you're only earning £1000, you'll only put in £250. At the same time, when it comes to paying ourselves, we'll establish an upper limit of £10,000 for any one producer, and a lower limit of £3000 below which no one can fall. Any excess we'll plough back into the business.'

Those were the broad parameters that we agreed. But the immediate problem was capital, or lack of it. To start a company you need money for wages, rent, stationery, furniture, typewriters. And money was what we didn't have. There had certainly been no golden, silver, or even lead handshake from EMI. When I left, Len Wood had said: 'What about your pension? When you're on your own you won't get that.' I got back all the contributions I had made over the years, which amounted to £1800. That was what I received for fifteen years with EMI.

Nevertheless, it was with EMI that we had to deal. The negotiations revolved around the Beatles, who by then were in full flood. I had, of course, told Brian Epstein that I intended to leave EMI, and he was very sympathetic, because he knew the problems. But I tried to put no pressure on him. 'This doesn't mean that you have to stay with me, Brian,' I told him. 'EMI may well choose another producer for the Beatles, someone on the staff. It'll be up to you to decide. I don't want my leaving to be an embarrassment. But I intend to leave whatever happens, whether I record the Beatles or not.'

The decision was really taken by the sheer logic of the situation. I was probably the most successful producer EMI had. I guess they were frightened of changing horses in midstream, of splitting a winning partnership. So they approached me on the subject. 'When you leave, you might lose the Beatles, mightn't you?' they said.

'That's up to them, isn't it?'

'Would you be available to record them if they wanted you to?'

'Yes,' I said, 'I'll make myself available, but only on a royalty deal. I'm not having any of your old rubbish at £3000 a year.'

Linked with that negotiation was a deal by which EMI would take any of our products they wanted. We should be discovering and producing new artists, and EMI would have first opportunity to issue them. The person with whom I was dealing was the very man who had finally driven me to leave, Len Wood; and when it comes to negotiation, he is very canny indeed.

I should add here that there's a curious ambivalence about my relationship with Len. I have bitter experiences from my negotiations with him. At the same time, the fact is that I grew up in the business with him. When I started with Parlophone, he was the sales manager for Columbia, and I've always been very fond of him. I think that the way in which he always conducted business is just his misfortune, part of the way he is made. He has a puritanical streak which has always disapproved of the raciness of the business, and he tries to exert his own restraint upon it. The irony is that he has been the most successful person in the record industry. At the Britannia Awards, made in 1977 to commemorate the Queen's Silver Jubilee, when I was given the award for being the best record producer of the past twenty-five years, the award immediately preceding mine was a special one for outstanding services to the British record industry. The man who mounted the rostrum to receive it was, you've guessed, Len Wood.

The contract I signed with him was enormously complicated. It took hours to study it, and the schedule attached to it which covered all territories and every kind of recording.

It seemed needlessly complex.

The nub of the contract was that if AIR made a record which it financed itself, it had to offer that record to EMI. If they accepted it, they would pay a royalty of 7% of the retail price. On the other hand, if we recorded any of EMI's artists for them, we would get a producer's royalty which I settled at 2% of the retail price. The highest royalty payable to an artist at that time was 5%, so we were asking for two-fifths of that. Considering that artists in those days were not making much of a living out of their records, and that record sales were not all that high, it wasn't an extortionate demand, and EMI agreed. To give us capital, I asked for and got an advance of £5000 against that contract.

As you might expect, there was one item not covered by these general terms—the Beatles. For them, 2% was a figure way out of court as far as EMI were concerned. They took the view, which some might find curious in the circumstances, that I was not entitled to cash in on something that was already established; they overlooked the thorny question of who had established it in the first place!

After months of negotiation, I finally settled on a series of producer's royalties on Beatle records—one for Britain, one for America and one for the rest of the world. They were extremely complicated, as usual. In England, we got 1% of the wholesale price, which became about ½% retail. America, however, yielded far less; we were to receive 5% of the pressing fee that EMI would get from their American licencees.

Although Capitol Records Inc. was a subsidiary of EMI, it was perfectly possible that other companies might issue Beatle records. The soundtrack of the film *A Hard Day's Night* had been issued on United Artists, and they had an option on the Beatles appearing in two further pictures. Nowadays, royalties are clearly outlined in percentages of the selling price in all territories. But in the 1960s, it was quite normal to receive a proportion of the pressing fee that the originating company received. Before the Beatle breakthrough in America very few records of British origin had been pressed in the USA in any case.

If this seems a crazy deal to which to have agreed, the fact was that I had no alternative. It came at the end of months of haggling, and it had come down to a matter of agreeing or giving up the Beatles. Nor was I even too sure how much I could count on their support at that time, because by then they were becoming resentful at their own royalty deal. They blamed me for that, and rightly so, since I had been the one who had signed them to it, working on EMI's hallowed principles. What they couldn't know is that after the first year, when we'd already had tremendous sales, I went back to Len Wood on their behalf.

'This is nonsense—we ought to tear this contract up and start again,' I told him. 'We've got them now. We have to exercise the first option on the contract in July 1963; at that point they're due to rise to a royalty of a penny farthing. I'd like to double their royalty immediately and make it twopence.'

'O.K.,' said Len, 'that's a good idea. Get them to sign for another five years.'

'No, you misunderstand me,' I said. 'I don't want to get anything from them. I just want to give them twopence.'

'That's not commercial sense, old chap. Give them more royalty, but get a further extension of time.'

I refused to do it. In a way, I washed my hands of it. I simply left him, saying: 'You *must* give them a twopenny royalty.' In the end they did get an increase, but only after long negotiation.

Now I, in turn, was feeling the weight of the EMI negotiating machinery, or perhaps I should say 'machinations'. On top of the main AIR contract, I had to sign a separate document concerning me personally, which stipulated that I would be available for recording the Beatles at any time during the next ten years, and on the same conditions.

That was to boomerang on me in a big way. Many years later, after the Beatles had disbanded, Paul came and said that he wanted me to work with him on 'Live and Let Die'. I was delighted, and at the outset didn't think about the money. I never do; I get too excited about the prospect of work that interests me. So we went ahead and made 'Live and Let Die', which I scored and produced with Paul. Then I rang up Len Wood and said: 'Look, Len, I've made this record with Paul, which he obviously wants to come out as a single. I want to know the royalty you're going to pay me for my work on it, since it only concerns Paul and is therefore outside the terms of our contract. I reckon 2% would be fair, because that's what everybody else gets, and is now a standard royalty, so I don't think I'm being greedy. My normal rate now is 3%.'

'My dear fellow,' said Len, 'you've forgotten that you signed a document saying you would operate on the same terms and conditions for a period of ten years from 1965, and we're still within that period.'

'But, Len, the Beatles don't exist any more,' I protested.

'You look at the wording on your contract,' he said. 'It says that you will be available to record the Beatles or any one of them.'

'That's true, but they *aren't* Beatles any more,' I said.

'Nevertheless old chap . . . I'm afraid . . . you can take it to court, but the fact is—'

'But, Len,' I interrupted, 'are you telling me that when this record gets to number one in America, which I assure you it will, I'm only going to get 0.15 of a cent per record? Apart from anything else, Paul's going to put one of his own pieces on the backing side, so I'll only get half my normal royalty even at that low level.'

'It's hard luck, old chap,' said Len, without managing to convey the feeling that he really meant it. Soon afterwards, he asked to see me at his office. 'It does seem a bit hard,' he said. 'I'll tell you what I'll do. I'll treat it as though you had both sides of the record.'

'What you mean to say is that you'll pay me double a pittance,' I said.

Ignoring that remark, he went on, 'But before I do that, I'll have to ring up Bhaskar and find out if he agrees, because it's him who's going to have to pay it.'

So, while I sat there in his office, he telephoned Bhaskar Menon in California. Even from where I was sitting I could hear Bhaskar laughing on the other end of the phone. Then he asked: 'What does this mean to me, Len?'

'For every hundred thousand records you sell, you'll have to pay another 155 dollars.'

I sat there seething. If I hadn't gone to Len Wood, my company would have received a princely $155 for every 100,000 sales. In his generosity he doubled it, and we got $310. It was the last straw. My relations with EMI were at their lowest ebb.

But worse was to come. We didn't get paid at all for the Beatles album *Let It Be*; and we decided to get really bloody-minded. We took counsel's opinion. While I was discussing it with him I happened to bring up the story of what had happened with 'Live and Let Die'. By then he had studied the contracts in great detail, and he told me that in his opinion, I should not have been bound by that Beatle contract at that time. That made it even more galling—to know that had I taken legal advice earlier I could have gone straight ahead and sued EMI, instead of bothering to try to 'negotiate' with Len Wood. I'm glad to say that I have, finally, learned that lesson.

Of course, AIR wasn't solely a matter of wrangling over contracts. We did spend some of our time doing what we set out to do, namely produce records! Our first signing was the group David and Jonathan. Their real names were Roger Cook and Roger Greenaway, and they were songwriters who had written quite a few numbers for my other artists, including the hit 'You've Got Your Troubles'. At that time they had been part of a group called the Fortunes. Now they were to be just a pair, we had to find a name. We couldn't call them The Two Rogers, and we didn't like Cook and Greenaway, so Judy hit on the idea of the biblical characters David and Jonathan, really as an example of two people who were very close friends. The first record I produced with them was 'Michelle', which the Beatles had not issued as a single. It became a big hit, here and abroad. Subsequently they had enormous success with the Coca-Cola song—Greenaway has been very strong on jingles—which went out as 'I'd Like to Teach the World to Sing'.

In spite of having to devote a great part of my time to the established artists like Cilla and the Beatles, I still managed to find room for some of my old 'nutty' ideas. There were the Mastersingers, for example, a group of four teachers from Abingdon School who specialised in a very good cathedral-plainsong approach to singing. I happened to hear their joke 'party piece', which was singing the *Highway Code* in a church style, and decided to record it. To a certain degree of surprise in the business, it became a hit, and I naturally wanted to follow it up. I asked them what else they could dream up, and they had the idea of recording the telephone directory. I thought that was marvellous. Sadly, the heavy hand of bureaucracy intervened. The Post Office declared: 'We won't allow you to do it. Joe Bloggs of Lanchester Drive might not want his address in a song.' My view was that Mr Bloggs would have loved it; but the Post Office would have none of it, and the idea came to nothing.

I was only to use the Mastersingers once more, on the B-side of Peter Sellers' Shakespearian single, which was a take-off of Laurence Olivier. The A-side was 'A Hard Day's Night', which he did in the manner of Richard III, following Olivier's version of that part. The B-side was 'Help!', which the Mastersingers rendered in their best ecclesiastical manner as a background to Peter delivering the lines like a preacher from the pulpit.

That record has become a kind of classic; the Mastersingers, I suppose, have gone back to teaching. But then, the record business is full of little incidents like that, of people doing one thing that's a bit exceptional, like Stanley Holloway's 'Albert and the Lion'. And there was a choir singing a number called 'Happy Wanderer', which became a huge success—the Obenkirchen Children's Choir. Who? Well, I assure you that they made a lot of records following that; but none came anywhere near that first success. It isn't even confined to pop music. The classics are full of examples, like Litolff's Scherzo from his Concerto Symphonique. I don't suppose that many people have ever heard anything else by Litolff.

Another facet of my new independence was that I was able to write more on my own account. One day in 1967 Dick James, manager of Northern Songs, the Beatles' company, rang me up and said: 'You know the BBC are starting their new Radio One? The man in charge is called Robin Scott, and he wants Paul McCartney to write a signature tune for it. But there's no way Paul is going to do it. If I can persuade him to use you instead, would you be interested?'

'Of course,' I said, 'but if he wants Paul McCartney and gets me, that's a poor substitute.'

'Well, why don't you meet him anyway?' said Dick.

So I did just that, and Robin Scott, a most charming man, gave me his specifications. The music had to be very English, very contemporary, with classical overtones, and strikingly unusual. It was a fairly tall order; but I went away and thought about it, and came up with 'Theme One'.

Since the idea was very much an orchestral one, rather than something to be knocked out on a piano, I decided the best thing to do was to make a record of it and send that to him. I wanted to use a cathedral organ to open it with, so, having done the main part of the recording, I did the introduction at the Central Hall, Westminster, where there is a large pipe organ, and cut that into the beginning of the record. That was quite an experience in itself, because I played the organ myself and found that the sound came out a good quarter of a second after I had placed my fingers on the keys. Playing in rhythm was really quite difficult, because it takes such a long time for the sound to go through the pipes. In fact the late Anna Instone, who was then the head of the BBC Record Library, is reputed to have said, on first hearing it: 'Good God, it sounds like William Walton gone mad!' But they were very pleased with it, accepted it, and put it out every morning and evening at the beginning and end of the programme. I guess, come to think of it, that a lot of people woke to the sound of the Martin fingers battling with that organ.

A couple of years later, in 1969, I had a call from Richard Armitage, one of my old friends in the music world, who handled my affairs in America for a while. One of his clients was David Frost, whom I knew very well from the old days of 'That Was the Week That Was', when I had recorded the whole show, with Lance Percival, Millie Martin and the others. Richard told me that David was to do a new series of TV shows in America, but was fed up with his old signature tune. Would I like to write a new one? 'Sure I would,' I said. The piece I wrote was a kind of send-up of the idea of David in America, because he was always the 'in' person—always trying to be the most swinging person imaginable, while really fairly square within himself. It was a kind of gentle mickey-take, with a Sinatra-ish swing to it. I called it 'By George, It's the David Frost Theme'. Well, why not?

But I suppose the most traumatic week of those early years of AIR, indeed probably of my whole life, came in June 1967. Judy was extremely pregnant. On the Tuesday my father died. We were in the middle of moving house. And at the end of the week, the Beatles and I were due to be the British contribution to a worldwide satellite television link-up called 'Our World'.

The show was to go out live to an expected audience of 200 million, and even the Beatles, who were seldom overawed by anything, were a bit bomb-happy about it. 'But you can't just go off the cuff,' I pleaded with them. 'We've got to prepare *something*.' So they went away to get something together, and John came up with 'All You Need Is Love'. It had to be kept terribly secret, because the general idea was that the television viewers would actually see the Beatles at work recording their new single—although, modern recording being what it is, we obviously couldn't do that for real; so we laid down a basic rhythm track first of all. I remember that one of the minor problems was that George had got hold of a violin which he wanted to try to play, even though he couldn't!

I did a score for the song, a fairly arbitrary sort of arrangement since it was at such short notice. When it came to the end of their fade-away as the song closed, I asked them: 'How do you want to get out of it?'

'Write absolutely anything you like, George,' they said. 'Put together any tunes you fancy, and just play it out like that.'

The mixture I came up with was culled from the 'Marseillaise', a Bach two-part invention, 'Greensleeves', and the little lick from 'In the Mood'. I wove them all together, at slightly different tempos so that they all still worked as separate entities.

The day of the performance came, with television cameras rolling into the big Number One studio at Abbey Road. But I was still worried about the idea of going out totally live. So I told the boys: 'We're going to hedge our bets. This is how we'll do it. I'll have a four-track machine standing by, and when we go on the air I'll play you the rhythm track, which you'll pretend to be playing. But your voices and the orchestra will really be live, and we'll mix the whole thing together and transmit it to the waiting world like that.'

The BBC's mobile control unit was set up in the forecourt at Abbey Road, and I was to feed them the mix from our control room inside the studios. Geoff Emerick, my engineer, was sitting right next to me but, even so, communication was rather hampered by the fact that a television camera was sitting right over us, watching our every move. To cap it all, at the last minute, just before we were due to go on the air, there was a panic call from the producer, sitting outside in the control van. 'George, I've lost contact with the cameras in the studio. They can't hear me. Can you relay my instructions to them?' So, apart from worrying about the vast audience who were going to be watching me, and worrying about the sound we would produce, and worrying about the orchestra in the studio, which Mike Vickers was conducting, I had, at the moment of truth, to worry about linking the TV cameramen to their producer. It became so complicated that I was on the verge of hysterical laughter. I remember thinking: If we're going to do something wrong, we might as well do it in style in front of 200 million people.

In the end the broadcast was a great success, and after some modifications to the tracks which I had recorded during the actual broadcast we put out 'All You Need Is Love' as a single. It duly went to number one. Unfortunately, there was a sting in the tail for me. I was being paid the princely sum of fifteen pounds for arranging the music and writing the bits for the beginning and ending, and I had chosen the tunes for the mixture in the belief that they were all out of copyright. More fool me. It turned out that although 'In the Mood' itself was out of copyright, the Glenn Miller arrangement of it was not. The little bit I had chosen was the arrangement, not the tune itself, and as a result EMI were asked by its owners for a royalty.

The Beatles, quite rightly I suppose, said: 'We're not going to give up our copyright royalty.' So Ken East, the man who had by then become managing director of EMI Records, came to me and said: 'Look here, George, you did the arrangement on this. They're expecting money for it.'

'You must be out of your mind,' I said. 'I get fifteen pounds for doing that arrangement. Do you mean to say I've got to pay blasted copyright out of my fifteen quid?'

His answer was short and unequivocal. 'Yes.'

In the end, of course, EMI had to settle with the publishers.

We've come a long way since then, but the journey hasn't been without its tribulations. People always seemed to want to buy me, to own me, and I didn't want to be owned. Way back, at the time I told Brian Epstein that I was thinking of leaving EMI, he had said: 'You know, it would be nice for us to go into business together. With you handling the recording side and Dick James doing the publishing, we'd have a great company.' But he wasn't thinking of a partnership. He saw himself as the pinnacle of a vast empire of talent, with myself employed to run the record division. I had no intention of leaving one company in order to join another. I, too, wanted to be my own boss. Besides, although he was quite prepared to set me up in a record company in whose profits I would share, there was no question of my partaking in the other sides of the business, the publishing and the management. So I simply said: 'I don't think that's a good idea. I'll stay as I am.' Those brief business talks were the only ones we ever had, and the subject was never mentioned again, for which I am glad. As I was to learn later, it's far better not to get into a business bed with friends.

The next approach came soon after we had opened our studios. This time it was from Gordon Mills, who had founded his Management Agency Music company (MAM) on the fortunes of Tom Jones and Engelbert Humperdinck. Peter Sullivan, while still working for Decca, had introduced Tom Jones to Gordon. Tom had come to Decca for a recording test, and was looking for a manager. Gordon was just beginning to get into management. Peter brought them together, and since that time he had been producing the

records of both Tom and, subsequently, Engelbert. Now Gordon
came to us with a breathtaking offer. 'I'll buy you for two million
pounds,' he said.

'But I don't want to sell,' I told him. 'It's silly, after all the effort
to build up our own company.'

On the other hand, none of us had a penny to his name, and
it was hard to resist the temptation of a cool half a million pounds
each. So we got into the inevitable discussion, which he left to his
'hatchet men' to sort out. Then the true details began to emerge.
'Of course we can't give you two million in cash,' they said. 'We'll
give you paper shares in MAM, which at current quotation we
think are worth such and such . . .' and so it went on. When it was
all boiled down, the offer was worth much less than two million,
though still more than a million.

Needless to say, there was a cat's cradle of strings attached, all
of which added up to the fact that we wouldn't be our own bosses.
But then came the final touch which really decided us. We were
given rather heavily to understand that if we didn't do the deal
and climb into bed with them, Tom and Engelbert would be taken
away from Peter. That did it. 'Fine,' I said, 'let it happen. To hell
with them!' That didn't bind Peter—he could have left AIR and
gone to work for Gordon; but he chose not to. Gordon, understandably I think, said in effect: 'Sod 'em. I'll take Tom and Engelbert
away from them and produce them myself. Why should I give
them the royalties when I can make their records myself?'

So that was that. Then, in 1972, along came Dick James—the
man to whom I had 'given' the Beatles, and who had become a
multi-millionaire as a result. I think the truth of the matter is that
he had never forgiven me for that. After all, it is a bit of a burden
to carry around. He once said to me: 'How many times must a man
say "Thank you"?' I never wanted him to say 'Thank you'; I didn't
want it to get in the way of our relationship. But in the end it did.

Dick offered us a million pounds, and this time it was real cash.
Since ours was a private company, the decision to sell had to be

unanimous among the four of us. But we were all still penniless, and with a quarter of a million each being dangled in front of our noses we decided to talk. The fact was that, apart from our individual problems, we had no capital assets except for the company itself, into which we had been ploughing back everything we made. We wouldn't have minded selling a bit of the company in order to raise some capital. But that was the problem; a little bit wasn't enough. From Dick James's point of view, it had to be what would eventually become a controlling interest.

The discussions went on throughout 1973, and finally ruptured at the start of 1974. The truth was that I got extremely annoyed, because I realised that he was trying to buy not only the company but also me and my future work. That was what he really wanted. Meetings became very acrimonious. He started to bang his fist on the table; I started to shout at him; and we went our different ways. It was the very thing I didn't want to happen—and I am sure in my mind that the underlying cause of it all was that nagging sense of guilty gratitude which went back to the day I suggested to Brian Epstein: 'Why don't you get Dick James as your publisher?'

The sale was off, but once again there was a sting in the tail for us. To our horror we found that the solicitors' fees (which were pretty high, since they had been involved in all the negotiations) had to be borne, not by the company, but by us individually as shareholders. Nor could they be set against tax. So we actually lost money over the whole non-deal, and were worse off than before.

It was against that background that, in October 1974, we finally succumbed, if that is the word, to yet another advance: this time from Chrysalis, the empire formed by Chris Wright and Terry Ellis. But it was a different bag of tricks altogether. Initially, they only set out to buy a small proportion of the company. That gave us the capital we needed. Then again, although they wanted the option of buying a controlling interest in the company, which they now have, it was on the clear understanding that they would not interfere with the way we wanted to run it. To all intents and purposes it was to remain ours. It has been an ideal marriage, based on mutual respect. They have left us alone, except to give financial advice and help in management. That in turn has freed me to develop my post-Beatle period of work in America, which has increased the revenue of the company—and myself, naturally—to a vast degree.

The brilliant thing about the deal, as far as I am concerned, is that it has not cost me my freedom. I can do exactly what I want. I'm as free as the wind. If I want to write music for a film, I can. If I want to go away and write a symphony, I can. If I want—no, *when* I wanted to take the time to work on this book, I could. Those freedoms are very important to me. Had I wanted to be a millionaire, which I am not but which I know full well I could have been had I so wished, it would have meant giving up some of them. All I seek is that when I get too old, or sick and tired of what I am doing now, my family and myself should be able to live comfortably. The idea of a string of yachts and private jets doesn't appeal to me. Those goals in life bring only worries.

Not that the building of AIR had been achieved without any headaches; and there was one more to come. While I was in America in 1976, I received a shock, the nature of which could truly be described as incredible. Because that's what it was: unbelievable. Each of the original partners in AIR, myself included, received a registered letter from EMI. It stated that EMI were terminating the original contract the following autumn, which they were entitled to do, but that notwithstanding the overall contractual arrangements, which clearly stated that royalties would be payable for twenty-five years, no more royalties would be paid from the termination date.

We were shattered. There was no question of anyone ringing us up to say: 'Look, old boy, this is what we're doing.' Just a registered letter. John Burgess was, to say the least, extremely upset, and once again we had to consult lawyers. We discovered that there was a clause in the contract which by virtue (or disgrace) of its devious ambiguity gave them an argument on which to base their action.

But the reason was different. We had been dissatisfied with the royalties we had been receiving, and we had not had a statement for eighteen months. Tiring of this continual delay, we had put an audit into EMI. The result was the registered letter. In the end it was all settled, but not without a good deal of rancour.

All in all, it is fair to say that relations between AIR and EMI have been less than cordial over the years since we first broke free of them. That is despite the many successful records we have made for them since we went independent. It is despite the fact that in 1967, two years after I had left, the Beatles and I made for EMI the record which some people have been kind enough to describe as the most influential in pop history: the record that went by the title *Sgt. Pepper's Lonely Hearts Club Band*.

11

A DASH OF PEPPER

THE TIME had come for experiment. The Beatles knew it, and I knew it. By November 1966 we had had an enormous string of hits, and we had the confidence, even arrogance, to know that we could try anything we wanted. The sales we had achieved would have justified our recording rubbish, if we had wanted to. But then, we wouldn't have got away with foisting rubbish on the public for long.

The single of 'Yellow Submarine' and 'Eleanor Rigby', and the album *Revolver*, had been issued in August that year. So it was several months since we had been in the studio, and time for us to think about a new album. 'New' was certainly how it was to turn out.

I suppose the indications were already there. 'Eleanor Rigby' and 'Tomorrow Never Knows', from *Revolver*, had been strong hints for those with ears to hear what was to come. They were forerunners of a complete change of style. Even I didn't realise at the time how significant it was, nor the reasons for it. Flower Power and the hippy and drug revolution had been taking place, affecting the boys in front of my very eyes, yet my own brand of naivety had prevented me from seeing the whole thing for what it really was. I hardly knew what pot smelled like, although it was right under my nose! But I did realise that something was happening in the music, and that excited me.

Strangely, the *Sgt. Pepper* album originated with a song which was never on it, 'Strawberry Fields'. That November John came into the studio, and we went into our regular routine. I sat on my high stool with Paul standing beside me, and John stood in front of us with his acoustic guitar and sang the song. It was absolutely lovely. Then we tried it with Ringo on drums, and Paul and George on their bass and electric guitars. It started to get heavy—it wasn't the gentle song that I had first heard. We ended up with a record which was very good heavy rock. Still, that was apparently what John wanted, so I metaphorically shrugged my shoulders and said: 'Well, that really wasn't what I'd thought of, but it's O.K.' And off John went.

A week later he came back and said: 'I've been thinking about it, too, George. Maybe what we did was wrong. I think we ought to have another go at doing it.' Up to that time we had never remade anything. We reckoned that if it didn't work out the first time, we shouldn't do it again. But this time we did. 'Maybe we should do it differently,' said John. 'I'd like you to score something for it. Maybe we should have a bit of strings, or brass or something.' Between us we worked out that I should write for cellos and trumpets, together with the group. When I had finished we recorded it again, and I felt that this time it was much better. Off went John again.

A few days later he rang me up and said: 'I like that one, I really do. But, you know, the other one's got something, too.'

'Yes, I know,' I said, 'they're both good. But aren't we starting to split hairs?'

Perhaps I shouldn't have used the word 'split', because John's reply was: 'I like the beginning of the first one, and I like the end of the second one. Why don't we just join them together?'

'Well, there are only two things against it,' I said. 'One is that they're in different keys. The other is that they're in different tempos.'

'Yeah, but you can do something about it, I know. You can fix it, George.'

John always left this kind of thing to me. He never professed to know anything about recording. He was the least technical of the Beatles. He had a profound faith in my ability to cope with such problems, a faith which was sometimes misplaced, as I certainly felt it was on this occasion. He had presented me with an almost insuperable task. But I had to have a go. I listened to the two versions again, and suddenly realised that with a bit of luck I might get away with it, because, with the way that the keys were arranged, the slower version was a semitone flat compared with the faster one.

I thought: If I can speed up the one, and slow down the other, I can get the pitches the same. And with any luck, the tempos will be sufficiently close not to be noticeable. I did just that, on a variable-control tape machine, selecting precisely the right spot to make the cut, to join them as nearly perfectly as possible. That is how 'Strawberry Fields' was issued, and that is how it remains today—two recordings.

The next song we recorded was 'When I'm Sixty-Four'; that was much simpler. It was the kind of vaudeville tune which Paul occasionally came up with, and he said he wanted 'a kind of tooty sound'. So I scored it for two clarinets and a bass clarinet. I remember recording it in the cavernous Number One studio at Abbey Road, and thinking how the three clarinet players looked as lost as a referee and two linesmen alone in the middle of Wembley Stadium.

Following that came 'Penny Lane', which started life as a fairly simple song. But Paul decided he wanted a special sound on it, and one day, after he had been to a concert of Bach's Brandenburg Concerti, he said: 'There's a guy in them playing this fantastic high trumpet.'

'Yes,' I said, 'the piccolo trumpet, the Bach trumpet. Why?'

'It's a great sound. Why can't we use it?'

'Sure we can,' I said, and at that he asked me to organise it for him. Now, the normal trumpet is in B flat. But there is also the D trumpet, which is what Bach mostly used, and the F trumpet. In this case, I decided to use a B-flat piccolo trumpet, an octave above the normal. To play it I engaged David Mason, who was with the London Symphony Orchestra. It was a difficult session, for two reasons. First, that little trumpet is a devil to play in tune, because it isn't really in tune with itself, so that in order to achieve pure notes the player has to 'lip' each one.

Secondly, we had no music prepared. We just knew that we wanted little piping interjections. We had had experience of professional musicians saying: 'If the Beatles were real musicians, they'd know what they wanted us to play before we came into the studio.' Happily, David Mason wasn't like that at all. By then the Beatles were very big news anyway, and I think he was intrigued to be playing on one of their records, quite apart from being well paid for his trouble. As we came to each little section where we wanted the sound, Paul would think up the notes he wanted, and I would write them down for David. The result was unique, something that had never been done in rock music before, and it gave 'Penny Lane' a very distinct character.

Then came Christmas, and we agreed to get together again after they had written some more material. But in the meantime EMI and Brian Epstein had told me that they needed another single, since they hadn't had one for a while. I said: 'O.K. It means we'll have to find extra material for the album, but let's couple the best two we have so far—'Strawberry Fields' and 'Penny Lane'—and issue them as a double-A-sided record.' To this day I cannot imagine why that single was beaten to the number-one spot, because for my money it was the best we ever issued. But there it was, and now we were left with 'When I'm Sixty-Four' on its own for the new album.

We started work again in February 1967, and the boys began bringing in the various songs they had written. But 'Sgt. Pepper' itself didn't appear until halfway through making the album. It was Paul's song, just an ordinary rock number and not particularly brilliant as songs go. Nor was there anything difficult or special about the recording of it. But when we had finished it, Paul said, 'Why don't we make the album as though the Pepper band really existed, as though Sergeant Pepper was making the record? We'll dub in effects and things.' I loved the idea, and from that moment it was as though *Pepper* had a life of its own, developing of its own accord rather than through a conscious effort by the Beatles or myself to integrate it and make it a 'concept' album.

'With a Little Help from My Friends', for example, was originally conceived as a separate entity, specially written for Ringo—we always felt there had to be some corner of each album that was forever Ringo! The boys backed him with vocal choruses and so on, since he never did have a very brilliant voice, but the song suited him admirably.

Again, George's contribution, 'Within You Without You', was, with all deference to George, a rather dreary song, heavily influenced by his obsession with Indian music at that time. I worked very closely with him on the scoring of it, using a string orchestra, and he brought in some friends from the Indian Music Association to play special instruments. I was introduced to the dilruba, an Indian violin, in playing which a lot of sliding techniques are used. This meant that in scoring for that track I had to make the string players play very much like Indian musicians, bending the notes, and with slurs between one note and the next.

But even such widely differing songs as these two seemed to merge into the whole once they had become the 'work' of Sergeant Pepper himself, from that first moment on the record when you hear the tuning-up noises of the band and the atmosphere of an audience. The way in which the record seemed to generate its own 'togetherness' became particularly apparent during the editing. A perfect example of that was 'Good Morning', an up-tempo, fairly raucous song with a curious, irregular metre to it. We normally faded out the music at the end of a song, but this time we decided to cover the fade with a host of sound-effects, particularly animals. We shoved everything in, from a pack of hounds in full cry to more basic farmyard noises. The order we had worked out for the album meant that that track was to be followed by a reprise of the 'Sgt. Pepper' song, and of course I was trying to make the whole thing flow. So imagine my delight when I discovered that the sound of a chicken clucking at the end of 'Good Morning' was remarkably like the guitar sound at the beginning of 'Sgt. Pepper'. I was able to cut and mix the two tracks in such a way that the one actually turned into the other.

That was one of the luckiest edits one could ever get. At other times, we could only fall back on our own mad ideas in order to achieve the effects we wanted: no more so than with 'Being for the Benefit of Mr Kite'. Like most of John's songs, it was based on something he had seen; he would often pick up a newspaper and see some item which was the spur to a song. In this case it was an old placard for a circus and fair, which he had hanging in his house. It announced, 'Being for the benefit of Mr Kite, a Grand Circus, the Hendersons, Pablo Fanques' Fair . . .' and included all the acts which would appear, including Henry the Horse. When we came to the middle section of the song, where 'Henry the Horse dances the waltz', we obviously had to go into waltz-time, and John said he wanted the music to 'swirl up and around', to give it a circus atmosphere. As usual, having written a great song, he said to me, 'Do what you can with it,' and walked away, leaving me to it.

In order to get a hurdy-gurdy effect, I got Mal Evans, the roadie, to play his enormous bass harmonica, while John and I did our thing on two electric organs, a Wurlitzer and a Hammond. John was to play the basic tune, and around it I was to play the swirly noises—chromatic runs based on it. Unfortunately, my digital capacities on an organ fall short of spectacular, and I found that I couldn't achieve the speed I wanted for these runs. So I told John: 'What we'll do is to slow the whole thing down by a half. You play the tune twice as slow and an octave down, and I'll do my runs as fast as I can, but an octave down as well. Then, when we double the tape speed, it'll come out all nice and smooth and very swirly.'

Of course, we could always have got a professional organist in to do it, but our attitude was 'Why the hell! Why should we let someone else in on our fun?' Besides, we were doing it all off the top of our heads: to bring someone else in would have meant delay and a lot of tedious explanation.

But even when we had done it this new way, it still didn't sound quite right, and I told John that I would think about it. Then I found the answer. I got together a lot of recordings of old Victorian steam organs—the type you hear playing on carousels at county fairs— playing all the traditional tunes, Sousa marches and so on. But I clearly couldn't use even a snatch of any of them that would be identifiable; so I dubbed a few of the records on to tape, gave it to the engineer and told him, 'I'll take half a minute of that one, a minute and a half of that one, a minute of that one,' and so on.

'Then what do I do with them?' he asked.

'You cut that tape up into sections about a foot long.'

'What?!!'

'Cut it up into little parcels about a foot long, and don't be too careful about the cuts.'

Clearly thinking I had lost my senses, he did it, leaving me with a bunch of pieces of tape some one foot long—about sixty in all. '*Now* what?'

'Fling them up in the air.'

Believing by now, I suppose, that the world had gone completely insane, he did as asked.

'Now,' I said, 'pick them up in whatever order they come and stick them all back together again.'

The poor chap couldn't contain himself. 'What did you do *that* for?!!'

'You'll see,' I said.

After he had laboriously stuck them all together again, we

played the tape and I said: 'That piece there's a bit too much like the original. Turn it round the other way, backwards.' We went on like that until the tape was a whole amalgam of carousel noises, but meaningless in musical terms because it was composed of fragments of tunes connected in a series of fractions of a second. It was an unreal hotch-potch of sound, arrived at without rhyme or reason; but when it was added as a background 'wash' to the organ and harmonica track we had already made, it did give an overall impression of being in a circus.

Compared with Paul's songs, all of which seemed to keep in some sort of touch with reality, John's had a psychedelic, almost mystical quality. 'Lucy in the Sky with Diamonds' was a typical John song in that respect, and a lot of analysts and psychiatrists were later to describe it as the drug song of all time. They were talking rubbish, but the tag stuck. I was very offended recently when I saw a television programme about the drug raid, Operation Julie, in which some major world suppliers of LSD were rounded up. The programme was prefaced with 'Lucy', as though it were *the* drug song—a 'fact' which people have taken as finally proven simply because 'Lucy', 'Sky' and 'Diamonds' happen to start with the letters LSD.

The gospel truth of the matter is that Julian, John's young son, came home from school one day carrying a picture of a little girl in a black sky with stars all round her. John asked if he had done the picture, and when Julian said he had, John asked him, 'What is it, then?'

Julian's best friend at school was a little girl called Lucy, and he replied, 'It's Lucy, in the sky, with diamonds.'

John's imagery is one of the great things about his work—'tangerine trees', 'marmalade skies', 'cellophane flowers'. I hope it doesn't sound pretentious, but I always saw him as an aural Salvador Dali, rather than some drug-ridden record artist.

On the other hand, I would be stupid to pretend that drugs didn't figure quite heavily in the Beatles' lives at that time. At the same time they knew that I, in my schoolmasterly role, didn't approve, and like naughty boys they would slope off into the canteen, lock the door and have their joints. Not only was I not into it myself, I couldn't see the need for it; and there's no doubt that, if I too had been on dope, *Pepper* would never have been the album it was. Perhaps it was the combination of dope and no dope that worked, who knows? The fact remains that they often got very giggly, and it frequently interfered with our work; never more so than in the episode with John.

We were overdubbing voices on one of the *Pepper* tracks, and John, down in the studio, was obviously feeling unwell. I called over the intercom, 'What's the matter, John? Aren't you feeling very well?'

'No,' said John.

I went down and looked at him, and he said, 'I don't know. I'm feeling very strange.'

He certainly looked very ill, so I told him, 'You need some fresh air. Let's leave the others working, and I'll take you outside.'

The problem was where to go; there were the usual five hundred or so kids waiting for us at the front, keeping vigil like guard-dogs, and if we had dared to appear at the entrance there would have been uproar and they would probably have broken the gates down. So I took him up to the roof, above Number Two studio. I remember it was a lovely night, with very bright stars. Then I suddenly realised that the only protection around the edge of the roof was a parapet about six inches high, with a sheer drop of some ninety feet to the ground below, and I had to tell him, 'Don't go too near the edge, there's no rail there, John.' We walked around the roof for a while. Then he agreed to come back downstairs, and we packed up for the night.

It wasn't until much later that I learned what had happened. John was in the habit of taking pills, 'uppers', to give him the energy to get through the night. That evening, he had taken the wrong pill by mistake—a very large dose of LSD. But Paul knew, and went home with him and turned on as well, to keep him company. It seems they had a real trip. I knew they smoked pot, and I knew they took pills, but in my innocence I had no idea they were also into LSD.

Paul's thoughtfulness in going home with John was typical of one of the best sides of his character. But during the making of *Pepper* he was also to give me one of the biggest hurts of my life. It concerned the song 'She's Leaving Home'. At that time I was still having to record all my other artists. One day Paul rang me to say: 'I've got a song I want you to work with me on. Can you come round tomorrow afternoon? I want to get it done quickly. We'll book an orchestra, and you can score it.'

'I can't tomorrow, Paul. I'm recording Cilla at two thirty.'

'Come on. You can come round at two o'clock.'

'No, I can't, I've got a session on.'

'All right, then,' he said, and that ended the conversation.

What he did then, as I discovered later, was to get Neil Aspinall, the road manager, to ring round and find someone else to do the score for him, simply because I couldn't do it at that short notice. In the end he found Mike Leander, who could. The following day Paul presented me with it and said, 'Here we are. I've got a score. We can record it now.'

I recorded it, with a few alterations to make it work better, but I was hurt. I thought: Paul, you could have waited. For I really couldn't have done it that afternoon, unless I had just devoted everything to the Beatles and never dealt with any other artist. Paul obviously didn't think it was important that I should do everything. To me it was. I wasn't getting much out of it from a financial point of view, but at least I was getting satisfaction. The score itself was good enough, and still holds up today, but it was the only score that was ever done by anyone else during all my time with the Beatles. However, it had happened, and there was nothing to be done about it.

Then we came to the major piece of the whole album, 'A Day

in the Life'. It started out very much as one of John's songs, culled from the pages of newspapers: 'I read the news today, oh boy.' For example, there was the bit where he referred to 'four thousand holes in Blackburn, Lancashire'. Some wizard of analysis claimed that this referred to the holes in a junkie's arm, but the truth was that John had read a little newspaper piece about the deplorable state of the roads in that town. A local councillor was quoted as saying: 'It's about time they did something. Do you know, I've been around Blackburn and I've counted four thousand holes.' John simply wrote that into the lyric.

Then John asked Paul if he had anything to go into the middle part of the song, and Paul came up with 'Woke up, got out of bed . . .', which is really a completely different song. But it merged into the other one, because it provided a sort of dream sequence. We divided the two sections with what was in effect a very long musical pause. When we recorded the original track it was just Paul banging away on the same piano note, bar after bar, for twenty-four bars. We agreed that it was a question of 'This space to be filled later'. In order to keep time, we got Mal Evans to count each bar, and on the record you can still hear his voice as he stood by the piano counting: 'One—two—three—four. . . .' For a joke, Mal set an alarm clock to go off at the end of twenty-four bars, and you can hear that too. We left it in because we couldn't get it off!

The question was, how were we going to fill those twenty-four bars of emptiness? After all, it was pretty boring! So I asked John for his ideas. As always, it was a matter of my trying to get inside his mind, discover what pictures he wanted to paint, and then try to realise them for him. He said: 'What I'd like to hear is a tremendous build-up, from nothing up to something absolutely like the end of the world. I'd like it to be from extreme quietness to extreme loudness, not only in volume, but also for the sound to expand as well. I'd like to use a symphony orchestra for it. Tell you what, George, you book a symphony orchestra, and we'll get them in a studio and tell them what to do.'

'Come *on*, John,' I said, 'there's no way you can get a symphony orchestra sitting around and say to them, "Look, fellers, this is what you're going to do." Because you won't get them to do what you want them to do. You've got to write something down for them.'

'Why?' asked John, with his typically wide-eyed approach to such matters.

'Because they're all playing different instruments, and unless you've got time to go round each of them individually and see exactly what they do, it just won't work.'

But he did explain what he wanted sufficiently for me to be able to write a score. For the 'I'd love to turn you onnnnnnnn . . .' bit, I used cellos and violas. I had them playing those two notes that echo John's voice. However, instead of fingering their instruments, which would produce crisp notes, I got them to slide their fingers up and down the frets, building in intensity until the start of the orchestral climax.

That climax was something else again. What I did there was to write, at the beginning of the twenty-four bars, the lowest possible note for each of the instruments in the orchestra. At the end of the twenty-four bars, I wrote the highest note each instrument could reach that was near a chord of E major. Then I put a squiggly line right through the twenty-four bars, with reference points to tell them roughly what note they should have reached during each bar. The musicians also had instructions to slide as gracefully as possible between one note and the next. In the case of the stringed instruments, that was a matter of sliding their fingers up the strings. With keyed instruments, like clarinet and oboe, they obviously had to move their fingers from key to key as they went up, but they were asked to 'lip' the changes as much as possible too.

I marked the music 'pianissimo' at the beginning and 'fortissimo' at the end. Everyone was to start as quietly as possible, almost inaudibly, and end in a (metaphorically) lung-bursting tumult. And in addition to this extraordinary piece of musical gymnastics, I told them that they were to disobey the most fundamental rule of the orchestra. They were not to listen to their neighbours.

A well-schooled orchestra plays, ideally, like one man, following the leader. I emphasised that this was exactly what they must not do. I told them 'I want everyone to be individual. It's every man for himself. Don't listen to the fellow next to you. If he's a third away from you, and you think he's going too fast, let him go. Just do your own slide up, your own way.' Needless to say, they were amazed. They had certainly never been told *that* before.

To perform this little extravagance, John and Paul had asked me for a full symphony orchestra. But although by then I had grown used to pretty lavish outlays where the Beatles were concerned, my sense of EMI-induced caution had not entirely deserted me. So I said: 'With all due respect, I think it's a bit silly booking ninety musicians just to get an effect like this.' So I settled on half a symphony orchestra, with one flute, one oboe, one bassoon, one clarinet and so on, instead of two of each. We ended up with forty-two players.

The recording was to take place in Number One studio at Abbey Road, and we all felt a sense of occasion, since it was the largest orchestra we ever used on a Beatles recording. So I wasn't all that surprised when Paul rang up and said, 'Look, do you mind coming in evening dress?'

'Why? What's the idea?'

'We thought we'd have fun. We've never had a big orchestra before, so we thought we'd have fun on the night. So will you come in evening dress? And I'd like all the orchestra to come in evening dress, too.'

'Well, that may cost a bit extra, but we'll do it,' I said. 'What are you going to wear?'

'Oh, our usual freak-outs'—by which he meant their gaudy hippie clothes, floral coats and all.

Came the night, and I discovered that they'd also invited along all their way-out friends, like Mick Jagger, Marianne Faithfull, and

Simon and Marijke, the psychedelic artists who were running the Apple shop in Baker Street. They were wandering in and out of the orchestra, passing out sparklers and joints and God knows what, and on top of that they had brought along a mass of party novelties.

After one of the rehearsals I went into the control room to consult Geoff Emerick. When I went back into the studio the sight was unbelievable. The orchestra leader, David McCallum, who used to be the leader of the Royal Philharmonic, was sitting there in a bright red false nose. He looked up at me through paper glasses. Eric Gruenberg, now a soloist and once leader of the BBC Symphony Orchestra, was playing happily away, his left hand perfectly normal on the strings of his violin, but his bow held in a giant gorilla's paw. Every member of the orchestra had a funny hat on above the evening dress, and the total effect was completely weird. Somewhere there is a film of the affair, taken by an Indian cameraman the Beatles knew.

The orchestra, of course, thought it was all a stupid giggle and a waste of money, but I think they were carried into the spirit of the party just because it was so ludicrous. In fact, it's worth mentioning that the only time we have had real objections from an orchestra was during the recording of 'Hey Jude', the biggest-selling single of all. I wanted them to sing and clap their hands as well as play, and one man walked out. 'I'm not going to clap my hands and sing Paul McCartney's bloody song,' he said, in spite of the fact that he was getting double rates for his trouble.

In the end, of course, the 'Day in the Life' party was not a waste of money, because it produced an incredible piece of recorded sound. In fact, looking back on it, I think I should have been more extravagant and booked a full orchestra. But even so, I ended up with the equivalent of not one but two full orchestras. After rehearsal, we recorded that sound four times, and I added those four separate recordings to each other at slightly different intervals. If you listen closely you can hear the difference. They are not quite together.

That sound was used twice during the song. The first time, we ended it artificially, by literally splitting the tape, leaving silence. There is nothing more electrifying, after a big sound, than complete silence. The second time, of course, came at the end of the record, and for that I wanted a final chord, which we dubbed on later. I wanted that chord to last as long as possible, and I told Geoff Emerick it would be up to him, not the boys, to achieve that. What I did was to get all four Beatles and myself in the studio at three pianos, an upright and two grands. I gave them the bunched chords that they were to play.

Then I called out, 'Ready? One, two, three—go!' With that, CRASH! All of us hit the chords as hard as possible. In the control room, Geoff had his faders—which control the volume input from the studio—way, way down at the moment of impact. Then, as the sound died away, he gradually pushed the faders up, while we kept as quiet as the proverbial church mice. In the end, they were so far up, and the microphones so live, that you could hear the air-conditioning. It took forty-five seconds to do, and we did it three or four times, building up a massive sound of piano after piano after piano, all doing the same thing. That chord was a fitting end to 'A Day in the Life'.

Well, almost the end. When we came to putting the record together, Paul said: 'You know, when these records are pressed, there's a run-out groove that takes the needle to and fro to get the automatic change working. Why don't we put some music in there? Something silly.'

'O.K.,' I said, 'if you want a bit of a joke. I don't think anyone's ever done it, but why not?'

'Let's go down and do something in the studio, then,' he said. So the four of them went down and chanted silly little things, each one different, without any sense; 'yum turn, tim ting' sort of sounds. I snipped about two seconds off the tape of that and put it into the run-out groove so that it went round and round forever.

Of course, when the record came out, all the fanatics heard this weird noise on the run-out groove and started wondering what it was, and why they had done it. Then the interpretations started. Finally, it came back to me as the craziest of all Beatle analyses: 'Hey, if you play that backwards, it says an obscene phrase.' Well, with a *huge* stretch of the imagination I suppose it did, but that was certainly never intended. It was simply typical of what the Beatle cult could produce, with every record being turned inside-out and upside-down in an effort to discern hidden meanings.

They even discovered the dog's recording, which *was* intended, but only as a private joke; it was never publicly announced. Not content with his nonsense in the run-out groove, Paul had said, 'We never record anything for animals. You realise that, don't you? Let's put on something which only a dog can hear.'

'All right,' I said. 'A dog's audio range is much higher than a human's. Let's put on a note of about 20,000 hertz.' It was a little private signal for dogs. They heard it, all right. But they weren't Beatle-lovers; they hated it, and they whined whenever it was played. I doubt very much if it's still there on modern pressings of the record. Knowing the EMI hierarchy, I expect they have said, 'It's a silly waste of time. Snip it off.' Not being a dog, however, I just don't know.

When it came to putting the record out, the boys were convinced, rightly, that they had done something really worthwhile, which no one else had ever tried. They were determined that the cover should be equally original. So they got a man called Peter Blake to stage it for them. It cost a great deal. They wanted the faces of all the people they had ever admired to be in the photograph with them, together, just for the heck of it, with a lot of people they didn't admire at all. They borrowed wax models of themselves from Madame Tussaud's, together with the effigies of Diana Dors and Sonny Liston. Well, why not? Marlene Dietrich was there as a cardboard cut-out, along with D. H. Lawrence. Then they added all the things that they felt were indicative of their times: musical instruments, a hookah, a television set . . . and marijuana plants. There was a row about that, naturally.

There was also a row about the cover as a whole. In fact, EMI were, to put it mildly, outraged. They rang me up and said: 'We can't have this cover. You can't put this record out.'

'Why not?'

'Because . . . do you realise? . . . all the faces on that cover . . . we've got to get permission from every one. We've even got to get permission from estates. We know Marilyn Monroe's dead, but we still have to ask the executors. Same with W. C. Fields. Mae West's still alive, so we'll have to ask her direct.' And so it went on. In some cases, they didn't know who the people on the cover were, and they would ring up to ask. EMI were worried sick, and I suppose they did have some reason for it. Someone like Marlon Brando might have taken exception. They had to write hundreds of letters all over the world in order to get all the clearances.

On top of everything else, the Beatles decided to have special uniforms made in fine silkwork by Douglas Hayward, a trendy tailor of the time. Having donned these uniforms for the photograph, they wanted to hold some very un-Beatle instruments—John a French horn, Ringo a trumpet, Paul a cor anglais, and George a flute. The only trouble was that they didn't know how to hold them!

But in the end everything turned out all right, like the best fairy stories, and the album was the biggest seller they had ever had. For my part, I felt it was the album which turned the Beatles from being just an ordinary rock-and-roll group into being significant contributors to the history of artistic performance. It was a turning-point—*the* turning-point. It was the watershed which changed the recording art from something that merely made amusing sounds into something which will stand the test of time as a valid art form: sculpture in music, if you like.

Technically, it was a bit of a nightmare. If I had had eight or sixteen-track recording facilities, I could have done a much better job. I only had four-track, and I had to stretch it to the limit. Anyone who listens to that record must realise that there have to be more than four tracks to provide the sounds on some of the songs, as indeed there were. What I did was to dub from one four-track machine on to another, sometimes not once but twice. Harking back to what I wrote earlier, that would mean, of course, losing up to nine generations of sound quality. The signal-to-noise ratio, if I dubbed down twice, would be nine times worse.

What I did was this. I would record the rhythm, the loudest part of the recording, on to four original tracks. These I would dub down to one track on a separate machine, leaving me three spare tracks. If I needed more once these had been recorded, I would dub the second lot of four tracks down to two tracks on a third machine, leaving me two more spare tracks. This meant that it was only the original rhythm sound which was impaired nine times in quality, and because of its essential loudness it was unlikely that the listener would be able to hear the quality difference. The second lot of three fresh tracks, when dubbed on to the third machine, would only lose four generations of sound quality. By this technique, I was able to prise up to nine tracks out of our four-track facilities.

That should have been the end of the *Sgt. Pepper* story as far as I was concerned. But in November 1976, nearly ten years after the album was made, I was approached by Robert Stigwood to do the musical score for the *Sgt. Pepper* film he was making.

My first inclination was to say no out of hand. I knew in my heart of hearts that the Beatles would not have approved, and, although I don't need their permission to run my life, I still wondered if it was right to go over old ground. On the other hand, Robert assured me that if I took the job on I would have complete artistic control over the music, and would be able to dictate exactly what it should sound like. In addition he was dangling a small fortune under my nose, more than I had ever had for a film before. Then I asked myself whether I was really thinking of doing it because of the money. If you do something for money which otherwise you don't want to do, you are doing it for the wrong reason and you shouldn't do it at all.

I was trying to be honest with myself, but one is seldom sure of one's own motives in situations like that. In the end it was Judy who made up my mind for me, as wives often do. She said: 'I understand the problems you're going through. You want to be sure that you're doing the right thing artistically. But have you ever considered that if you don't do it, someone else will, and you will hate what they've done? So you won't be defending the music's integrity—and on the other hand, if you do it, you'll be in a position to ensure that the music isn't maltreated.' That, and Robert's promise of total freedom, which in the event was fully honoured, finally decided me.

Shooting was planned to start in April 1977, but then they started having difficulties in getting the right artists. The Bee Gees and Peter Frampton were signed up, but no one was cast for the other roles, and all sorts of names, some plausible, others highly implausible, were being bandied about. Then there was trouble with the director. The first one they hired was a television director, who proved to be unsuitable, and it took some time to find a replacement.

When they did find him, it was absolutely the right choice— Michael Schultz, who had shot to fame through his direction of the film *Car Wash*. He and I hit it off from the moment we met. I found him very easy to get to know, and, more importantly, we were of one mind about the way the music should be handled. That was fine, but to make a film you need artists, and casting was going very slowly. They got George Burns to play Mr Kite; then there was talk of Mick Jagger for another role, eventually filled by Aerosmith, the American 'heavy metal' group. With all these delays, the shooting didn't finally start until October 1977.

Before that could happen, I had to prepare all the music tracks. Since it was a musical film, all the musical sequences had to be mimed to existing recorded performances. It didn't mean making finished tracks, but providing them with the nucleus, the rhythm and voices. With nearly two hours of music in the film, there was obviously a mountain of material to record before they could even start shooting. I started work in Los Angeles on 1 September. For the rhythm section, I engaged Max Middleton, an old friend from the Jeff Beck group, as the keyboard man; Wilbur Bascombe, also from Jeff Beck, on bass; Bernard Purdie, a great drummer out of New York; and Robert Awhai, a guitar player who had worked a lot with Max.

Although I prepared certain scores for them, we mainly worked from what are called 'head arrangements'. That meant that I would give them chord symbols and bass lines, but the actual style was decided on the studio floor. I would tell them: 'This is the feel I want, this is the rhythm I want, this is the style of playing, these are the modulations, this is how we go from here to there. We need so much instrumental here, and so much vocal there . . .' and so on.

In laying down those tracks I had to work very closely both with the film director, who would tell me how long the scene was going to be and what was going to happen in it, and with the choreographer, who had to decide how people were going to move during the scene. In many cases, they would say, 'This song isn't long enough as it stands. We need a section here where they strut through the town hall'—or wherever it was. I would have to add so many bars of rhythm, working to their specifications. Then, with the rhythm tracks recorded, we would bring in the artist to make the final vocal tracks.

Working with the Bee Gees and Peter Frampton was very easy. The Bee Gees are extremely professional, and in a curious way there was a sense of *déjà vu* for me. Although I had never thought of them as being like the Beatles, they do have the same irreverent sense of humour, and it was strange how certain situations and experiences seemed to be revived, ten years on.

When it came to harmony singing, they were incredibly facile.

The film was not limited to songs from the *Pepper* album, and when we came to 'Because', from the *Abbey Road* album, I decided that the backdrop should be the authentic *Abbey Road* sound; that is, the choral structure of the voices, the electric harpsichord which I played on the original album, and the generally very thin backing. So I again laid down the electric harpsichord track myself, and then gave the Bee Gees the notes of all the very complicated harmonies. There were three tracks, each bearing three voices, and the way the lines moved was quite complex, but they got them almost as easily as the Beatles had done. That was surprising. A group of professional singers would have had more difficulty with it, but the Bee Gees had an innate sense of where it should go.

With some of the other songs and singers, though, there was more of a problem. Many of the songs had been written for either John Lennon or Paul McCartney to sing, and they have very distinctive voices. Without those there is inevitably something lacking, particularly if the new voices are very different from theirs. 'Strawberry Fields', for example, originally written and sung by John, was sung in the film by Sandy Farina. The key in which she sang it was a good fourth away from John's original key, and I found it intriguing to hear how that altered the whole character of the song. It had a completely different texture.

Even then it had to be altered, as did a number of the tracks, because what Michael had done visually sometimes didn't fit the music. So then the music had to be made to fit the picture. I had originally intended doing 'Strawberry Fields' in a very raunchy and hypnotic sort of way. But in the film she sings it at a very tender moment between herself and Peter Frampton, and I had to soften it, adding strings and so on to make it more suitable as a love song. There was quite a lot of other deviations from the original Beatle concepts of the songs, but it was done with a definite idea in mind. My basic premise was that where the group in the film, played by the Bee Gees, were starting out in their raw state, the song should be reproduced as near as possible to the original. But as they got more successful and sophisticated in the film, the music changed too, becoming more 'hip' and sophisticated.

Where artists outside the group were performing, I didn't regard myself as being confined to the original at all. For example, Mr Mustard, the malevolent electronic genius played by Frankie Howerd, has two female robot assistants. They sing the song 'Mean Mr Mustard' from *Abbey Road*, which was originally a kind of quick, throwaway number. I slowed it down, and made it a bit more groovy. But there was also the problem that the singing voices of these two androids should sound like—well, singing androids. I did this with an instrument called a Vocoder, which takes the syllables and consonants of a human voice, but leaves out the tone. You can then superimpose its output over the tone of a synthesiser, which you can play, producing a distinctly eerie and robot-like voice.

Making the film was a lot of fun, and a challenge. There was one sequence where the band marches through the streets, symbolising the different periods from the First World War onwards by the style in which it is playing. So I had to arrange the tune 'Sgt. Pepper' in ragtime, Charleston, Gershwin, swing, big-band and present-day style—all to be performed in the course of three minutes!

The film has not been a huge success, although the soundtrack album was a multi-platinum seller. I enjoyed the enormous amount of work involved in the film, but the irony for me is the adverse comparisons which have been made with *Yellow Submarine*. In that cartoon film, apart from the many Beatle tracks, I had to write an original film score of about an hour's length. That was very rewarding, both artistically and financially. In the *Pepper* picture, no original music was allowed to be included, but I had to prepare two hours of music with many different artists, involving far more work than *Yellow Submarine*.

Yellow Submarine has been lauded as a work of art; *Sgt. Pepper* has been received less kindly. I think perhaps its very title was a disadvantage. It certainly was not a film of the record. But then, I do not think anyone now could ever make a film of *Sgt. Pepper's Lonely Hearts Club Band*. It was, and is, unique.

12

WRITE IN THE PICTURE

THE DREAM of my childhood had been to write music for films. When, in 1962, my first chance finally came, it was more like a minor nightmare.

It was a small-budget British B movie starring the Temperance Seven. Because I had been making records with them, I was asked to write the music for the film, for the princely fee of £112. Not that I really cared about the money. This was my Big Chance.

The songs I wrote for them, and the incidental music, in a typical twenties style, worked out fine and suited the mood of the film very well. But when we came to fitting the music to the picture my troubles started. It was done at Shepperton, and provided my first experience of a film studio; I had no conception of how hard it would be. I was not helped by the fact that the Temperance Seven were seen to be playing in the picture, and that I therefore had to fit the music to what they were doing on film. That was a basic error on the part of the producers. They should have recorded the music first, and then the band should have mimed to it on film, which would have been far easier. As it was, I was landed with having to do the thing back to front, with no idea as to how. It was the most exhausting, nerve-racking experience of my life, and I got through it by sheer hit-and-miss, trial-and-error methods.

My problems were not alleviated by the fact that the Temperance

Seven fell short of being well-trained musicians. They didn't follow my conducting very well anyway, and it hardly helped when they started watching the picture instead of me! Again, the facilities at Shepperton were antiquated in the extreme. There was no 'rock-and-roll' machine for running the film forwards and backwards, as there is today. Instead, if we muffed something, which we did continually, the whole reel had to be rewound; this necessitated a delay of about ten minutes before we could try again, which was less than soothing to my already well-frayed nerves.

The film was called *Take Me Over*, but that was the reverse of what I felt about it. At the end of the recording, I remember going home and saying: 'I never want to do another film again. If that's film music, you can have it!' What's more, I didn't think anyone would require my services after that little débâcle; so I was astonished when, soon after that, I was approached by Muir Matheson, a huge name in the industry, who probably had more experience than anyone else in conducting orchestras for British pictures. A fine man, and a Scot, he had been asked to provide the music for a comedy film called *Crooks Anonymous*, starring Wilfred Hyde White, Leslie Phillips and James Robertson Justice. As it happened, I was recording Leslie Phillips at that time.

Muir, though a fine conductor and arranger, was not a particularly strong composer, and felt that he couldn't write a whole score. So he came to me and said: 'Why don't you write a song for Leslie Phillips? We'll get him singing it over the opening titles, and then you can work with me on the film score. You do all the commercial bits, and I'll do all the snippety bits of fitting.' That's what we did. It was a happy little partnership, and I learned a great deal from him about the techniques of film writing.

The only small problem was that, as he himself was the first to admit, Leslie Phillips didn't sing too well, and at the last minute the director and producer decided they didn't like him singing the title song. For some reason, however, they failed to invite us back to do a new opening. The result was that, when I first saw

the picture at the Odeon Acton, I was utterly amazed. The opening titles were accompanied by the score I had done for the brash
opening music for the song. That was fine. But when the voice
was due to appear—nothing. Not a word. All I could hear was the
accompaniment to a missing voice. It must have been a very full
accompaniment, because no one else seemed to notice. The film was
a moderate success.

My next offer came, to my surprise, from the producers of my
first film. It was to write the music and supervise the scoring for
a film called *Calculated Risk*. It was aptly named, both from their
point of view and from mine, but I accepted, and that gave me more
valuable experience. Perhaps it wasn't such a gamble, because I had
learned a lot from working with Muir. I had learned how to fit music to film. I had found out about the frames on a film, and the
speed at which the film ran through the 'gate' in the camera. I had
learned how to make my own measurements of music related to
film, and how to cope with other people's measurements.

All this, of course, took place while I was still working at EMI,
and was done in my own spare time; but it was time well spent, a
valuable grounding which stood me in good stead when my first
real breakthrough came in 1964. The film was *A Hard Day's Night*,
the first Beatles film and probably their most successful.

Dick Lester was the director, and I made special recordings
with the Beatles of songs which were going into the film, producing them specifically with the film in mind. Then I had to knit it all
together, and write the incidental music. That worked pretty well.
What is more, whereas I had been disappointed that the film was
to be in black and white, feeling that the first Beatles film ought to
be in glamorous colour, in the event that worked very well too. Dick
Lester's zany editing, and especially his experience in commercials,
which enabled him to snap everything into tight, hard-packed little sequences, was excellent.

The only trouble was that he was something of a musician himself. He is the sort of person who, at a night-club or a party, will go

to the piano in the corner and play his idea of jazz to amuse people. He plays jazz piano tolerably well, and he gave me the impression that he considered me inferior to him musically. The adage that a little learning is a dangerous thing was borne out, and it led to a nasty split between us. There was one of my scores which he particularly disliked. That I wouldn't have minded, but he waited until the actual recording to tell me so. I was on the rostrum in front of the thirty-piece orchestra when he came roaring up and tore me off a gigantic strip. 'This is absolute rubbish you've written,' he ranted. 'What the hell do you think you're doing? You're a bloody fool. What do you call this—this—crap?'

I was very embarrassed, and very angry. 'This is what you asked me to write in the first place,' I told him. But it did no good, and there ensued one of those stupid arguments which can benefit no one. So I did some quick revision there and then, and recorded something along his new line of thinking. After that, we were hardly on speaking terms.

The irony was that when the film came out the Americans gave it two Academy Award nominations. One was for the script, by Alun Owen. The other was for the musical direction, by me. Dick got not a mention. Perhaps it was poetic justice. It was also the only Oscar nomination I have had, but I didn't even go to the ceremony. I knew I had no chance, because the opposition included *Mary Poppins* and *My Fair Lady*. In the event, it was the latter for which André Previn got the musical-direction Oscar.

There were no aggravations with the next people I worked with, the Boulting brothers. The film was called *The Family Way,* and they had got Paul McCartney to write the basic themes. I was to score them and write the incidental music. The film was set in the North, with steep cobbled streets and so on, and Paul had the good idea of using a sort of northern brass sound. But I needed more material than he had given me. So I went to see him and said: 'I need a wistful little tune. You're supposed to be writing the music for this thing, and I'm supposed to be orchestrating it. But to do that I need a tune, and you've got to give me one.'

His reply was, 'All right, what do you want?'

I told him again, but he was still prevaricating; so I said: 'If you don't give me one, I'm going to write one of my own.' That did the trick. He gave me a sweet little fragment of a waltz tune, which was just what was needed, and with that I was able to complete the score.

As with my first film, the recording was to be done at Shepperton; but I was so unhappy with the inefficiency of the place, compared with proper recording studios, that I went to see John Boulting and told him: 'I don't want to work at Shepperton. I'd rather do it at CTS.' CTS, down in Bayswater, was at that time the best film-recording studio in London.

'Why? What's the point?' he asked. 'We've got a very good recording studio out at Shepperton.'

'I've worked there,' I said, 'and I think it's absolutely ghastly!'

The trouble was that the Boulting brothers were part of British Lion, and part-owners of Shepperton, and to record there would cost them very little. So he was naturally reluctant to go outside. I could understand that, but I pressed the point.

I told him, 'I'm going to use a brass quintet and a string quartet in most of the scoring, and that's not many musicians. I'll be saving you money doing it that way, even though we'll be using very good players. But recording a string quartet or a brass quintet is very clinical, and very difficult. The balance is extremely important. There's no room for error, because everything's magnified. With a large symphony orchestra, someone can make a squawky noise somewhere in the back desk of the violins and no one's ever going to notice it. But with a string quartet you can hear everything—and I want the recording to be perfect.'

That, at least, persuaded him to a compromise. 'I'll tell you what we'll do,' he said. 'Do a session down at Shepperton with me.

I promise you that'll be a trial. If it comes off well, as I'm sure it will, we'll do the rest of the score there. But if you can convince me that the studio's lacking what you need, I promise you'll have every right to go elsewhere.'

So we did our session at Shepperton, with the string quartet led by Neville Marriner, of the Academy of St Martin-in-the-Fields. Neville, a marvellous musician, was a tremendous help to me, but when I walked into the studio and saw the set-up I could hardly believe my eyes. They had grouped the string quartet like a chamber orchestra at a Wigmore Hall recital. The microphones were suspended about fifteen feet up in the air. 'Well, honestly, that's not going to do,' I said. 'I want to hear the resin on the bow of the cello when he's biting away. I don't want to hear all the ambience of this room.' Looking over at the brass players, I went on, 'What's more, you're going to pick up an awful lot of brass on the string mikes. It's just not going to work.'

My remarks were not met with any electrifying burst of co-operation. The studio personnel clearly felt that, having been in the business for about sixty-five years, they didn't need some young man coming along to tell them how to do it. Their attitude was, frankly, bloody-minded. When I said that the mikes had to be nearer the instruments, especially the cello, I was in the studio when the talk-back came over from the control room: 'Ernie . . . er . . . would you mind moving the boom down about four feet for Mr Martin, please?' The engineer wouldn't dream of coming out to do it himself. He had to get the appropriate union man, who was Ernie. And even after Ernie had lowered it a bit, it still didn't make much difference. It was, you might say, an unhappy session.

John Boulting was convinced. 'I know you haven't sabotaged it,' he said. 'Go and do a session at CTS, and see if that comes out any better.' So we did, and it did. It worked brilliantly, and we ended up recording the whole thing there. It was an eye-opener for John. At lunch in Bayswater, after one of the CTS sessions, he asked: 'What's the difference, George? I can see things have been going better for you here. Why can't our studios at Shepperton be like that?'

'Honestly, John,' I said, 'I think the subject's a bit long! You've got the wrong equipment. It's out of date. We don't use the microphones you're using any more. What's more, we don't use the people you're using any more. It's all about the basic attitude to the job.' I knew I was on pretty safe ground saying that anyway—Roy and John's film *I'm All Right, Jack* had been a fair indication of their attitude to union pettiness. Happily, film studios have improved a great deal since those days.

On the Beatle front, the next film was *Help!*, and that was done without my help! I produced all the Beatles recordings for it, of course, and they certainly thought I was going to do the film music; but since the director was Dick Lester again, it was hardly surprising that, to quote Sam Goldwyn, I was included out. The music was done by Ken Thorne, a buddy of Lester's.

Then, in 1966, came *Yellow Submarine*. That film was a whole package of problems, not least the fact that the Beatles were against the idea from the beginning. At that time they were suspicious of anything that wasn't their own idea, and this was a deal which had been worked out between EMI, Brian Epstein, and the producers. It was to be a cartoon film, and the producers were King Features, the American syndication outfit whose main claim to fame was the strip *The Flintstones*. The Beatles clearly thought it was going to be yet another rip-off, and wanted nothing to do with it.

But Epstein had contracted not only for the film to use about a dozen of the Beatles' old songs, but also for them to write four brand-new titles. Their reaction was 'O.K., we've got to supply them with these bloody songs, but we're not going to fall over backwards providing them. We'll let them have them whenever we feel like it, and we'll give them whatever we think is all right.'

The result was that, as we recorded songs for future albums, they would try out some little bit of nonsense at the end of the session, and, as long as it worked moderately well, they would say: 'Right, that's good enough for the film. Let them have that.' So the film scraped the bottom of the Beatle music barrel as far as new material was concerned, the songs they produced being 'Only a Northern Song', 'All Together Now', 'Hey Bulldog', and 'It's All Too Much'.

The other great problem was the speed at which the film was being made—a year from start to finish, compared with the minimum of two years that Disney always took to make a full-length animated feature. Normally, in the case of such a film, they like to score all the music first and then animate to that, as in the case of *Fantasia*. But with *Yellow Submarine* that was just not possible. The director was George Dunning, a brilliant Canadian animator, and since he wanted, in view of the time allowed, to get writing and visualising straight away, we had to work out a system by which I would work side-by-side with him and his team. He told me: 'We can't take time for you to write the music before we start, and we can't take time for you to write it when we've finished, so the answer is that you'll have to write it while we're making the picture.'

'How on earth am I going to do that?' I asked him.

'Well, I'll send you a reel at a time, whenever a reel's near completion, and you'll just have to write and record as quickly as you can. I haven't got time to consult with you where the music should go. You just write it where you think it should go, and we'll fit it in afterwards.'

It was nice enough to be given *carte blanche* like that, but it was an incredibly chaotic way to work. I might get reel 4 followed by reel 7—and even then there might be a couple of scenes missing, with a little notice on the reel to tell me how long the scene would be. I spent a frantic month writing the music, fifty-five minutes of it, in this haphazard way, and there was no room for mistakes. Everything had to be tailor-made to the picture. If a door opened or a funny face appeared at a window, and those moments needed to be pointed up, it was the musical score that had to do the job. Luckily, one of my very earliest experiences in the world of film music had given me the tool with which to accomplish that.

I had gone down to Elstree to see Nelson Riddle doing a film-recording session for a Peter Sellers picture, *Lolita*. What struck me in particular was a section where Peter was driving off with this young girl. Nelson Riddle had scored it with one of his typical rhythm sections, a cushion of strings rather than any particular tune. You saw Peter looking in the rear-view mirror, and then suddenly his eyes opened wide in the mirror because he realised that he was being followed. It happened twice, and on each occasion there was a jarring note from the orchestra to emphasise what was happening. That note had nothing to do with the basic rhythm. It didn't even happen on the downbeat, but in the middle of a bar, yet it fitted exactly on the first run-through. I wondered how on earth Nelson Riddle had achieved that.

The answer was really very simple. You plan whatever tempo your rhythm is going to be, and then you lay down what is called a 'click track'. That is, a separate track which simply contains a click sound which appears every so many frames of film. You know that 35-mm film runs at twenty-four frames a second, so, knowing what tempo you want, you simply ask the film editor to put on a click at whatever interval you want. Then, while conducting the orchestra, you wear headphones through which you can hear the clicks, and by keeping to that particular beat you 'lock in' the orchestra to the film. In that way you can write your score knowing that, even if something happens a third of the way or halfway through a bar, you can safely put in whatever musical effect you want, with the absolute certainty that it will match the picture. That was how Riddle did it, and that's how I did it with *Yellow Submarine*. I wrote very precisely even with avant-garde and weird sounds like 'Sea of Holes', keeping to bar-lines, knowing that the click track would ensure it fitted.

Yellow Submarine saw some pretty strange experiments, too. In one sequence, in the Sea of Monsters, the yellow submarine is wandering around and all kinds of weird little things are crawling along the sea floor, some with three legs, some rolling along like bicycle bells. One monster is enormous, without arms but with two long legs with Wellington boots on. It has a huge trunk with a head sticking out of the top of it, and in place of a nose there is a kind of long trumpet. This is a sucking-up monster; when it sees the other little monsters, it uses its trumpet to suck them up. Eventually it sucks up the yellow submarine, and finally gets hold of the corner of the screen and sucks that up too, until it all goes white. I felt, naturally, that that scene required special 'sucking-up' music! The question was, how to do it with an orchestra?

Suddenly, I hit upon the obvious—backwards music. Music played backwards sounds very odd anyway, and a trombone or cymbal played backwards sounds just like a sucking-in noise. So I scored about forty-five seconds for the orchestra to play, in such a way that the music would fit the picture when we played it backwards. The engineer working at CTS at that time was a great character named Jack Clegg, and when I explained the idea to him he said, 'Lovely! Great idea! I'll get the film turned round, and you record the music to the backward film. Then, when we turn the film round the right way, your music will be backwards.' It sounded like something from a Goon script.

We did that, and at the end of the take, instead of the usual yell for me to come into the control room, I heard Jack speaking on to the tape in some weird, Japanese-type language. I could hear this in my headphones, and had no idea what was going on. Then, when the time came to play the film back to hear what it sounded like, I understood. At the start of the take you could hear Jack's voice saying something like 'Myellah summarin, teek tree'. While we had been recording, he had carefully worked out what his announcement should be if he spoke it backwards, so that when it was played forwards it would sound English. Well, roughly English! It was a very difficult thing to do, and we all fell about—laughing, amazed, but also full of congratulation—when we heard it.

Once all the music had been recorded, we dubbed it on to the film, and even then there was more messing about. In some places we cut out the music because sound-effects worked better; in others, we eliminated the sound-effects because what I had written sounded better. Yet, in spite of everything, that score proved enormously successful and earned me a load of fan mail. Jimmy Webb even asked me if he could use the opening 'Pepperland' sequence for a Ringo Starr TV special in America.

When it came to making the soundtrack album which the producers wanted, there were more problems. The Beatles were still holding themselves remote from the whole enterprise, and simply left us to our own devices. So I told the film people: 'Obviously the thing to do is to let the Beatles issue whatever they want of their own songs. I'll issue my stuff separately, because I don't want to ride on their backs.'

The Beatles decided to issue an EP of their four new songs from the film. For their part, the film people wanted me to put out an LP of the background score, with voices from the film and with narration. This was to tell the story of *Yellow Submarine*, and was to be assembled by the man who had written the original story—Erich Segal, later to make his name and find fame with *Love Story*. I had worked very closely with him on the script of the film, and the record was to be a combination of words and music, rather like *Peter and the Wolf*. We were about to start work on that, when suddenly the Beatles changed their collective mind. 'No, we don't want to do that,' they said. 'We want to have a long-playing record.' What they had realised, of course, was that EPs didn't sell in America, while LPs did. What's more, they probably realised by then that, in spite of their lack of interest or co-operation, the film was likely to be the success it eventually proved to be.

So it was decided that the album should have their music on one side and mine on the other. To their four new songs they added 'Yellow Submarine', which had originally been a single, and 'All You Need Is Love'. On my side there were 'Pepperland', 'Sea of Time',

'Sea of Holes', 'Sea of Monsters', 'March of the Meanies', 'Pepper-land Laid Waste', and 'Yellow Submarine in Pepperland', all of which I re-recorded. It was more convenient to do so—and no more costly, since the original orchestra would have had to be paid twice anyway if we had used the soundtrack for the record.

The success of *Yellow Submarine* soon paid dividends for me. Out of the blue, a film director named Mike Hodges rang up Shirley Burns, my long-time, long-suffering assistant, and asked, 'Can I come and see George Martin?' He appeared in my office, told me that he was making a film in Malta with Michael Caine, and asked me if I would like to do the music. To be truthful, I was astonished.

'There are many writers who do nothing but film music,' I said. 'When I get asked to write film music, it's generally to orchestrate a song that Paul McCartney's written, or in some connection like that. Why have you chosen me?'

'I think your *Yellow Submarine* was the best thing I've heard in ages, and that's why I want you to do the music for my picture.'

'Well, thanks. It's lovely of you to say that. I hope I can justify your faith,' I said.

Hodges was great to work with, and I was pretty happy with the score, but sadly the film was a minor failure—a result, I believe, of bad distribution as much as anything else. It was called *Pulp*, and was about a paperback writer who got involved in a scenario that he could have written himself. It had a good cast, with Michael Caine, Mickey Rooney, Elizabeth Webb and Lionel Stander; it was well constructed and well directed. What's more, when I saw it I enjoyed it! But that doesn't alter the fact that it 'bombed'.

From that bomb, I went to Bond. Paul McCartney had been asked to write a song for the film *Live and Let Die*, and I or-chestrated and recorded it for him. After the producers, Albert 'Cubby' Broccoli and Harry Saltzmann, had heard it, I got a call from Harry's assistant, Ron Cass, saying that they would like to meet me. Ron and Cubby took me to lunch at the Tiberio in Curzon Street, and made it clear that I was being considered for doing the score for the film, since they had been impressed by the orchestration on the record. Would I, they asked, be willing to fly at their expense to Jamaica, to meet Harry Saltzmann who was on location there?

'I don't mind. I might put myself out,' I said.

They were doing all the location work at Ocho Rios, and my first meeting with Harry was straight to the point. He sat me down and said, 'Great. Like what you did. Very nice record. Like the score. Now tell me, who do you think we should get to sing it?'

That took me completely aback. After all, he was holding the Paul McCartney recording we had made. And Paul McCartney was—Paul McCartney. But he was clearly treating it as a demo disc.

'I don't follow. You've got Paul McCartney . . . ,' I said.

'Yeah, yeah, that's good. But who are we going to get to sing it for the film?'

'I'm sorry. I still don't follow,' I said, feeling that maybe there was something I hadn't been told.

'You know—we've got to have a girl, haven't we? What do you think of Thelma Houston?'

'Well, she's very good,' I said. 'But I don't see that it's necessary when you've got Paul McCartney.'

Perhaps I was being a bit obtuse. The fact was that he had always thought of a girl as singing the lead song in his films, like Shirley Bassey in *Goldfinger*, and Lulu; and whoever it was, he wanted a recognisable voice rather than Paul's.

As gently as possible, I pointed out that, first of all, Paul was the ideal choice, even if he wasn't a black lady, and that, secondly, if Paul's recording wasn't used as the title song, it was very doubtful whether Paul would let him use the song for his film anyway. This required some degree of diplomacy, because, if I had said what I thought with any hostility, Harry would probably have taken umbrage, to say the least. He would have chucked it out and blown the whole thing with Paul. As it was, he agreed.

I hadn't done myself any harm, either, because when I got back to London I was given the job of writing the music for the picture. The director was Guy Hamilton, a very easy man to work with. Like Roy Boulting, who had directed *The Family Way*, he was not a musician, which is always a help. But he was always very concise in his specifications and his brief. He would tell me exactly where he wanted the music, and the kind of effect he wanted from it.

He would say something like: 'Now in this sequence, you see, Bond's climbing the hill. He doesn't know what's over the hill. He's getting to the top of it. We're seeing him, and we see that he's being watched on a TV monitor screen by the baddie. Something's going to happen. When he gets to the top of the hill and looks down, we know what's there. Now, I want you to build up the suspense as he's going up the hill and being watched by the baddie. He gets to the top, and you see his face looking all around, and you've got to think that you're about to see some disaster area. Then, and only then, do you finally see it for yourself, and realise that there's nothing there except fields. That's what I want you to convey in the music.'

When the score was finished, he came to the recording session, and listened as I played it with the orchestra. Having listened, he asked me for only a few very minor changes. I was naturally pleased about that, and felt that it said as much for his accurate briefing as for my scoring. There were about fifty-five minutes of music in the film; I used Paul's song twice, once his own version in the opening, and a second time sung by Brenda Arnau.

Then came *Sgt. Pepper*, of which enough already.

In many ways, film music has become a part of our culture. The audience know, for instance, when a murder is about to happen, or the cavalry are on their way, or the lovers are about to kiss, because the music tells them so, and the convention is understood. Without that musical build-up, most films would seem clinically sterile. But the audience need not necessarily be aware of the music.

There was a very exciting car chase in *Live and Let Die*, in which another driver tries to kill Bond with a poisoned dart, but only succeeds in killing Bond's driver. The car goes out of control, with the accelerator jammed under the dead driver, and Bond is fighting to control it as it weaves in and out of the traffic. Finally he does manage to bring the car to a halt, gets out, brushes himself down, and mentions something about a close shave. The whole thing has been incredibly exciting and as he speaks the whole audience inevitably goes 'Phew!' Now I'm certain that if you had asked any member of the audience what the music was like in that sequence, he would have proved unaware that there was any music at all. But there was—and without it, and the sound-effects, most of the excitement would have been stripped from that scene.

The trouble with film music today is that so much is written, particularly with the enormous output of television, that clichés will inevitably arise and be constantly used, because there are only so many ways of doing a particular thing. When you've seen one car chase, you've seen them all, and visual clichés tend to have aural clichés as their companions.

That's not so surprising when you realise that in Los Angeles they actually have musical factories. I discovered that many years ago, when I went there with Brian Epstein. I went to look up a young songwriter named Randy Newman, who has since achieved fame but was then unknown. His publisher had sent me some of his songs; I thought they were very good indeed, and had recorded one with Cilla Black. I knew that he was related to Alfred Newman, a great film writer, and that Lionel Newman, head of music at Twentieth Century-Fox, was his uncle. So I went first to see Lionel, whom I knew, and he told me: 'Randy's working in the arranging and copying department. You'll find him over there.' 'Over there' was a building that was just part of the whole township of a typical Hollywood studio. The music section was a vast area like a typing-pool, with men sitting at anonymous desks writing music. At one of these was a little dark-haired chap who had glasses and a slight squint. This was Randy Newman.

We introduced ourselves, and I told him how much I liked

his work. But at the same time I was wondering to myself what on earth he was doing in this place, when he had such talent. Then, glancing along the rows of desks, I spotted an English writer I knew, who had done a lot of music for Tony Newley and Leslie Bricusse. I was astonished. Of course they were earning a good living at it, but it was so tedious: exactly like a typing-pool, a musical factory production line. They would be asked to write seventeen seconds of car chase music, or forty-five and three-fifths seconds of music for moonlight romance. Sometimes they would not know what film they were writing for. But again, so many TV films were being churned out that they contained stock situations, and therefore stock lengths of music had to be written.

The click tracks I mentioned earlier were so much a part of the scene that they had a whole library of them, giving every tempo from a beat every five seconds to one every micro-second. It really was a machine process. As soon as the music was written, it was taken into the studio, where musicians were waiting to record it. Nor did they even have to record it to the picture. If the right click track had been selected, the music would fit.

The whole attitude, the whole process, explains why television music is so unexceptional—always the same kind of music, the same kind of scoring. Occasionally good tunes emerge, but with so much material being used, boredom is the rule. To be fair, I am sure that all those people, writing all those bits of music, are trying to do something different. But if you are doing it all the time, it must become harder and harder.

That is one reason why I am glad that my dream did not come true, that film music has not become my career. If I did it all the time, I don't think I would be much good at it. One picture a year is fine, but keeping to that is very difficult, because it is a kind of golden treadmill. To be accepted by the film people entails having film credits. You have to go from one success to another, and that means doing nothing but film music. John Williams is a good example. He wrote the music for *Jaws*, followed that with *Star Wars*, and followed that with *Close Encounters of the Third Kind*. He gets offered more film work than he can possibly handle, so he does nothing else.

I consider myself lucky because, as well as writing for films, I am still able to produce records, build recording studios, write other kinds of music and even write this book (with a little help from my friend). I may even be able to take time to attempt a lifelong ambition, that of writing music for the ballet. I don't just have to write music for films; if I did, I think I would soon become bored with it, and my music, in consequence, would become very boring too.

But I would hate this to be taken as meaning that I believe all film music to be workaday. On the contrary, much of it is highly creative and inspirational. That's not to say that when I write music for films I want to write tunes that will appeal to everyone in the world. I try to write good ones, and when they don't sell a million I am not bothered.

For a start, songs sell much more easily than orchestral tunes, because the human voice projects music much more readily and finds a quicker route to people's gut feelings. There have, of course, been instrumental hits, like 'Love Is Blue', and 'A Walk in the Black Forest', but they are few, probably less than one in a hundred of the totality of hits. To write hit tunes, therefore, you have to be a songwriter, which I am not. But the fact is that writing film scores is basically writing instrumental music, and men like John Williams and Lalo Schifrin are tremendously good at that without writing any hit tunes. Nor does that lack of hit tunes prevent albums like the music from *Star Wars* from selling in enormous quantities.

Films use all sorts of musical sounds, but the staple diet is a symphony orchestra. Today, of course, rhythm sections, electric guitars, synthesisers and so on are also used. But ever since the transition from the piano in the pit of the silent movies to the early version of *Ben Hur*, through Victor Young and Dimitri Tiomkin, and up to today, the backbone of film music has come from a miniature symphony orchestra. So, base logic to the fore: if you want to write for films you have to know how to orchestrate for a symphony orchestra.

Orchestration is an enormous subject, on whose various aspects many, many books have been written. There are certain rules which, if followed, happen to work out very well. In spite of that, and in spite of all those books, many people don't follow those rules. They seldom, if ever, get away with it.

One of the easy traps, when writing for strings, is to think of the string section as being like a piano. People who do that write the cello parts as if they were the left hand, and the violas and violins as if they were the right hand. Then they bunch them all together with a gap in between, which is what happens when you play the piano. I have found that the secret of good string writing—and I claim no original thought in the matter—is to write for four parts. That may sound rather obvious, but if you can keep it down to four parts and not indulge yourself in too many harmonies, you get a much better string sound. It also helps if you balance those string parts within themselves, so that they are not too far apart. Think of the cellos, the violas, the second violins and the first violins as being like four human voices, equivalent to the bass, the tenor, the alto and the soprano, and you can't really go wrong.

The best way to learn to write for a string orchestra is to write first of all for a string quartet. Then you *have* to be economical. In a full orchestra, there are desks of violins, at each of which two people sit. The second person turns over the music for the first, because they only have one piece of music in front of them. Mostly they play the same notes. But sometimes what the composer does is to 'divisi' the notes. That means splitting the violins into two parts. The leader of the orchestra, and all the others sitting on the right-hand side of the desks, play the top line, and those on the left play the bottom line, so that the section as a whole plays two lines instead of one.

You can't do that with a string quartet, because there is only one person per musical line, so that writing for a string quartet teaches you real economy. It also teaches you the value of each particular instrument. The importance of that is that another easy trap into which people fall, when writing for strings, is to write too many parts. They think that they must cover every note in the harmonies. When you play the piano, you play up to ten notes at a time, simply because you have ten fingers and piano composers make use of that fact. But inexperienced people tend to write that for a string orchestra, and a combination of ten different notes among strings sounds horribly thick. Think of just four notes, two in each hand. Then you will write cleanly for strings, and each line you write will mean something because it will have to weave its own particular direction. Each is a single line weaving among three others. That is the way to write for strings.

Writing for brass is rather different, because trumpets like to be fairly close together. If you spread them out too much, they become a bit thin. In addition, the range among brass instruments is not as wide as that among stringed instruments. The range from the bottom note of a cello to the top note of a violin is much wider than that from the bottom note of an ordinary trombone to the top note of a trumpet. So brass writing has to be a little more compact—though much depends on how many instruments you are using, since each plays only one note at a time. Woodwind has problems and limitations similar to brass, but the important thing there is to know the texture of the instruments, of the sound they make.

When writing for an orchestra, it really does help to know what an instrument can do. That may sound obvious; after all, a textbook on orchestration will tell you that the range of an oboe starts at the B flat below middle C and rises two and a half octaves to round about G, and will supply you with similar information about every instrument in the orchestra, so that you can know, in theory, exactly what each can do. But what the textbook does not tell you is which notes sound better than others, and on which instruments. That information will only come from experience, and from knowing the instrument.

The ideal way of achieving that, of course, is by playing it. But it is just not possible for everyone to go and learn every instrument in the orchestra. Music students, however, would do well to get as much of that practical experience as possible. When I studied orchestration at the Guildhall, I took oboe as my second subject, so I learned that very thoroughly, even if my peak performances were only to be in public parks! But I also took violin for a term. That was pretty painful for anyone within earshot, but I did learn what I could do with it, what the bow could do, what the range of the fingers was.

I learned, for example, that it is quite difficult to play open fifths double-stopped on a violin, because the fingers get in each other's way. That lapse into musical jargon does not mean this is about to become a technical treatise. It merely serves to indicate the importance of knowing the capabilities of each instrument. To put it more simply, most people are familiar with a piano. Even if they know nothing about composition, they realise that it would be absurd to write a piece of music in which the thumb of the right hand had to play middle C while the little finger of the right hand played the C two octaves above—not unless they were writing for giants!

And for most people, of course, playing the piano is the closest acquaintance they ever make with a musical instrument. They simply never get the chance to learn any other. For them, the majority, the key thing should be to listen to the instruments, and try to work out which is which. If you are really interested in orchestration, do a mental analysis of what you are hearing when you listen to a record. Most people, when listening to an orchestra, let it flow over them like a homogeneous mass, a beautiful sound. They don't really care about what makes its constituent sounds.

But the serious musician who wants to orchestrate will listen to it very clinically. He will ask himself: Is that a flute I can hear there, doubling thirds on the violins? Is it the bassoon I can hear reinforcing the cellos? He may not know for sure, but he will get a good idea. If he can see the actual score, which he can when classical music is being played, he will find out for himself what is doing what, and he will learn from that. Then, he can set out expectantly towards the golden treadmill of a career in film music.

But if he wants variety, he should hope to become a record producer.

13

THE RECORDING ANGEL

THE typical 'Day in the Life' of a record producer does not exist. He may be doing different things on every day of the week. And that activity is multiplied ten-thousandfold, for the simple reason that the world is *full* of record producers, or aspiring record producers. It has struck me forcibly that, especially in the United States, the majority of young people with ambitions in the field of recording want not to be top pop stars as one might have imagined, but top record producers.

When, in 1977, I won the Britannia Award for being the top British record producer of the last twenty-five years, I was asked after the presentation: 'What's your secret? What's the key to success in producing records?' There was no answer I could give. There is no single answer, and there is no simple answer. All I can offer, as I do now, is a series of sometimes disconnected observations, based on what those years have taught me, in the hope that they may be helpful to all those young aspirants.

But I must add a caveat: what has worked for me may be quite different from what has worked for other, equally successful producers. There is no magic formula.

When I joined the business in 1950 there was no such thing as a record producer. People like Oscar Preuss and myself were A and R men—Artists and Repertoire men, artists' managers.

The making of a record would start with myself and, say, Sidney Torch having lunch together and talking for a couple of hours about what should be on his next record. Leroy Anderson was very popular in those days, and we recorded numbers like 'Musical Typewriter', 'Sleigh Ride', and 'Serenata'. The suggestions might come from him, or I might give him something from all the material that the publishers used to bring us. One I gave him was 'Ecstasy', a Spanish-sounding piece which proved quite a hit.

Then we would discuss who would be orchestrating the pieces, when the recording would take place and what size of orchestra he wanted. It would be my job to organise all those things, find the orchestrator, book the studio and arrange for the musicians to be booked. But when the appointed day came, it was really the engineer who was in charge. The pop end of EMI studios was run by Charlie Anderson and Laurie Bamber, and Charlie in particular was one of the very top engineers. They were of a generation who really flew by the seat of their pants. They knew nothing of electronics, but they had great experience in the placing of the microphones and the acoustics of the studio.

Charlie's technique for handling strings in Number One studio was unequalled, but he was terribly jealous of his secret, and wanted no one to know how he did it. If a journalist wanted a photo of an artist, Charlie would go into the studio and re-arrange all the mikes in impossible positions, lest the world should discover his brilliant layout. Nor was it only the outside world he feared. If anyone, like myself, was in the control room with him, he would hunch over the control panel, covering the knobs with his hands, so that you never knew exactly what he was doing. It was rather like a schoolboy trying to stop his work being cribbed during an exam.

My function at the recording was very limited. Settling the way the piece was performed was the prerogative of the performer, Sidney Torch or whoever it was. The recording was Charlie's baby, and the ultimate aim of an engineer in those days was simply to recreate the sound as faithfully as possible. All that I could say would be something like: 'I think we might do with a bit more strings on that passage, Charlie,' or 'Can you keep the timps down? I think they're a bit heavy.' Or I might go out to Sidney, or whoever it was, in the studio and say, 'That seemed a bit slow to me. Can you speed it up?'

If it was a question of balance, I might ask Charlie if he could get anything better, and he might say: 'No, that's all I've got. I can't give you any more. They've got to play up from there.' In that case I would have to go and explain the problem to Sidney, and ask him if he would keep the timpani down and get the trumpets to play a bit louder, or whatever. Then he would listen to the playback and judge for himself. It was in those days that I learned that one of the most important aspects of record production is the ability to handle people. Tact is *the* prerequisite. That and patience come far above musicianship in the list of elements essential to being a good producer.

Tact had to apply to my dealings with the engineers, too. Officially, of course, Charlie Anderson was supposed to do what I wanted. I *could* say, 'I'm sorry, Charlie, but I don't like what you're doing with the strings.' He would have to do something about it, and would probably mutter under his breath as he left the control room to move the mike about six inches, knowing full well that it would make not the slightest difference. In naval terms, I was the Midshipman, a young whipper-snapper of twenty-four, while Charlie was the Master-at-Arms, a man of fifty with vast experience. The midshipman does not argue too often, if he has any sense, with the Master-at-Arms.

But all that was about to change. Starting in the business at the same time as myself was a new generation of young engineers, who had studied electronics and who were ready to adapt to the new techniques of tape-recording. The revolution was under way around the time I came back from my first trip to America. The youngsters had begun to be given their heads. Cliff Richard was being recorded by Peter Bown, an electronics wizard in his twenties;

Malcolm Addey was recording Adam Faith; and working with me was a bright young engineer named Stuart Eltham.

Along with the new techniques came another change. In the United States, the capital of the record kingdom, with the largest record industry in the world, they started to talk about 'record producers'. That usage soon crossed the Atlantic. It was an indication of the changing role of the A and R man/producer, and of the increasing importance that was being attached to him. For the first time he started to get a bit of status, whereas previously he had been just another Joe Gubbins working in the factory.

Today, the producer's role has completely changed. He works with the engineer to create something which, in terms of normal acoustics, is not possible, something which is larger than life. He is there to superimpose his will on the artist, to steer the recording into the particular musical direction he wants.

He has become, in a sense, a star in his own right.

But not all record producers become stars. Today, anyone can be a record producer, and the awful thing is that practically everyone is! When I started, I joined an élite band of about a dozen people in the United Kingdom who produced records. Now, every third person I meet seems either to be a producer, or trying to be one. It has become *the* desirable thing to do. A student is more likely to go to music college with the idea of becoming a producer than of becoming a concert pianist. And for every one who goes to music college, there are ten thousand who don't, but who still want to become producers, and still do become producers.

All you need is the necessary money to go into a studio with a group of musicians. You will find Fred Flange, who lives at 29 Acacia Villas, down the road. Fred has got his own little group. Fred and you agree that the group is the bee's knees, and you sign him up, saying: 'I'll be your manager; I'll take 30%, and I'll make a record with you.' You rustle up something between £600 and £1000, and take the group into a studio. Whether you know anything about it at all, or (as most probably) not, you emerge at the end of the day with a little tape, usually with some ghastly noise on it. If you are extremely lucky, you can sell that tape to a record company. If you are luckier still, it could become a hit. It is that huge element of chance, rather like the pools, which attracts people to the idea. But it has nothing to do with the true *profession* of being a record producer, where the element of chance is not part of the game.

Not only can anyone become a record producer, but anyone can start his own label. When I started, there were very few record companies in this country. They were old-fashioned, almost feudal institutions; although they ground their employees into the dust, they were very strait-laced, and exceedingly honourable in their dealings with recording artists and others. Then came the revolution, with the influx of American companies, the breakaway of independent producers, and the setting-up of small record organisations. The power of the original companies has been dissipated to such an extent that they have almost become distributors of other people's records, and factories to produce them.

Today, a combination of will, energy and a certain amount of money is all that is required for starting a label. It is even easy to get records produced. You can hire a recording studio, either using an independent producer or settling for a do-it-yourself job. You can then take the master tape and have it processed, for a price, by any record company. You can order, say, five thousand discs, get the sleeves made up, and set out on your own. Of course, that does cost money, and if you don't know what you're doing you will burn your fingers. You also have to have distribution, which you can arrange by going to any shop, or chain of shops, and saying: 'Right, I'm marketing records. Will you stock them for me?' They usually will, whereas in the old days only recognised record dealers dealt in records.

In fact, most people don't go to all the trouble of starting a label, but organise licensing deals with the large record companies. Even a company like AIR, before it actually makes a record, will first make an arrangement with a large company for the issue of that record. We made our own records and licensed them, through EMI, to Columbia, Parlophone, or whoever it was: a record would go out as, say, a Parlophone record, but also as an AIR production. We would pay the cost of recording and would recover it in the form of an advance and a royalty, out of which we would pay the artists. That is how many of the smaller production companies operate. But in 1976, we changed all that in our own case when we started the AIR label, and we will issue our records only on that label.

Anyone wanting to become a professional producer has two basic options open to him. He can become a staff producer with one of the large companies, in which case he gets a salary. Or he can become an independent producer, and forage for himself. The independent hires himself out to the highest bidder. He generally expects to get a royalty on the sale of the records, and he gambles that his skill will make that record sell. If he is good enough, he will demand an advance against those royalties, rather like an author's arrangement with a book publisher.

When we started AIR back in 1965 we set the standard for what royalties should be. We said that 2% was the normal, basic royalty to which a producer should be entitled. Today, that varies. Top producers get much more. I may get 4% or even more, depending on the circumstances. The irony is that, when we achieved that breakthrough for the independent producers, we also won the battle for the staff producers. On top of his salary, any staff producer worth his salt will nowadays also receive a very handsome royalty.

When an independent producer is approached to make a record, that approach may come either directly from the artist or group, or it may come from the record company. But we learned long ago that it is wiser not to deal with individual performers, however important or friendly they may be, on the question of money. So, if a group approaches me, my manager, who handles all negotiations, will say to their manager: 'These are our terms: so many per cent royalty; so many thousand dollars advance.' There is a fairly standard form of contract, by which the producer gets royalties and statements of account every three months, every six months, or whatever it is. But we always insist that, whatever the deal may be, we must be paid directly by the record company concerned. They send us the statements, and they send us the royalties, regardless of any payments they make to the artists.

The whole field is very negotiable. There might, for instance, be a group contracted to produce so many records for a company. That group might want to use their favourite independent producer, while the company might prefer to use one of its staff producers, which would probably mean they have to pay less in royalties. The outcome will depend on the particular situation. If, as in the case of the group America whom I record, the producer is recognised as being a vital link in the chain, in the sound of the final product, the record company will tend not to argue. In other circumstances, if it comes to a head-on disagreement, the group, if they believe a particular producer is essential to their success, may agree to take a lower royalty themselves in order to accommodate the producer's demands.

It is all a matter of sale and demand, the original marketplace. If you are in demand, you will obviously command a higher royalty than if you are just starting. And when you are just starting, it is the devil of a job to win acknowledgement in the business. Make no mistake, while it may be true that anyone can become a record producer, success as a professional producer is very hard to achieve. But once the breakthrough comes, you will be asked again; that is certain. There tends to be a fashion in producers. I have known cases where people have tried to sell records on the strength of their being 'A George Martin Production'.

But I think that that fashionable side of the business can be very dangerous. I have known many record producers who have been, like recording acts, mere flashes in the pan. They make a tremendous hit. Everybody wants to use them. Then they take a nose-dive and sink without trace. It is stamina, the ability to do a professional job year in, year out, that is hard to achieve. You can't rest on your laurels. You can't let up for a moment in seeking the best result of which you are capable. After more than a quarter-century in the business, I still always expect that next week people will say: 'George Martin! That old fuddy-duddy! We don't want him any more.'

But as long as one is wanted, the rewards can be very great indeed. If an album in America 'goes gold'—that is, sells half a million copies—it will earn the producer a small fortune. The retail price of an album is about eight dollars. A 3% royalty works out at something over twenty cents an album. So a 'gold' album means $100,000 for the producer.

With the successes that I have had in producing the group America—records like *History, Hideaway, Holiday* and *Hearts*—I was bringing something like half a million dollars a year into this country. That money, of course, went to my company, AIR, rather than to me, because it was for my work as producer. It is only when I score, arrange, write film music or conduct a concert that the fees or royalties for my work come to me personally. I think *History* was the single album which made us the most money. It was a compendium of America's hit singles—songs like 'Horse With No Name'—which they had asked me to put together as a special package. That didn't stop at gold. It went platinum. I believe they ended up selling something like two million copies; we made about $200,000 out of it, even though I had not produced all the tracks.

The other rewards of being a successful record producer are those which go on to the mantelpiece rather than into the bank balance. They are, of course, awards.

I often feel that, although winning is nice, the very fact of being nominated is almost as good, because by then the whole field has been narrowed down to about five names, and those five people must all have done pretty well. To me, an Oscar nomination was a great honour, even though, as I wrote earlier, I knew I had no chance of winning.

Mind you, that sort of attitude can backfire. In 1976 Don Kirschner and the American CBS television network started the Rocky Awards, to honour people in the rock music industry. It was held in Los Angeles, and I actually flew from there to London the night before the ceremony, never dreaming that I could be in the running. I thought the 'producer of the year' award would go to Gus Dudgeon, who produces Elton John, or to John Lennon, Stevie Wonder, or Peter Asher, Jane's brother, who is probably the most successful producer in America right now. To my astonishment, I had hardly set foot back in England when I got a call to tell me that I had won, and that someone else had had to collect the award on my behalf. Apart from that, the whole thing was rather funny to me since I don't really regard myself as a rock producer at all.

That's the thing about these awards: you really don't know who has won until they open those envelopes. You just have to sit there and quake. Nor do I think that there is any question of it being 'his turn this year', where awards are concerned. They tend to be based on the hard facts of sales and so on.

Apart from the Rocky Award and the Britannia Award, I have won four Grammies, which are the music business's equivalent of Oscars. They are given by the National Academy of Recording Arts and Sciences in America. In England I have won an Ivor Novello Award for special services to music, though they are normally given to writers for their compositions.

The other kind of memento, of course, is the gold, silver, or platinum disc. I have rather a large collection of those, and it is with no disrespect, or lack of pride in them, that I now reveal the use to which they are put. They 'paper' the walls of the smallest room at my London home!

One of the main problems for the record producer is finding suitable material.

This is especially true when you are recording someone like

Matt Monro or Shirley Bassey, who don't write their own songs. It is the job of the producer to find them the right ones. If you are a professional producer and people in the business know that you record Matt, or Shirley, or Cilla Black, they will send you songs with those people in mind. Even the public sends offerings. But that is not enough. You still have to search. You still have to ring up the publishers' offices.

You might think that they should be smart enough to send the stuff without being asked. But everyone isn't smart all the time. Sometimes, if you push them enough, they may produce something which they have not thought of as suitable anyway, because they tend to send you only the obvious ones. If you have had a hit with Cilla Black called 'You're My World', the next three months' mail will consist of songs exactly like 'You're My World'. It will not occur to anyone that you and Cilla might be interested in 'You've Lost That Loving Feeling' or 'Baby, It's Cold Outside'.

Ideally, the producer should try not to stick to the same thing. He should give the artist the chance of doing something different. He must keep his mind open. And he must keep the publishers' minds open, too.

It is not necessary to have a degree in physics in order to be a record producer. I am certainly no electronics expert, though I have inevitably picked up basic knowledge, like what a valve does and how a transistor operates.

Electronic wizardry is a matter for the engineer, and it is ironic to me to see those young engineers who came up with me—the generation after Charlie Anderson and his friends—now seeming rather old-fashioned, for all the enormous help they gave in improving our studios and our techniques. Today, there is a new brand of engineer pushing his way up in the business.

There are no set rules for the relationship between the producer and the engineer. It is entirely a question of what works best. Geoff

Emerick and I, for example, work very well as a team, because we work together so much, and respect what each other does. We keep our separate areas of responsibility quite definite. Our long collaboration has led to a deep understanding, so that I know in advance what he is going to do and he knows in advance what I want. With other engineers, especially in America, I have to give detailed instructions. I must say what kind of echo I want on the voice, what equalisation I like on the strings, the nearness or distance of sound that I require, the drum sound I like, the bass sound I prefer. It all has to be spelled out.

There is a race of men who are producer-engineers; they combine both functions. In theory I could do that. But I do not think it is a very good idea. I would not be able to see the wood for the trees. The essence of a producer's job is to be impartial. He must be able to see the whole picture, and make a value-judgement as quickly as possible. But when you are playing about with equalisation knobs, trimming limiters and compressors, varying the amounts of echo or reverberation time, and involving yourself in a million other technical activities, you tend not to listen to the music. And I am rather single-minded about that.

A producer's function is to listen to the sound, and to the music as an overall unit together, and from that he must judge the recording. An engineer's function is to ensure that, technically, it is the very best recording obtainable. If they are worrying about each other's area of responsibility, they are not doing their own jobs properly.

Equally, there can at times be a legitimate overlapping of function. In spite of the understanding that Geoff and I have built together, he won't know exactly what my score is like. He won't know precisely how I visualise the relationship of the backing to the voice and the rhythm. He won't know that, although I have written the strings in a very high passage at one point, I do not want them to be very loud. Conversely, I may have written them in a very low passage elsewhere, and he cannot know that I want them not too soft. And since the dynamics of scoring a modern recording are such that many of these effects have to be artificially manipulated, I might well tend to override his controls in such cases.

He will get the main balance, according to his normal standards and to what he has come to expect with me, and I will put the fine touches in afterwards. That speeds up the whole process, and is better than if I said to him: 'That was a good run-through, Geoff. But next time, when the voice hits the word "told", will you pull back the strings . . . ?' It is much quicker, simpler, and more accurate if I do it myself. Nor does Geoff mind at all. It's a far cry from those early days, when the engineers hated your touching a thing. 'Keep your bloody hands off my controls!' It was almost a union matter.

I am in no way a typical record producer. I am a jack-of-all-trades and master of none, and it is fortunate for me that I have found a line of business which accepts versatility rather than genius.

One of the ways in which I am fairly unusual among producers is the degree to which I arrange and orchestrate. For the actual job of producing, that is not important. A top record producer does not in any way need the ability to translate everything literally into precise musical terms, into the precise technical language. He can hire an arranger to do that. But I do believe that he should have a working knowledge of music in an appreciative sense, a feeling for shape and form. He should be able, for example, to say to the arranger: 'I like your arrangement, but I think it's a bit heavy-handed, a little too ponderous.'

If he is not a musician, he will have to talk in broad terms like that. He won't have the vocabulary to say: 'You shouldn't have doubled the contrabassoon there.' Equally, there are many non-musician producers who have acquired at least a part of that vocabulary through sheer experience. They are often very successful.

They have worked all their lives in the record industry; they have clawed their way up, starting perhaps as messenger boys, moving up to the A and R department, listening all the time to record programmes and what the disc jockeys have to say, so that they know what people want and form a clear idea of what they like themselves. And over the years they have picked up the details in the fine print of musical language.

If they are lucky enough to have learnt their craft in a studio, starting as an assistant's assistant, they can gain by sheer observation. They can watch the violas and the violins playing and listen to their distinct sounds, and they will know from that when it is preferable to use the one rather than the other. Typical in this field are the engineers who have become producers in their own right. Geoff Emerick himself produced an album with the Campbelltown Pipers, on which he worked with Paul McCartney. Glyn Johns is another. There is also Phil Ramone, a very fine producer, who recorded all the music for Barbra Streisand's film *A Star Is Born* and made many records with Paul Simon and Billy Joel.

Then again, there are record producers who do not pontificate on music at all. Norman Newell at EMI, for example, was most successful with records of shows. If something like *Mame* or *Seven Brides for Seven Brothers* came to town as an English production and EMI wanted an original-cast album of the English show, Norman would do it. He became expert at it. He was not a musician, but he was an excellent producer.

There are no set rules. I even knew one very famous record producer who made it his sole function to sit with his feet up in the control room, watching the group in the studio below. Occasionally he would press the mike button to communicate with the studio and say, 'Absolutely fantastic!' Then he would release the button and beam all over his face. With this heavy chore behind him, he would get out his pot, roll a joint, light up and offer it round when the boys came out of the studio. That was his entire contribution. Having achieved all this, he would walk away with a hit record!

I will refrain from mentioning his name, but, believe me, it is extremely well-known.

The choice of recording studio is a matter for the artist and the producer. Every producer will have his own favourite, one in which he can work happily.

I naturally prefer to work at AIR Studios, not only because they are owned by my company, but more because I happen to think they offer better facilities and quality than can be found in most other places. The only reason for going outside would be if, for instance, I were using an eighty- or ninety-piece orchestra. Then I would prefer to use the Number One studio at Abbey Road, because of its ambience and long reverberation period.

But if, say, Cilla Black were to tell me that for some reason she would rather work at EMI, then at EMI we would work. Provided the studios were up to good modern standards, I would never quarrel with an artist on those grounds.

The advent of multi-track working, as I have described, was a great blessing to the professional producer. It gave him freedom to re-think. Like a painter in oils who doesn't like a couple of lines in his picture, he can go back over his work, erasing it and filling in with something new.

But as the hard core of professional producers swelled into a vast army of amateurs, multi-track working assumed far greater importance. As records became better, musicians themselves became more involved in the studios, more aware of studio techniques. They also began to have more say in what the sounds should be like. I would think that today only about 20% of records are made by professional producers. The great majority are made by the groups themselves. As producers, they are amateurs; they simply do not have the experience. And as the multifunction power drill is for the home handyman, multi-track is the ideal tool for do-it-yourself recording.

Perhaps the classic example of what could be achieved with that tool is Mike Oldfield's creation, *Tubular Bells*. When he made that record he was a complete amateur, though the experience itself has turned him into a professional. But he had the genius to know the sound he wanted. He achieved that record by working away in a studio, laying down a basic track, adding to it, subtracting from it, adding something else—putting a little bit of synthesiser here, a bit of strings there. He was painting a picture, but gradually. If you like, he was painting by numbers, slowly adding colours here and there, taking away a colour that didn't work once the other shades had been added.

For him, multi-track working was an absolute necessity. He had neither the experience nor the discipline to say in advance what he wanted. At the same time, it is probably true to say that if he *had* had that experience and discipline, it is unlikely that *Tubular Bells* would have emerged as such an imaginative work.

To a certain extent, it was a hit-and-miss way of working. But then, that was how someone as great as Picasso often worked. I remember a film which showed Picasso painting on a ground-glass screen. The cameraman used stop-frame photography, and you could see how the artist would start with his basic lines, then fill them in, a colour here and a colour there, until the picture became very full and very complex. Suddenly there came a point at which you realised that he was wiping out what he had done before, because it had given him the inspiration for something else. The whole picture was changing, and the final result was quite different from his original thoughts.

Rock musicians tend to work that way. The degree of pre-thought, the extent to which ideas are worked out before the recording, varies with the group, but a lot of creativity happens on the spur of the moment. That must also apply to the producer. If I am doing something of my own, and especially if I am working with a large orchestra, which is expensive, I have to work the whole picture out in advance. I have to get it right on the manuscript, even though there may still be small alterations on the day. But when the producer is working with a group, he is creating in the studio. He uses his own thoughts and those of the group, collating and assembling them and rejecting the ones that are no good. So another element in the make-up of a good producer becomes the ability to choose: to choose between what works and what does not work—and, what is most important, to choose quickly.

That is, if there *is* a producer. Today, particularly in America, there are three reasons why most groups are reluctant to engage one. First, because the producer's importance is so widely recognised today that they want the glory of saying they produced their record themselves. Secondly, since the producer now gets so much money in royalties, they would rather keep that income 'in the family'. Thirdly, they may feel that an experienced producer will inhibit their genius. They don't want some old fuddy-duddy slowing them down, especially if they are looking for something that no one has thought of before.

The consequence of all this is that many groups spend an enormous amount of time in the studio just playing around, 'doing their thing'. Two people from the group Deep Purple, for example, invented an instrument called a Gizmo. Closeted with this new toy, they spent no less than *eighteen months* in the studio making one record. Some said this was a trifle self-indulgent, but the fact was that they were trying to plumb the depths of their brainchild, and wanted to show off all the Gizmo's potential.

It is this sort of exercise which makes it essential that studio technology should be first-class—a technology at whose core lies multi-track working. If you were to record Shirley Bassey with a forty-piece orchestra, you would have three songs on tape within three hours, and as near a final mix as makes no difference. After the recording you might need a few hours just to titivate it a bit, but that's all. With a group, three tracks in three hours would be quite impossible.

We have come a long way from that first Beatle album, *Please*

Please Me, which I started at ten o'clock one February morning in 1963, and which was all mixed and ready for issue by eleven o'clock that night!

Often, when a producer has to work with a group over a period to bring out an album, the general ambience of the place where they work is as important as the more obvious needs of good studio facilities. Occasionally, it may even be more important, and the producer may have to use a little ingenuity in order to work in a good location.

In 1970, I was asked to record Sea Train, a folk-rock group whose sounds I liked very much. They wrote their own songs, which three or four of them sang, with lots of harmonies. I was asked to record them in New York, in July, but I said: 'There is really no way that I want to go to New York and record in July. It gets so hot there, and one way and another we're going to be in a heavy city.' Besides, my youngest son, Giles, was still only a year old, and I did not want to be away from my family for too long.

The group's manager was Bennett Glotzer, who used to be in partnership with Albert Grossman, who handled the Band and Bob Dylan. He said, 'Look, most of the group live up in Massachusetts. If you thought it was a good idea, we could probably record up there. What do you think?'

The idea intrigued me, and I flew up from New York to have a look at Marblehead, the little town where they lived. I discovered that there were houses to rent in the summer, and I started working on the notion of equipping our own studio in one of them. I soon found the ideal house. It was huge, empty, almost derelict, and stood in its own grounds on Marblehead Neck, which was effectively an island, connected to the town by a causeway. It had a very large sitting-room, about twenty-five feet by sixteen, which we could use as a studio, and right next door to that was another room which was suitable for a control room.

To help me I brought over Bill Price, one of AIR's best engineers at that time, who now runs Wessex Studios, and he ordered the felt boards we would need to make the place acoustically right. From a firm in Rhode Island we hired a very good recording desk. The 3M company rented me a sixteen-track machine. Dolby Laboratories generously lent me the Dolby units free, in return for publicity on the venture; and I shipped my own loudspeakers over from London, since I was used to their sound. Then we hired a good piano locally, and spent about a fortnight setting the whole thing up.

It was an idyllic summer, and we stayed there from July until October. Bennett had rented another house near the 'studio', for Judy and me and the children, Lucy and Giles, and we would spend most mornings on the beach. Then we would start recording at two in the afternoon, with a break at seven, when I would cycle home for supper, returning to work until about two in the morning.

But there were a few problems locally. Marblehead is a charming New England town, famous for yachts and boating, but there was an extremely right-wing WASP—white Anglo-Saxon Protestant—element among its inhabitants. We discovered this early on, when the owner of the house we lived in told us that when he had first moved into the district he had been asked to sign a document declaring that he would not sell his house to a Jew, a Catholic, or a coloured person.

He had refused. But when we descended on this bigoted backwater, a rock group whose bass and fiddle players were Jewish and whose keyboard player had a black girlfriend, one can understand how there came to be a certain amount of opposition. This first showed when Judy and I and the kids were sitting on the beach one day, a perfectly public beach, and a woman came up and told us to get off it. 'We don't want your sort here at all,' she thundered. The irony was that she was the wife of a man Norman Newell knew very well. Norman had written to him to tell him we were coming, and he had been looking forward to it. His wife, not knowing who we were, blew it completely, of course, establishing an immediate atmosphere of discord, not to say intense hatred!

It is true that we were, I suppose, acting illegally, and should not have been making a record in a private house, but we were not disturbing anyone. It was the fact that we were there at all which really offended the populace.

The houses were all detached, and stood in their own grounds, but there were no fences between the plots, and the well-mown lawns ran into one another. Our next-door neighbour was an eye specialist, and before we moved in our landlord told us, 'The man next door has heard all about you, Mr Martin. He's very anxious to meet you. He admires your work immensely, and I'm sure he'll be calling on you before very long.'

'Thank you very much,' I said. 'I'm not really looking for that, but it's nice to know that people do appreciate what one is doing.'

Well, we moved in, and a week went by, two weeks, a month. We saw them across the lawns, but they ignored us completely. We weren't worried. If that was the way they felt, then fine.

But one Sunday Lucy, who was a precocious child of four, wandered across the lawn to talk to the man as he was cleaning his car, and we could hear her little voice piping across the stretch of green. 'What car have you got?' asked Lucy.

'This is a Lincoln Continental.'

'Oh.'

There was a pause, and then—shamed into conversation, I suppose—he asked her, 'What car does your daddy have?'

'Oh, we've got a Rolls-Royce.' Now, at the time, this was perfectly true, though it happened to be a rather old Silver Cloud. Not that *they* knew that!

Lucy persisted. 'Do you have a boat?'

'No, but I suppose you do,' said the man, obviously feeling his sense of superiority slipping.

'Oh, yes,' said Lucy. 'Daddy always takes the boat to Greece, every summer.'

This also happened to be perfectly true. We had a nine-foot

inflatable dinghy, which we took on our package tours to Greece. Not that *they* knew that!

Within an hour there was a knock on the door, and we were invited round for cocktails. But we never disillusioned them about the age of the Rolls or the nature of the boat!

Since the whole operation had been rather expensive, I had agreed with Bennett Glotzer to do a second album while we were there, so after Sea Train I set to work with Winter Consort. It was a semi-classical group, and a very unusual combination. It was led by Paul Winter, who played a sort of classical saxophone, as well as being a folk writer. Then there was Paul McCandless, who played oboe, and cor anglais and other wind instruments. Ralph Towner played classical guitar, piano, and pipe organ. The cello was in the hands of David Darling, whose brother was a space scientist at Cape Kennedy. There was a Fender bass player. And to complete the line-up there was a man playing what they called 'traps'—drums, that is—which was their only concession to rock-and-roll. He had the most incredible collection of weird instruments: bongos, conga drums, African urdus, marimbas, and an enormous twelve-foot-long xylophone called an amarinda, which required three people, sitting cross-legged, to play it.

The album was called *Icarus,* and was, I think, the finest record I have ever made. It didn't sell particularly well, but a lot of people took notice of it. And it had one special distinction. The title song, 'Icarus', also went out as a single, and David Darling's brother gave a copy to one of the Apollo crews.

That was how it came to be the first record taken to the moon, though I don't think they had the facilities for playing it!

One of the great virtues of a good record producer is patience. But impartiality is almost equally essential.

That may be one reason why I have never gone out of my way to write tunes or songs with the specific aim of making them hits, although I think I could do so. There are ways of manufacturing a hit. There is a kind of dictionary of good bits to put in a song; you take those and juggle them around, and you have a hit. But, just as film work becomes what I called a golden treadmill, so the making of hits tends to turn one into a machine. Again, it means giving up everything else. Most important of all, I am certain that if I had started aiming for hits, I would not have been as good a record producer, because then I would have become biased.

What is more, although I enjoy making my own records from time to time, I would be embarrassed if they were to transform me into a recording star, because that would lead to ambivalence in my relationships with the artists I produce. It is very difficult to work with somebody else. You have to be in tune with that person, and you have to get over any ego problems. If one side always takes, and the other is always giving, talent is suppressed. If a very talented artist browbeats a very talented producer into such a state that he cannot express himself, the producer's talent is wasted; he is ineffective. The same is true the other way round. A successful record has to be a real expression of *everyone's* talent. That was true when I recorded Ella Fitzgerald, and it is true when I work with Jimmy Webb. It was true when I made successful recordings with Jeff Beck; it is true when I get together with my friends Cleo Laine, John Dankworth and that marvellous classical guitarist John Williams.

And it was never more true than in all those years I worked with the Beatles. There were no clear lines of demarcation. It was more a question of being a good team than of isolating individuals as being producer, arranger or songwriter. When I arranged, I worked closely with John, Paul or whoever it was, and they arranged with me. To hark back to an example—the use of the piccolo trumpet on 'Penny Lane': it is true that I arranged it, but equally true that Paul was thinking up the notes. If I had been left to myself, I honestly do not think I would have written such good notes for David Mason to play.

I must emphasise that it was a team effort. Without my arrangements and scoring, very many of the records would not have sounded as they do. Whether they would have been any better, I cannot say. They might have been. That is not modesty on my part; it is an attempt to give a factual picture of the relationship. But equally, there is no doubt in my mind that the main talent of that whole era came from Paul and John. George, Ringo and myself were subsidiary talents. We were not five equal people artistically: two were very strong, and the other three were also-rans.

In varying degrees those three could have been other people. The fact is, we were not. Although you could say of a successful football team that it might have done as well with another goalkeeper, or another centre-forward, the fact remains that that goalkeeper and centre-forward *are* in the team, and as part of it they cannot be discounted.

And I did win one battle in the industry—not only for myself, but for all who take a pride in their ability to produce good records. After our first successes, the labels and sleeves bore the legend 'Produced by George Martin'.

14

BUILDING ON AIR

IN THE early years of AIR, we had no studios of our own. We had
to rent whatever studio was available and suitable for the particular recording. The more work we got, the more money was being
spent on other people's studios. It didn't take a genius to work out
that if we had our own studios the trend would be reversed—not
only would that money not have to be paid out, but some might
even start coming in. In addition, the company was enjoying an
ever-increasing income from royalties, which was likely only to be
fodder for the taxman. So it made sense for us to keep our belts
tightened, not pay ourselves very high salaries, and plough back
the money into our own company, quite legitimately, to finance
the building of our own studios. Someone who knew a great deal
about that side of the business advised me against it. 'You'll burn
your fingers. You'll lose your money,' he said. But being pigheaded,
we went ahead with the idea.

The most difficult job was to find a suitable site. London is a
very expensive place, and none of the major studios was actually
in the centre, such facilities as existed being confined to poky little
places. It became a straight choice between 'out' and 'in'. If we went
to the fringes of London, we could build much more cheaply and
have a big car park. I found that the dividing line was a circle
whose radius from the centre stretched about as far as Finchley.

Beyond that was cheap. Once inside that line, expanding parking restrictions and uniformly high prices meant that there wasn't much to be gained unless we went right to the centre. The choice was greatly affected by the fact that I wanted a multi-purpose studio, one that could be used for dubbing films as well as making records. To make that pay we would have to attract the American trade. I wanted the best American film and record producers to use the studios. That indicated somewhere within easy distance of Claridges and the Connaught. So we started to look for sites right in the centre of London. All suffered from one disadvantage or another.

Finally I heard about the top of the Peter Robinson building at Oxford Circus. You certainly couldn't get more central than that. Peter Robinson is one of the big old London multi-purpose department stores. Like many of them, it had at the top a huge restaurant—a banqueting-hall, in fact—in which the gentry had been wont to take their china tea, cucumber sandwiches and cakes after making their purchases. The gentry having been whittled away, or absorbed into a world of T-shirts and hamburgers, it had fallen into disuse, and for two years the store, which still occupies the building, had been trying to let the floor as offices. Lack of success in this enterprise was hardly surprising, as conversion would have cost a fortune. To walk into that place was to step back half a century into the high Edwardian era. It had a huge vaulted ceiling with neo-classical frescoes, marble columns, and kitchens at each end. It was enormous, and very tall.

'It's certainly got the space,' we said. 'It's certainly got the height. And the rent is very reasonable. So why don't we investigate the difficulties of building a studio in it?' Those difficulties were very real, not least the fact that we were looking directly down on one of the world's busier traffic junctions. In addition, we were in a steel-framed building directly above three Underground railway lines (which today have become four, with the new Victoria Line). There were clearly going to be acoustic problems!

Although we had been in studios all our working lives, building one was quite another matter, and that we had never done. Nor, in fact, had our architects, Bill Rossell Orme and his assistant Jack Parsons, though they had designed a few cinemas. The important thing was that Bill was used to doing big contracts, with county councils and so on. That meant he was accustomed to assembling many different talents for a project, which in the case of a recording studio was clearly going to be necessary. To work with him from our side I recruited Keith Slaughter as studio manager, and later Dave Harries who had worked with Keith at EMI. Their job was to liaise on problems like wiring—something like twenty miles of wire had to be brought into the place—and the ordering and placing of equipment. After all, we didn't want to be obsolete before we started.

As our acoustics expert we employed Kenneth Shearer, a real sound boffin, who can tell you more about acoustics than anyone else in this country. He is the man who designed all those 'flying saucers' in the Albert Hall. The answer to the rumble up through the building from the Underground was drastic, and dramatic. The whole works—studios and control rooms—would be made completely independent of the main building. Essentially, a huge box was to be built inside the banqueting-hall, and mounted on acoustic mounts.

Then there was the problem of air-conditioning; obviously you can't have windows open in a studio! You have to be able to supply air to appropriate parts of it, and not only does that supply have to be at the right temperature and humidity, but it must also be completely silent. In order to keep it fresh, especially with the amount of oxygen consumed by loud-lunged rock groups, a large volume of air has to be exchanged. And a large movement of air through small channels creates a great deal of noise; you only have to listen to the extractor in the kitchen to know that. The system we installed was a large-volume/low-speed air exchange, mounted in sound-proof baffles, so that no sound could enter from outside— nor, equally importantly, could we expel any sound.

That may sound very elementary, but it is surprising how many recording studios do not have proper air-conditioning. EMI, for example, for all their sophistication and history of brilliant recordings, had continual problems with sound escaping. At times, this used to drive the studio manager to the brink of despair. We often recorded at night, especially with the Beatles; the police would come round and we had injunctions flying in all directions. For a while the authorities stopped us recording after midnight, and on one occasion threatened to close the studios down unless we complied. The curious side of it was the particular effect of this escaping sound. It would come out of the echo-chamber, go straight up in the air and then, by some freak combination of acoustic, weather, and possibly architectural conditions, land again about a mile away in Swiss Cottage.

With these and other problems to contend with, the planning and design of our studios took a year. Finally we got an estimate of £66,000 for the work, and decided to go ahead. Unfortunately, it didn't end there. A few weeks later Bill Orme rang me to say: 'I want you to come to a meeting. I'm afraid I've got some bad news for you.' As I entered, all the experts were sitting round a table—fourteen of them: quantity surveyors, sub-contractors, architects, air-conditioning people and the rest. 'You'd better sit down first,' said Bill, 'because I don't want you to take the shock standing up. As you know, the original estimate was £66,000. The fact is that there now seems no way we can make it less than £110,000.'

Retrieving my limp body from the floor, I expostulated: 'How can you do this to me? I haven't *got* £110,000!'

'Well, we can always cancel it,' he said, deeply apologetic. 'But things are costing more. For instance, we didn't know, until we got into the building and took that beam out, that it had to be underpinned.'

I felt as if I were on the set of the film *Mr Blandings Builds His Dream House*; we had been trying to build AIR on a shoestring—and it seemed the string had just snapped. The whole business shook me to the core, to the extent that when I held an immediate meeting with my partners I even said: 'All those critics who said we should never do it were probably right. It's costing far more than we ever dreamed. What do you think?'

But it was only a moment of doubt. The fact was that we were already in far too deep to back out, and we simply had to go ahead. Even then costs continued to rise, and in the end we settled for about £136,000. On top of that was a £200,000 bill for equipment. It was an enormous effort; we had to strip our company to the bone, and were in what the jargon calls a 'serious cash-flow situation' for a while. It very nearly bankrupted us, and, if the studio hadn't turned out a success, that would certainly have happened, because at the start money was going out far more quickly than it was coming in. But in the end we managed, and we survived.

We even held a party in true showbiz tradition for the opening in October 1970, to which we invited all our friends and enemies from EMI, people from other record companies, and—with a certain magnanimity, I thought—the architects, with whom we had had a major falling-out over the spiralling costs. The saddest thing was that, soon after the studios were completed, Bill Orme's assistant Jack Parsons suffered a paralysing stroke. Since the project began he had done little else than work on the design, and I have always felt that without his devotion we would never have had the fine studios we enjoy today.

The opening party was on 7 October. And on 9 October I made the first recording at AIR Studios; the artist—Cilla Black, godmother to our daughter Lucy.

Not long afterwards, the acoustics of the studio, with its floor 'floating' two feet above the original floor and its walls and ceilings suspended from acoustic mounts, were put to a severe test. We were approached by Argo Records, who specialise in the spoken word. It seems that they had been recording *Julius Caesar* with Laurence Olivier at Decca's studios in West Hampstead, and in the middle of a key passage had got the sound of a jet flying overhead. It's well-known and generally found acceptable that there are certain anachronisms in Shakespeare, such as cannon going off when cannons hadn't even been invented; but it was felt that a Boeing 707 was taking things a little too far!

So they wanted to see if they could do better with us. Their chief engineer came to our Number One studio and placed a very sensitive microphone in the centre of it. Then they shut all the doors, went into the control room, and turned up the gain to the maximum on all the amplifiers, so that if someone had whispered in one corner of the studio it would have sounded like a lion's roar. Then they just listened to the ambient sound, to hear if there was any spillage from the air-conditioning, or any other extraneous noise. They could hear nothing, and it's true to say they were amazed. But they weren't satisfied with that. They next ran a tape off that mike for two hours, at a speed of 7½ inches per second. Then they played it back at 30 inches per second, which would have the effect of quadrupling the frequencies of any rumbles or other noises that might otherwise have remained inaudible. Still they could hear practically nothing.

So they were satisfied, and we gained the first of many customers for recording the spoken word. There was only one embarrassment. Their first session with us was to record a jet-less version of *Julius Caesar*. Just as Olivier was delivering a speech from the steps of the Roman Forum, he moved, and we discovered to our horror that we had a squeaky floorboard! Stone steps just don't squeak, and we soon got *that* repaired.

AIR today has many functions. We have our own record label. We have our own artists, whom we record. We record artists for other labels. We hire out our studios to other producers—who may either use our own recording engineers, or bring their own as is current practice in America; and we hire out producers and engineers to others. But most often, because we now have a worldwide reputation, people come to us not only for the studios themselves but also to use our staff, knowing they are backed by AIR's training and high standards. That may sound like a sales pitch, but it happens to be true, to the extent that we have a very live agency which actually exports the talents of AIR's creative people—men such as Geoff Emerick, Peter Henderson, Mike Stavrou, Steve Nye, Jon Kelly and myself.

Once AIR Studios in London became a reality and gained its reputation of being the finest recording complex in Europe, my thoughts turned to other ideas.

The concept of a 'total environment' studio had always appealed to me. I had worked at Jimmy Guercio's Caribou studio in the American Rockies about sixty miles from Denver, and I loved the creative freedom it gave. You were there to make an album, and the studio was yours for as long as you wanted it, any time of the day or night. It was very comfortable, with individual homely log cabins and a good studio with a Neve console. The only thing wrong was the time of year that I was there. In February Colorado can be pretty cold, and a macabre sense of humour could easily label it as an expensive labour camp! Our nickname for it was Stalag Luft III. However, it was a great idea that worked well. In England Richard Branson was having some success with his studio The Manor, installed in an old Oxfordshire manor-house. There is certainly a great deal to be said for working in congenial surroundings when the pressure is high.

I had the temerity to think of building a studio on a ship. It could go anywhere—preferably the Mediterranean or the Caribbean—and it would certainly give the groups their get-away-from-it-all feeling. I suppose I spent two years developing the idea and sorting out the problems. Keith Slaughter, who had been running our London studios, was put in charge of the project, and I started boat-hunting. After a great deal of looking, as far afield as Iceland and Yugoslavia, the choice narrowed to two vessels. The smaller (and more expensive) was the SS *Albro*—a yacht, converted from a Scandinavian freighter, which I found in Malta. It was about 120 feet long, with most of the superstructure at the back, driven by a

slow single-shaft engine with feathering prop. It had been beautifully converted, and the living accommodation was spacious and
luxurious. But the studio would have had to go in the hold, and that
was not quite large enough for my ideal.

The alternative ship I found in Yugoslavia. This one, of about
160 feet overall, had twin engines and seemed to give us all the room
we needed. She was a passenger ferry named *Osejevik* that plied her
trade up and down the Dalmatian coast. With the building of a new
coast highway, trade had fallen off, and the Yugoslav government
had decided to offer her for sale. Of course, a ship studio presents
enormous problems. Running costs would obviously be high, power
supplies had to be stable, and the acoustic problems presented by
a large steel box made the building of AIR London a picnic by
comparison. Still, our experience stood us in good stead, and we
believed we had all the answers. It is difficult to believe now, but
it should have been possible to have completed the project in 1974
at a cost of around $750,000. Today it would cost at least twice
as much. But with great regret the idea was abandoned. The real
killer was the economic crisis which hit Britain—the three-day
week—and the world oil crisis, all of which made risky ventures
downright foolhardy. So it became an unrealised dream, and I
turned my thoughts to a land studio.

Of all the places I had been to, I loved the atmosphere of working in Hawaii. But that was much too far away from London, and
while we were based in England it did not make a lot of sense to
build on American soil. Canada was tempting; Mexico more so.
I knew the Caribbean fairly well, but never seriously considered it
because of its political instability. There always seemed to be under-
currents in the Bahamas and Virgin Islands, and beautiful Jamaica
is sadly an unhappy place.

Then I discovered Montserrat. It is still a British colony (one of
the few left), and I was delighted to find a luscious green tropical
island with a population that seemed happy to be living together,
black and white. I was struck by the natural friendliness of the

place, which I am sure has a lot to do with the lack of progress in 'civilised' developments. I am happy to say Montserrat does not have a casino, high-rise hotels, or concrete sunbathing pads beside huge chlorinated swimming-pools. But it does have a fresh charm of its own. What clinched the whole thing was finding an ideal site for our purpose. In short, we now have a super new studio on a thirty-acre farm overlooking the Caribbean Sea, five hundred feet up. The clients live in villas nearby and it has become my ideal working place. My only complaint is that I cannot get in because of other people wanting to book it!

The studio has both twenty-four- and thirty-two-track machines, but I personally am not over-enthusiastic about thirty-two-track. I can cope quite nicely, thank you, with twenty-four; and, if more are really needed, I prefer to use our locking device to harness two twenty-four-track machines together, giving up to forty-six tracks. Cost is a great factor to be taken into account. Our first console at AIR London, built by Rupert Neve who makes the Rolls-Royce of recording desks, was sixteen-track, and cost $35,000. At the time, we thought that was a lot of money. The Montserrat console, by contrast, cost $210,000. Even though it is hand-made, and designed to our own specifications, that is still a lot of money! It has fifty-two inputs and twenty-four or thirty-two outputs, with twenty-four separate monitors. It is about as advanced as any console can be today without changing from what is called the analogue system.

And the chances are that within a couple of years it will have to cope with 'digital recording'. But that is part of things to come. . . .

15

TOMORROW NEVER KNOWS

IF THE history of recording stays true to form, we are about to embark on a new era, another quarter-century of new techniques.

So much progress has been made in the past twenty-five years that one wonders how far the technology will take us. The explosion of computer development and automation in industry in general will have its effect on our record business, and the silicon chip is not going to be ignored in the future recording studio. Digital recording is already here and working. It is still crude and expensive, but it tells us the way we are going.

With our present systems, making a record is rather like making a movie. The tape is the medium (like film) which receives an imprint of sound, which is recorded and replayed. Because the sound is an imprint, it suffers from similar defects to a photograph—distortion, lack of clarity, background noise, tape hiss and so on. It can never be a *perfect* reproduction of the original. Digital recording is another matter entirely; it is a literal duplication of the original. Computer technology has given us this new system. How does it work?

Most people know that computers do very simple sums extremely quickly. They store information which is either yes or no. Your little pocket calculator is capable of solving incredibly complex problems which would take a human brain ages to work out, but in fact it works very simply (though very fast). If you want to multiply 17 by 32 it will in fact add 32 17s together—at the speed of light.

Digital recording essentially breaks sound down into numbers, stores the information in a memory bank and re-assembles it when it is replayed. If you were to take a magnetic tape at any one point, you would not get anything very useful from it. But if you take a cross-section of a computer recording, like cutting a tree across the trunk and examining its rings, you can look at it and find out exactly what is happening. In a segment of sound lasting, say, 1/50,000 of a second, every frequency in the spectrum has a particular volume level; 30 cycles might have 58 decibels, 150 cycles might have 62 decibels, 2500 cycles might have 79 decibels, and so on. And, if every frequency were scanned, its volume accurately measured and the information stored, it would be a simple matter to recreate these frequencies in the same pattern.

Now, think of that particular segment as one frame in a cine film. If the same process were repeated very quickly—in this case 50,000 times every second—and the results played back, you would not know that it was not a continuous sound: just as the human eye is tricked into seeing as one continuous image the twenty-four new pictures a cine film flashes on to the screen each second. In effect, the original sound would be rebuilt.

Digital recording is not recording in the normal sense—it is analysis and re-structuring; making a template and building an identical image. Therefore, because recording tape is not used in the ordinary way, we do not suffer from its disadvantages. There will be no hiss, no distortion, no cross-talk between tracks. (Tape is used, of course, but only as a computer uses it—merely to store binary-coded information.) Nevertheless, we will still be able to do all the things we do now—and more. We will be able to allocate the sound from one particular microphone to a particular section on the computer, and tell it, 'I want that sound kept separate.' You can add sounds *ad infinitum*. At the moment, this new system is linked to the kind of analogue recording desk which exists today. Only the tape recorder is digital. But its real value will come when desks are specially designed for digital recording.

Automation has been with us for some time. We installed in our AIR studios in London the very first Neve automated mixdown desk. Unlike the other systems in operation, NECAM (which is what Neve christened it) not only remembers all the movements of the faders, but physically moves them when asked to reproduce the mix. To watch it at work is rather like seeing the invisible man in the studio.

It works wonderfully well. I believe that we shall see a new design of desk which will contain everything that a studio needs. There will be no need for a separate tape machine—the desk will incorporate the terminal to the computer, which will not only store the recording information but do many other things besides. It will edit; it will mix one set of sounds with another. It will copy other sounds. Suppose you wanted to reproduce the type of echo used on an old Elvis Presley recording. You would play the record on your terminal and instruct it: 'Remember the echo on voice, and give it to me on the recording I am making now.' It should be able to do that by calling up the right sequence of extra frequencies, without any need for an echo-chamber of its own.

Another great advantage will come from its speed of operation, as users of pocket calculators will understand. Even with modern techniques, a lot of time is used in running magnetic tape to and fro. With digital recording you will be able to go to wherever you want on the recording almost instantaneously.

What else is waiting for us in the future? Well, obviously video records will be as common as sound records are today; the record producer is going to have to become a visual as well as an aural maker of images. The disc played by a needle will soon become archaic; discs will still be made—but they will be scanned by a laser beam, which will eliminate the surface noise, pops and crackles that one gets in present-day discs. And of course with the high-quality sound will come a superb colour picture. Such systems already exist, even if they have not reached the wide marketplace. There is even an ordinary record turntable which can be operated by cordless remote control—you can order it to skip certain tracks on a long-player if you don't want to hear them. You can sit in your armchair and tell it, 'Play tracks one, three and nine, and then go back and play track four'—and I do not think even H. G. Wells thought of that one!

Video-recorders are becoming normal domestic appliances. Soon there will be plenty of pre-recorded videocassettes of popular films and plays, and eventually prices will fall to make the video album a truly economic proposition. But of course with laser technology and the allied invention of holography it will be possible to have video recordings in 3D. A three-dimensional projected image, rather as R2D2 gave us in *Star Wars,* is well within the bounds of possibility for our coming quarter-century. At the moment holography is only possible in monochrome, but it cannot be long before full-colour transmission will be developed.

These are just some of the changes I foresee. For the rest, it is anybody's guess. I dare say that if, on my first day at EMI studios, back in 1950, I had been told that I would be using twenty-four tracks or more on a computer-automated mixing console to make a high-fidelity stereophonic record, I would have raised at least one eyebrow.

Of course, there has been rapid progress in all fields of technology in this last quarter-century, but few have known the transformation undergone by the record industry. Nor does the speed of change seem to have faltered. It so happens that all my children, Alexis, Gregory, Lucy and Giles, enjoy making music as well as listening to it. And if my crystal ball could tell them what will be available to them twenty-five years from now, I dare say their eyebrows, too, would be raised. It's all theirs!

Index

SIR GEORGE MARTIN (1926–2016) was a legendary record producer, arranger, and audio engineer. He is best known for working with the Beatles, among many other famous recording artists. He was made a Commander of the British Empire in 1988 and was awarded a knighthood in 1996.